What Critics and Professionals Say About the "Impact Guides"

"*THE DEFINITIVE GUIL* [...]
Frommer, The Arthur Fron[...]

"*THE BEST* travel book I've e[...]
West[...]

"*AN EXCELLENT, EXHAU!* [...] *FASCINATING* look at shopping in the East . . . it's difficult to imagine a shopping tour without this pocket-size book in hand."—**Travel & Leisure**

"*BOOKS IN THE SERIES* help travelers recognize quality and gain insight to local customs."—**Travel-Holiday**

"*THE BEST GUIDE* I've seen on shopping in Asia. If you enjoy the sport, you'll find it hard to put down . . . They tell you not only the where and what of shopping but the important how, and all in enormous but easy-to-read detail."—**Seattle Post-Intelligencer**

"*ONE OF THE BEST GUIDEBOOKS* of the season—not just shopping strategies, but a Baedeker to getting around . . . definitely a quality work. Highly recommended."—**Arkansas Democrat**

"*WILL WANT TO LOOK INTO* . . . has shopping strategies and travel tips about making the most of a visit to those areas. The book covers Asia's shopping centers, department stores, emporiums, factory outlets, markets and hotel shopping arcades where visitors can find jewelry, leather goods, woodcarvings, textiles, antiques, cameras, and primitive artifacts." —**Chicago Tribune**

"*FULL OF SUGGESTIONS*. The art of bartering, including every-day shopping basics are clearly defined, along with places to hang your hat or lift a fork."—**The Washington Post**

"*A WONDERFUL GUIDE* . . . filled with essential tips as well as a lot of background information . . . a welcome addition on your trip."—**Travel Book Tips**

"*WELL ORGANIZED AND COMPREHENSIVE BOOK.* A useful companion for anyone planning a shopping spree in Asia."—**International Living**

"*OFFERS SOME EXTREMELY VALUABLE INFORMA-TION* and advice about what is all too often a spur-of-the-moment aspect of your overseas travel."—**Trip & Tour**

"*A MORE UNUSUAL, PRACTICAL GUIDE* than most and is no mere listing of convenience stores abroad . . . contains unusual tips on bargaining in Asia . . . country-specific tips are some of the most valuable chapters of the guidebook, setting it apart from others which may general-ized upon Asia as a whole, or focus upon the well-known Hong Kong shopping pleasures."—**The Midwest Book Review**

THE TREASURES AND PLEASURES
OF SINGAPORE AND BALI

By Drs. Ron and Caryl Krannich

TRAVEL AND INTERNATIONAL BOOKS
Click and Easy Travel Planning on the Internet
International Jobs Directory
Jobs For People Who Love to Travel
Mayors and Managers in Thailand
Politics of Family Planning Policy in Thailand
Shopping and Traveling in Exotic Asia
Shopping in Exotic Places
Shopping the Exotic South Pacific
Treasures and Pleasures of Australia
Treasures and Pleasures of China
Treasures and Pleasures of Egypt
Treasures and Pleasures of Hong Kong
Treasures and Pleasures of India
Treasures and Pleasures of Indonesia
Treasures and Pleasures of Israel and Jordan
Treasures and Pleasures of Italy
Treasures and Pleasures of Paris and the French Riviera
Treasures and Pleasures of Rio and São Paulo
Treasures and Pleasures of Singapore and Bali
Treasures and Pleasures of Singapore and Malaysia
Treasures and Pleasures of Thailand

BUSINESS AND CAREER BOOKS AND SOFTWARE
101 Dynamite Answers to Interview Questions
101 Secrets of Highly Effective Speakers
201 Dynamite Job Search Letters
Best Jobs For the 21st Century
Change Your Job, Change Your Life
The Complete Guide to International Jobs and Careers
The Complete Guide to Public Employment
The Directory of Federal Jobs and Employers
Discover the Best Jobs For You!
Dynamite Cover Letters
Dynamite Networking For Dynamite Jobs
Dynamite Resumes
Dynamite Salary Negotiations
Dynamite Tele-Search
The Educator's Guide to Alternative Jobs and Careers
Find a Federal Job Fast!
From Air Force Blue to Corporate Gray
From Army Green to Corporate Gray
From Navy Blue to Corporate Gray
Get a Raise in Seven Days
High Impact Resumes and Letters
Interview For Success
Job-Power Source CD-ROM
Jobs and Careers With Nonprofit Organizations
Moving Out of Education
Moving Out of Government
Re-Careering in Turbulent Times
Resumes & Job Search Letters For Transitioning Military Personnel
Savvy Interviewing
Savvy Networker
Savvy Resume Writer
Ultimate Job Source CD-ROM

THE TREASURES AND PLEASURES OF

Singapore and Bali

BEST OF THE BEST

RON AND CARYL KRANNICH, PH.DS

IMPACT PUBLICATIONS
MANASSAS PARK, VA

Cover photo: "Breakfast With the Orangutan," Courtesy of the Singapore Tourism Board.

Library of Congress Cataloging-in-Publication Data

Krannich, Ronald L.
    The treasures and pleasures of Singapore and Bali: best of the best / Ron and Caryl Krannich.
        p. cm.—(Impact guides)
    Includes bibliographical references and index.
    ISBN 1-57023-133-8 (alk. paper)
        I. Shopping—Singapore—Guidebooks. 2. Shopping—Indonesia—Bali (Province)—Guidebooks. 3. Singapore—Guidebooks. 4. Bali (Indonesia: Province)—Guidebooks.
I. Krannich, Caryl Rae. II. Title. III. Series.

TX337.S55 K72   2000
380.1'45'0095957—dc21   00-023076

Publisher: For information, including current and forthcoming publications, authors, press kits, and submission guidelines, visit Impact's Web site: *www.impactpublications.com*

Publicity/Rights: For information on publicity, author interviews, and subsidiary rights, contact the Public Relations and Marketing Department: Tel. 703/361-7300 or Fax 703/335-9486.

Sales/Distribution: For information on distribution or quantity discount rates, call (703/361-7300), fax (703/335-9486), e-mail (*singapore@impactpublications.com*) or write: Sales Department, Impact Publications, 9104 Manassas Drive, Suite N, Manassas Park, VA 20111. Bookstore orders should be directed to our trade distributor: National Book Network, 15200 NBN Way, Blue Ridge Summit, PA 17214, Tel. 1-800-462-6420.

Contents

PART II
Acquiring Treasures With Ease

CHAPTER 3
Shopping Rules and Bargaining Skills 35

PART III
Surprising Singapore

CHAPTER 4
Singapore 57

PART IV
Exotic Bali

Liabilities and Warranties

WHILE THE AUTHORS HAVE ATTEMPTED TO provide accurate and up-to-date information in this book, please be advised that names, addresses, and phone numbers do change and shops, restaurants, and hotels do move, go out of business, or change ownership and management. Such changes are a constant fact of life in ever-changing Singapore and Bali. We regret any inconvenience such changes may cause to your travel and shopping adventure.

Inclusion of shops, restaurants, hotels, and other hospitality providers in this book in no way implies guarantees nor endorsements by either the authors or publisher. The information and recommendations appearing in this book are provided solely for your reference. The honesty and reliability of shops can best be ensured by **you**—always ask the right questions and request proper receipts and documents. Chapters 2 and 3 provide insights on how to best do this in Singapore and Bali.

The Treasures and Pleasures of Singapore and Bali provides numerous tips on how you can best experience a trouble-free adventure. As in any unfamiliar place or situation, or regardless of how trusting strangers may appear, the watch-words are always the same—*"watch your wallet!"* If it's too good to be true, it probably is. Any *"unbelievable deals"* should be treated as such. In Singapore and Bali there simply is no such thing as a free lunch. Everything has a cost. Just make sure you don't pay dearly by making unnecessary shopping mistakes.

Preface

WELCOME TO ANOTHER IMPACT GUIDE ON the treasures and pleasures of shopping and traveling to two very special places—Singapore and Bali. Join us as we explore these two fascinating islands from a very different perspective than what is normally found in other travel guidebooks or, for that matter, in any other book written on Singapore and Bali.

Have you ever wanted to escape to a unique tropical island of sand, surf, sun, and shopping? Better still, would you love to visit two fabulous islands that also offer some of the world's best hotels, resorts, and restaurants?

Welcome to surprising Singapore and seductive Bali, two of the world's most exciting travel and shopping destinations, where paradise is both lost and found. If you've never visited these islands, you're in for a real treat. Singapore, like Hong Kong, is all about making and spending money. High-rise, sanitized, orderly, and efficient, this city is one huge shopping and gastronomic center. You can easily "shop 'til you drop" in Singapore's many shopping malls, hotel shopping arcades, department stores, and markets. Bali, on the other hand, seems a world apart with its distinctive culture, beautiful tropical setting, and fascinating people. In Bali, life tends to imitate art in many different ways, including its richly rewarding shopping culture. Shopping in Bali is both fun and rewarding as you discover wonderful arts, crafts, antiques, furniture, jewelry, and textiles. If you're like many other visitors to Bali, you'll fall in love with this intriguing place . . . and want to return again and again to explore its many treasures and pleasures.

If you are familiar with our other Impact Guides, you know our books are very different from most guidebooks. We operate from a particular perspective and we frequently show our attitude rather than just present you with "the travel facts." We're not budget travelers who are interested in taking you along the low road to Singapore and Bali; we don't find that to be an attractive road nor particularly enlightening. We've been there, done that. If that's the way you want to go, you'll find lots of great guidebooks on budget travel to these two islands. At the same time, we're not big on immersing ourselves in local history and taking in lots of sightseeing. We get just enough history and sightseeing to make our travels interesting rather than obsessive. And we're not preoccupied with hotels, restaurants, cultural shows, and other forms of entertainment.

What we really enjoy doing, and think we do it well, is shop. Indeed, we're street people who love "the chase" and the serendipity that comes with our style of travel. We especially enjoy discovering quality products; meeting local artists and craftspeople; unraveling new travel and shopping rules; making new friendships with local business people; staying in fine places; and dining in the best restaurants where we often meet the talented chefs and visit their fascinating kitchens.

Like Winston Churchill and many other focused travelers, our travel philosophy is very simple: *"My needs are very simple—I simply want the best of everything."* When we travel, we seek out the best of the best—just like we often do back home. In the cases of Singapore and Bali, we want to discover the works of the best artists, craftspeople, and jewelers. In so doing, we learn a great deal about Singapore and Bali and their talented populations. For us, shopping makes for great travel adventure.

The chapters that follow represent a particular perspective on travel to Singapore and Bali. We purposefully decided to write more than just another travel guide with a few pages on shopping. While other books briefly examine the "whats" and "wheres" of shopping, we saw a need to also explain the "how-tos" of shopping in Singapore and Bali. Such a book would both educate and guide you through these islands' slippery shopping maze as well as put you in contact with the best of the best in accommodations, restaurants, and sightseeing. Accordingly, this book focuses primarily on the shopping **process** as well as provides the necessary details for making excellent shopping **choices** in specific shopping areas, arcades, shops, and markets.

Rather than just describe the "what" and "where" of travel and shopping, we include the critical "how"—what to do before you depart on your trip and when you are in Singapore and Bali. We believe you are best served with a book which leads to both **understanding and action**. Therefore, you'll find little in these pages about the history, culture, economics, and politics of Singapore and Bali; these topics are covered well in other types of books. Instead, we focus on the whole shopping process in reference to these islands' major shopping strengths.

The perspective we develop throughout this book is based on our belief that traveling should be more than just another adventure in eating, sleeping, sightseeing, and taking pictures of unfamiliar places. Whenever possible, we attempt to bring to life the fact that Singapore and Bali have real people and interesting products that you, the visitor, will find exciting. These are countries of talented designers, craftspeople, traders, and entrepreneurs who offer you some wonderful opportunities to participate in their society through their shopping process. When you leave Singapore and Bali, you will take with you not only some unique experiences and memories but also quality products that you will certainly appreciate for years to come.

Our focus on **the shopping process** is important for several reasons. The most important one is the fact that few travelers are prepared for different shopping cultures. Shops may be filled with familiar looking goods, but when there are no price tags on items, the process of acquiring them can be difficult if you do not understand such basic processes as bargaining, communicating, and shipping. What, for example, should you do when you find a lovely painting, antique, or piece of jewelry but no price tag is displayed? How do you know you are paying a "fair" price? More importantly, how do you know you are getting exactly what you bargained for in terms of quality and authenticity? And if you buy large items, how will you get them back home? These "how" questions go beyond the basic "what" and "where" of shopping to ensure that you have a successful and rewarding trip to Singapore and Bali.

We have not hesitated to make qualitative judgments about the best of the best in Singapore and Bali. If we just presented you with shopping and traveling information, we would do you a disservice by not sharing our discoveries, both good and bad. While we know that our judgments may not be valid for everyone, we offer them as **reference points** from which you can make your own decisions. Our major emphasis is on quality shopping, accommodations, dining, and sightseeing, and in that order. We look for shops which offer excellent quality and styles. If you share our concern for quality shopping, as well as fine restaurants and hotels, you will find many of our recommendations useful to your two-island adventure.

Buying items of quality does not mean you must spend a great deal of money on shopping. It means that you have taste, you are selective, you buy what fits into your wardrobe and home. If you shop in the right places, you will find quality products. If you understand the shopping process, you will get good value for your money. Shopping for quality may not be cheap but neither need it be expensive. But most important, shopping for quality in Singapore and Bali is fun and it results in lovely items which can be enjoyed for years to come!

Throughout this book we have included "tried and tested" shopping information. We make judgments based upon our experience—not on judgments or sales pitches from others. Our research was quite simple: we did a great deal of shopping and we looked for quality products. We acquired some fabulous items, and gained valuable knowledge in the process. However, we could not make purchases in every shop nor do we have any guarantee that your experiences will be the same as ours. Shops close, ownership or management changes, and the shop you visit may not be the same as the one we shopped. So use this information as a starting point, but ask questions and make your own judgments before you buy.

We wish to thank the many public relations managers and concierges who shared their insights into travel and shopping in Singapore and Bali as well as Northwest Airlines who took us safely to and from Singapore in exceptional comfort and with excellent service.

We wish you well with your Singapore and Bali adventure. The book is designed to be used prior to and during your stay on these two islands. If you **plan your journey** according to Chapter 2, **handle the shopping process** according to Chapter 3, and **navigate the streets** of Singapore and Bali based on our tips in Chapters 4 and 5, you should have a marvelous time. You'll discover some exciting places, acquire some choice items, and return home with many fond memories. If you put this book to use, it should become one of your best travel friends— the ultimate passport to the unique treasures and pleasures of Singapore and Bali!

Ron and Caryl Krannich

THE TREASURES AND PLEASURES
OF SINGAPORE AND BALI

Welcome to Fabulous Singapore and Bali

WELCOME TO TWO OF THE WORLD'S BEST kept shopping and traveling secrets. Situated in the heart of Southeast Asia, these two small but vibrant islands are jam-packed with a dazzling array of exciting shopping treasures and travel pleasures. You can easily shop 'til you drop, but you'll want to do a lot more than just shop these islands.

Located only two hours from each other by air, Singapore and Bali at times seem worlds apart given their geographic, cultural, ethnic, economic, and political differences. But on closer examination, these are two complimentary places that make a perfect travel combination for those who enjoy high density shopping, dining, sightseeing, beaches, sailing, culture, entertainment, fine hotels and resorts, and exotic sights and sounds.

As many seasoned travelers to Southeast Asia learned long ago, shopping and traveling don't get much better than in Singapore and Bali. Whether you want to experience a stimulating adventure or just get away from a stressful world by escaping anonymously to some tranquil tropical paradise, both places seem to have it all. For shoppers, Singapore and Bali offer a motherload of exciting products and many unique shopping adventures involving interesting shopkeepers, artists, and craftspeople. Here you can shop for exquisite jewelry, antiques, furniture, handicrafts, tribal artifacts, fashionable clothes, electronic gadgetry, and souvenirs. If you are a collector, home decorator, souvenir hunter, fashion lover, or high-tech buyer, you can easily spend days and weeks exploring Singapore's and Bali's many shopping centers, department stores, hotel shopping arcades, shophouses, markets, and warehouses—and still not cover it all.

But there's a lot more to these places than just shopping treasures. As you'll see in the following chapters, both Singapore and Bali are great travel adventures offering a wide range of things to see and do. High rise, high tech, and high energy Singapore is a traveler's smorgesboard where you can arm yourself with maps, brochures, subway tickets, and a proactive list of "101 Things to Do" within three days! Bali is wonderfully exotic and chaotic, a place that captivates visitors with its art, culture, people, natural beauty, and street-level drama. In serendipitous and seductive Bali you can easily wile away a couple of weeks, indeed many months, doing whatever seems to come your way. Singapore and Bali are perfect places to experience exotic cultures, meet interesting and accommodating people, and shamelessly pamper yourself. Spend a week or two exploring the treasures and pleasures of these two places and you may think you've discovered paradise. You'll most likely want to come back for more!

EXOTIC WORLDS OF WONDERS

Best of all, Singapore and Bali are convenient, comfortable, and intriguing places to visit. **Singapore** is all about convenience, order, money, and shopping, and to a much lesser degree about celebrating history and culture. Focusing primarily on the future rather than being captivated and hobbled by its past, Singapore loves "infrastructure," both physical and electronic. Be it airports, roads, subways, ATMs, fast food, parks, hotels, convention facilities, computers, or the Internet, the infrastructure here works with incredible efficiency. Not surprisingly, its tourism has a decided "eat, drink, and be merry" entertainment character which at times contrasts sharply with its neighboring countries. Singapore is one of those unique cutting-edge societies that rightfully views itself as a world leader in manufacturing, technology, and finance which spills over to its tourism; it likes to be the very best by doing everything right, the Singapore way, including being wired for the 21st century via the Internet. Just visit the Singapore Tourism Board's Web site, and you'll see what the "being wired" and "doing it right" ethic is all about: *www.travel.com.sg* or *www.newasia-singapore.com*.

Above all, like its counterpart Hong Kong, Singapore is Southeast Asia's enviable economic powerhouse. Energetic and modern, it works hard at what it does best—create a convenient city-state for making lots of money. In Singapore, hotels, restaurants, and transportation are simply outstanding. Standards of health and cleanliness are some of the best in the world. Most people speak English, and they are friendly, helpful, delightful, and interesting to meet. This is a highly educated, talented, and innovative country that welcomes appropriate imports from everywhere, including Borders Bookstore and its attendant sidewalk cappuccino culture. If nothing else, Singapore simply looks and feels good. You can shop, eat, and disco 'til you drop. It has a lot to offer visitors.

Bali is a contrast in many ways. It's not neat, tidy, and antiseptic nor is it into "being wired" or "doing it right," although it is beginning to link itself to the rest of the world via the Internet: *www.bali-paradise.com* and *www.balitravelforum.com*. While things don't work as well as in Singapore, Bali has its own strengths and charms that will touch you forever. Here you'll discover some of the world's most fabulous resorts and immerse yourself in a truly unique and exotic culture associated with a totally integrated Hindu society. Challenging at times, you should have few problems getting around with English. One of nearly 14,000 Indonesian islands, Bali shares much of Indonesia's crowded, chaotic, and worn Third World character while offering Indonesia's best tourist infrastructure and facilities. While Bali lacks the variety of tourist sites, shopping venues, fine food, and restaurants found in Singapore, and its sanitation and transportation standards and other convenience factors are less than stellar, it more than makes up for these deficits in terms of its unique people, culture, beauty, and atmosphere. In the end, you may find less familiar and convenient Third World Bali more intriguing and fun than orderly and antiseptic Singapore. Seductive Bali is the type of adventure many travelers love to encounter; some become so captivated with this place that they stay for months and years.

CONTRASTING ADVENTURES

When you visit Singapore and Bali, you encounter a variety of fascinating communities, from vibrant cities to tranquil villages. Each offers delightful treasures and pleasures for those who know what, where, and how of navigating these unique islands. Each also offers many contrasting adventures.

Singapore is known for many things. Above all, it's one of the world's great shopping paradises. Stroll down Orchard Road, the city's "Golden Mile," and you will quickly discover why so many people come here to indulge their shopping and gastronomic fancies. This is a city of outstanding hotels, restaurants, and miles and miles of shopping centers, department stores, supermarkets, shophouses, and market complexes selling an infinite variety of fashionwear, jewelry, electronics, antiques, handicrafts, and home decorative items. In one moment you can be shopping in an ultra modern shopping center with hundreds of exclusive shops and the next moment—just a few blocks down the street—bargaining for antiques, handicrafts, gems, and fabrics in the shophouses of Singapore's traditional ethnic enclaves of Chinatown, Little India, and Arab Street. But shopping doesn't stop in the highly touristed areas of downtown Singapore. There's even more shopping in the many suburban areas frequented by local residents—the Chinese, Malays, Indians, and European and North American expatriates. When not shopping, Singapore has many interesting things to see and do that should entice you to stay here for more than the average three days. It's especially noted for its wonderful international cuisines and restaurants as well as numerous entertaining museums, parks, gardens, temples, theme attractions, landmarks, monuments, and island excursions.

Bali also is a shopper's paradise but of a different kind and character. It's a complete social and cultural experience. An island of charming chaos, it lacks the hectic and high rise character of Singapore. Don't expect to find in Bali air-conditioned shopping malls filled with imported fashionwear, electronics, and jewelry sold at fixed retail prices. And it's not a place that has a central shopping district. Shopping is dispersed throughout the island. Indeed, while you will find some good shopping in the capital city of Denpasar, the best shopping for visitors is found in small towns, villages, and resort communities, such as Kuta, Legian, Ubud, Batubulan, Mas, Celuk, Sanur, and Jimbaran Bay. These towns and villages, each with their own unique character, are lined with shops, factories, and warehouses that are filled with a large variety of hand-crafted items—from carvings and paintings to stone sculptures and furniture—produced by local artisans. Shops at the major hotels offer some of the best products from Bali as well as from other parts of Indonesia. While a few shops have fixed prices, most prices are subject to bargaining which can result in a 20 to 60 percent discount, depending on the shop and your bargaining skills. And prices tend to be excellent in Bali—a true bargain destination. While you can walk to most of the major shops in Singapore, in Bali you'll need to hire a car with driver to visit the various towns, villages, and resort communities. In Bali, shopping is truly a travel adventure that also is a personally rewarding experience. While you will meet numerous salaried retail clerks in Singapore, in Bali you'll often go directly to the production source where you will have an opportunity to buy directly from artists, craftspeople, and shop owners. For many visitors in Bali, shopping on this island is as much a cultural experience as it is an exercise in acquiring unique products. Bali is truly a shopping adventure that may forever enrich your life.

If you are like many visitors, you may quickly get bored with all of Singapore's comforts and conveniences. After five days of conquering perhaps 25 of the "101 Things to Do" in Singapore, you may feel it's time to move on to a more exotic and challenging place, such as Bali. While you'll initially marvel at Singapore's efficiency, you also may feel you've "been there, done that" because Singapore is so orderly and predictable, and many of the goods are expensive "duty free" imports from Europe. Indeed, Singapore can be expensive for everything from hotels and restaurants to shopping; you'll find few real bargains in Singapore.

Wherever you go in Singapore or Bali, you'll find plenty of special shopping opportunities as well as many travel pleasures associated with great hotels, restaurants, sightseeing, and entertainment. If you are like others who have preceded you, shopping on these two islands will seem both familiar and exotic. You should return home with a treasure-trove of purchases and many exciting memories.

FOCUS ON QUALITY AND VALUE

The Treasures and Pleasures of Singapore and Bali is a different kind of travel book for a very special type of traveler. It's designed to provide you with the necessary knowledge and skills to enjoy the many treasures and pleasures of these two fascinating destinations. Like other volumes in our Impact Guides series, we designed this book with three major considerations in mind:

- Learn a great deal about Singapore and Balinese society and culture by meeting their many talented artists, craftspeople, and shopkeepers and by exploring their many cities and towns.

- Do quality shopping for items having good value.

- Discover unique items that can be integrated into your home and/or wardrobe.

As you will quickly discover, this is not a book on how to find great bargains in inexpensive Singapore and Bali, although we do show you how to bargain as well as where and how to find bargains. Rather, this book primarily focuses on quality shopping for unique items. As such, we are less concerned with shopping in Singapore and Bali for imported goods or to save money and get great bargains than with shopping for unique local products that can be taken home, integrated with one's wardrobe and home, and appreciated for years to come. Rather than find a cheap tailor or purchase an inexpensive piece of jewelry or art, we prefer finding the best of what is available and selectively choose those items we both enjoy and can afford. Buying, for example, one finely tailored suit, a piece of exquisite jewelry, or a valuable artifact or work of art that can be nicely integrated into your wardrobe and home will last much longer and you will appreciate it for many more years to come than to purchase several cheap pieces of jewelry or tourist kitsch that quickly lose their value and your interest.

Our general shopping rule is this: A good buy is one that results in the exchange of money for something that has good value; when in doubt, go for quality because quality items will hold their value and you will enjoy them much more in the long run.

Indeed, some of our most prized possessions from shopping in exotic places are those we felt we could not afford at the time, but we purchased them nonetheless because we knew they were excellent quality items and thus they had great value. Our decisions to buy quality items in the long run were wise decisions because these items are things we still love today.

We have learned one other important lesson from shopping abroad: Good craftsmanship everywhere in the world is declining due to the increased cost of labor, lack of interest among young people in pursuing the traditional crafts, and erosion of traditional cultures. Therefore, any items that require extensive hand labor and traditional skilled craftsmen—such as ikat textiles, handcrafted jewelry, woodcarvings, paintings, furniture, and tribal artifacts in the case of Singapore and Bali—are outstanding values today because many of these items are quickly disappearing as fewer craftsmen are trained in producing quality arts and crafts. As elsewhere in the world, the general trend in Singapore and Bali is to move from producing high quality traditional arts and crafts to mass producing contemporary handicrafts for tourists and export markets as well as importing name brand goods from Italy, France, England, Japan, Korea, Taiwan, and the United States. Singapore has already made this transition to "modern" shopping in a big way; Bali is slowly moving in the same direction. Although many traditional handcrafted items may seem expensive, especially tribal artifacts and textiles, they are still good buys considering their labor content, workmanship, significance, and scarcity.

Throughout this book we attempt to identify the best quality shopping in both Singapore and Bali. This does not mean we have discovered the cheapest shopping or best bargains. Our search for unique shopping and quality items that retain their value in the long run means many of our recommended shops may initially appear expensive. But they offer top value that you will not find in many other shops. So, for example, when we take you through the art and antique shops of Singapore, we visit several of Singapore's finest quality shops—Tatiana, Tiepolo, Harvest Straits, and Mata-Hari in Tanglin Centre; Kwok Gallery in the Far Eastern Shopping Centre; and Tomlinson and Exotica in the Raffles Hotel Arcade. We also visit some of our favorite home decorative and furniture shops.

In Bali, we'll venture into the best shops and markets of Denpasar, Kuta, Legian, Batubulan, Celuk, Mas, and Ubud and the major hotels in Nusa Dua, Sanur, and Jimbaran Bay. We'll visit fabulous furniture and home decorative shops, jewelry stores, art galleries, textile emporiums, and arts and crafts markets. In Kuta and Legian, you'll discover the treasures of Warisan, Polos, Jonathan Gallery, and Anang's Place. In Ubud we'll explore the many shops that line Main Street and Monkey Forest Road, visit famous art galleries, and explore the unique treasures offered by Shalimar Gallery. We know these shops well because these are the places we have made some of our most important purchases. They offer both unique and quality items we will cherish for many years to come.

MUCH MORE THAN JUST SHOPPING

While the primary focus of this book is on quality shopping in Singapore and Bali, we also recognize the importance of integrating other aspects of quality travel with shopping. Indeed, what better way to shop than to also discover great hotels, restaurants, sites, and entertainment along the way?

Wherever possible, we include the best of the best in travel pleasures to accompany your search for shopping treasures. For over the years, with limited time and resources, we've discovered how important it is to experience the best a country has to offer its visitors. Consequently, we'll explore some of the world's greatest hotels in Singapore and Bali, especially the Four Seasons, Ritz-Carlton, and Raffles, along with some very good value accommodations for those who prefer spending money on less than stellar places. We'll take a gastronomic tour of both Singapore and Bali where we'll discover fine dining with terrific views along with some great hawker stalls and cooking schools.

As you'll quickly discover, this is not another budget guide to inexpensive Singapore and Bali where most of the pleasures of travel are free and where hotels and restaurants are decidedly low class. We want you to budget well so you'll have a great time discovering the best of the best in these two terrific destinations. We'll walk the streets, meet the people, try some cheap eats, and visit the sites. But we're also going to spend some money experiencing the best of the best in Singapore and Bali. Remember, you can always go back home and make more money. But chances are you won't be able to find that wonderful antique or unique piece of furniture, art, or jewelry you passed up because you wanted to "think about it" or it seemed too expensive at the time. It's probably gone forever, and went to someone who understood the value of buying quality now.

You may occasionally want to splurge on a fine restaurant as well as pamper yourself in a five-star hotel or resort. As you'll quickly see, we have nothing against such places! They are as much a cultural experience as a budget hotel or cheap restaurant, and without the arrogance that often accompanies budget travel. If you are like us, you'll want to experience the best of the best a country has to offer its visitors. To do less is to miss out on many of the great treasures and pleasures of travel.

APPROACHING THE SUBJECT

The chapters that follow take you into the best shops, hotels, restaurants, and sites in Singapore and Bali. In so doing, we've attempted to construct a complete user-friendly book that first focuses on the shopping process but also includes the best of Singapore's and Bali's many other treasures and pleasures, especially their many fine hotels and restaurants.

The chapters are organized like one would organize and implement a travel and shopping adventure to these two destinations. Each chapter incorporates sufficient details, including names and addresses, to get you started in some of the best shopping areas and shops in each city, town, or village.

Indexes and table of contents are especially important to us and others who believe a travel book is first and foremost a guide to unfamiliar places. Therefore, our index—a separate one for each destination—includes both subjects and shops, with shops printed in bold for ease of reference; the table of contents is elaborated in detail so it, too, can be used as another handy reference index for subjects and products. By using the table of contents and index together, you can access most any information from this book.

The remainder of this book is divided into three parts and four additional chapters which look at both the process and content of shopping in exotic Singapore and Bali. The next chapter in Part I—"Traveling Smart"—assists you in preparing for your Singapore and Bali shopping adventure by focusing on the how-to's of traveling and shopping in these two countries. Chapter 2, "Plan and Manage Your Adventure," examines how to best prepare for your trip to Singapore and Bali, including what best to pack as well as how to best manage your money, identify your shopping needs, and ship your purchases home with ease.

The chapter in Part II—"Acquiring Treasures With Ease" —focuses on basic skills and information one needs in order to be an effective shopper in Singapore and Bali. Chapter 3, "Shopping Rules and Bargaining Skills," prepares you for Singapore's and Bali's distinct shopping cultures where knowing important shopping rules, pricing practices, and bargaining strategies are keys to becoming an effective shopper.

Part III—"Surprising Singapore"—examines the how, what, and where of shopping and traveling in Singapore. Here you will discover Singapore's major shopping strengths and learn how and where to best shop for different products. This section also covers Singapore's major hotels, restaurants, sightseeing, and entertainment.

Part IV—"Exotic Bali"—focuses on the how, what, and where of shopping and traveling in Bali's major cities, towns, villages, and resort communities. This section also includes Bali's major hotels, restaurants, sightseeing, and entertainment.

RECOMMENDED SHOPS

We hesitate to recommend specific shops since we know some of the pitfalls of doing so. Shops that offered excellent products and service during one of our visits, for example, may change ownership, personnel, and policies from one year to another.

This is especially the case in Bali which has experienced a great deal of economic turmoil due to the recent collapse of the Indonesian economy. Many shops have gone bankrupt or are still struggling to survive; they may be eager to take your money but slow in delivering the goods! As we'll see in the section on Bali, shopping and shipping remain problematic in such a strained economic situation. In addition, our shopping preferences may not be the same as your preferences.

Our major concern is to outline your shopping options in Singapore and Bali, show you where to locate the best shopping areas, and share some useful shopping strategies that you can use anywhere in Singapore and Bali, regardless of particular shops we or others may recommend. Armed with this knowledge and some basic shopping skills, you will be better prepared to locate your own shops and determine which ones offer the best products and service in relation to your own shopping and travel goals.

However, we also recognize the "need to know" when shopping in unfamiliar places. Therefore, throughout this book we list the names and locations of various shops we have found to offer good quality products. In some cases we have purchased items in these shops and can also recommend them for service and reliability. But in most cases we surveyed shops to determine the quality of products offered without making purchases. To shop in all of these places would be beyond our budget, as well as our home storage capabilities! While we believe you should have the advantage of this information, we also caution you to always evaluate a business by asking the necessary questions to determine if it's right for you. Should you encounter any problem with these recommendations, we would appreciate hearing about it. We can be contacted as follows:

Ron and Caryl Krannich
IMPACT PUBLICATIONS
9104 Manassas Drive, Suite N
Manassas Park, VA 20111-5211 USA
Fax 703-335-9486
E-mail: *krannich@impactpublications.com*

While we cannot solve your problems, future editions of this book will reflect the experiences—both positive and negative—of our readers.

You also may want to stay in contact with the publisher's travel Web site:

www.ishoparoundtheworld.com

This comprehensive site is designed to complement the Impact Guides with numerous additional resources and advice. The site includes travel and shopping tips, updates, frequently asked questions, links to useful travel sites (airlines, hotels, restaurants, tourist offices, tour groups, maps, publications), recommended resources, a message board, and an online travel bookstore. If you have questions or comments, you may want to address them to us at this site.

Whatever you do, treat our names and addresses as **orientation points** from which to identify your own products and shops. If you rely solely on our listings, you will miss out on one of the great adventures of shopping in these places—discovering your own special shops that offer unique items and exceptional value and service.

EXPECT A REWARDING ADVENTURE

Whatever you do, enjoy Singapore and Bali. These are two very interesting destinations that are surprisingly easy and enjoyable to get around in—more so than many places in Europe. Better still, they offer unique items that can be purchased and integrated well into many western homes and wardrobes.

So arrange your flights and accommodations, pack your credit cards, ATM card, and traveler's checks, take your sense of humor, wear a smile, and head for two of Asia's most delightful destinations. Two to three weeks later you should return home with much more than a set of photos and travel brochures and a weight gain attendant with new eating habits. You will acquire some wonderful products and accumulate many interesting travel tales that can be enjoyed and relived for years to come.

Searching for treasures and pleasures on these two islands only takes time, money, and a sense of adventure. Take the time, be willing to part with some of your money, and open yourself to a whole new world of treasures and pleasures. You are about to encounter the best of what these countries have to offer international visitors. If you are like us, your shopping adventure will introduce you to an exciting world of quality products, friendly people, and interesting places that you might have otherwise missed had you just passed through these places to eat, sleep, see sights, and take pictures. When you combine shopping with traveling in Singapore and Bali, you learn a great deal about the people, products, and places that define Singapore's and Bali's many treasures and pleasures.

PART I

Traveling Smart

Plan and Manage Your Adventure

WHILE SINGAPORE AND BALI ARE RELATIVELY comfortable and convenient places to travel, they do require some basic pre-trip preparation if you plan to travel and shop these places properly. You will especially want to anticipate the most important aspects of any trip to this part of the world by budgeting overall costs, gathering information, checking on Customs regulations, managing your money, gathering essential shopping information, packing right, and anticipating shipping alternatives, arrangements, and potential problems.

PREPARATION

Preparation is the key to experiencing a successful and enjoyable shopping adventure in Singapore and Bali. But preparation involves much more than just examining maps, reading travel literature, and making airline and hotel reservations. Preparation, at the very least, is a process of minimizing uncertainty by learning how to develop a shopping plan, manage your money, determine the value of products, handle Customs, and pack for the occasion. It involves knowing what products are good deals to buy in Singapore and Bali in comparison to similar items back home. Most important of all, preparation helps organize and ensure the success of all aspects of a shopping adventure.

ANTICIPATE COSTS

Traveling and shopping in Singapore and Bali can be as inexpensive or expensive as you want them to be. You will find the cost of round-trip air transportation to be relatively inexpensive compared to costs 5 or 10 years ago or current costs of domestic airfares in the U.S. or international airfares from the U.S. to Europe. Indeed, Asia still has some of the most inexpensive airfares in the world. For example, you can fly round-trip from New York City to Singapore or Bali on major airlines for under US$1,000, and many excellent package tours will include 5 days of hotels and some ground arrangements for that same price!

Hotels, resorts, and local transportation in Bali and Singapore are also some of the best buys in the world. Bali, for example, is rated by many travel professionals as one of the best travel values with excellent buys on first-class and deluxe resorts. Indeed, you may want to upgrade your accommodations in both Bali and Singapore given their price advantages and excellent service and facilities. Budget accommodations for under US$50 a night in Bali are often surprisingly comfortable.

Singapore and Bali offer some wonderful cuisines, both local and international. Dining out in these two places can be very pleasant—and at times an exciting cultural experience—as well as relatively inexpensive. While many restaurants in Singapore are expensive, others also are good value. Bali offers very good value given favorable exchange rates between the U.S. dollar and the Indonesian rupiah. You can easily get by on US$15 a day for excellent local foods or splurge at fine Continental restaurants for under US$50 per person—restaurants that might cost more than US$120 per person in other major cities of the world.

Your major traveling costs will most likely be the cost of shopping for local products. Here, we cannot give you specific guidelines other than the general observation that you should take enough cash, personal checks, and traveler's checks, as well as sufficient credit limits on your credit cards, in anticipation of finding plenty of treasures on these two islands. If you prefer using ATMs when traveling, you'll find Singapore to be most convenient for using your card. If you are a serious collector of antiques, tribal artifacts, and jewelry, you may quickly find yourself in financial trouble given the large number of quality items you will probably want to buy in both Singapore and Bali!

DEVELOP AN ACTION PLAN

Time is money when traveling abroad. The better you plan and use your time, the more time you will have to enjoy your trip. If you want to use your time wisely and literally hit the ground running, you should plan a detailed, yet tentative, schedule for each day. Start by doing the following:

- Identify each city, town, and area you plan to visit.

- Block out the number of days and/or hours you plan to spend in each place.

- List those places you feel you "must visit" during your stay, including may of the "best of the best" shops we identify for both Singapore and Bali.

- Select accommodations that are conveniently located near the places you plan to visit.

- Leave extra time each day for unexpected discoveries and for rewarding yourself.

Keep this plan with you and periodically revise it in light of new and unexpected information.

WELCOME SERENDIPITY AND LUCK

Planning is fine, but don't overdo it and thus ruin your trip by accumulating a list of unfulfilled expectations. Both Singapore and Bali, but especially Bali, lend themselves to a very relaxed and open style of travel—basic planning with allowances for many unexpected discoveries. If you are an inquisitive traveler who asks questions, you'll probably receive many recommendations and discover many new shops—unexpected developments that take time and thus require altering well laid out plans. As seasoned travelers and shoppers quickly discover, planning needs to be adapted to certain realities which often become the major highlights of one's travel and shopping experiences. Good luck is a function of good planning: you place yourself in many different places to take advantage of new opportunities. You should be open to unexpected events which may well become the major highlights of your travel and shopping experiences.

If you want to have good luck, then plan to be in many different places to take advantage of new opportunities. Expect to alter your initial plans once you begin discovering new and unexpected realities. Serendipity—those chance occurrences that often evolve into memorable and rewarding experiences—frequently interferes with the best-laid travel and shopping plans. Welcome serendipity by altering your plans to accommodate the unexpected. You can do this by revising your plans each day as you go. A good time to summarize the day's events and accomplishments and plan tomorrow's schedule is just before you go to bed each night.

Keep in mind that your plan should be a means to an end—experiencing exciting travel and shopping—and not the end itself. If you plan well, you will surely experience good luck on the road to a successful trip!

CONDUCT RESEARCH AND NETWORK FOR INFORMATION

Do as much research as possible before you depart for your Singapore and Bali adventures. A good starting place is the Internet. You'll discover several gateway sites that lead to all types of travel information, including many useful chat groups that discuss the latest travel developments in these two places. You may want to start with these large travel gateway sites and then explore more specific sites for Singapore and Bali:

www.citynet.com	*www.yahoo.com*
www.mytravelguide.com	*www.travel-guide.com*
www.travel.com	*www.Travel-Library.com*
www.travelnotes.org	*www.vtravel.com*

We cover these and several hundred additional travel Web sites in our forthcoming companion volume, *Click and Easy Travel Planning on the Internet* (Impact Publications, 2000).

When you begin focusing specifically on Singapore, start with these two gateway sites:

www.newasia-singapore.com   *www.sg.com*

If you're interested in restaurants, you'll want to visit this entertaining site that reviews the best and the worst of dining out in Singapore: *www.makansutra.com*. For visitors from the United States, the Singapore Tourism Board maintains a separate tourist information site: *www.singapore-usa.com.*

In the case of Bali, explore the linkages and discussion found on these two useful sites:

www.bali-paradise.com   *www.balitravelforum.com*

We identify several additional Web sites in the chapters on Singapore and Bali.

If you're not using the Internet, you may want to write, call, or fax the Singapore Tourism Board (STP) for information. The STP (in North America, call 312-938-1888, 323-852-1901, 212-302-4861, or 416-363-8898), for example, puts together an excellent package of materials which outline the highlights of traveling and shopping in Singapore. Unfortunately, Indonesia does not provide comparable information on Bali.

We also recommend **networking for information and advice**. You'll find many people, including relatives, friends, and acquaintances, who have traveled to Singapore and Bali and who are eager to share their experiences and discoveries with you. They may recommend certain shops where you will find excellent products, service, and prices. Ask them basic who, what, where, why, and how questions:

- **Where** (cities) did you find the best shopping?
- **What** shops did you particularly like?
- **What** do they sell?
- **How** much discount could I expect?
- **Whom** should I talk to?
- **Where** is the shop located?
- **Is** bargaining expected?
- **Do** they pack and ship?

List serves, news groups, and travel discussion groups on the Internet can provide a great deal of useful information and advice. Explore these groups for starters:

Newsgroups: *www.deja.com*
                     www.digiserve.com

List Serves: *www.liszt.com*
                     www.egroups.com

Travel sites: *www.fodors.com*
                     www.lonelyplanet.com
                     www.ishoparoundtheworld.com
                     www.balitravelforum.com

Once you arrive in-country, be sure to gather information from local sources. In the case of Singapore, contact the Singapore Tourism Board office at the Raffles Hotel Arcade. In Bali, you will need to acquire local information at the airport or through your hotel concierge, fellow travelers, and travel agencies; the Indonesian government is not organized to provide such information to travelers.

CHECK CUSTOMS REGULATIONS

It's always good to know Customs regulations before leaving home. If you are a U.S. citizen planning to return to the U.S. from Singapore or Bali (Indonesia), the United States Customs Service provides several helpful publications which are available free of charge from your nearest U.S. Customs Office, or write P.O. Box 7407, Washington, DC 20044.

- *Know Before You Go* (Publication #512): outlines facts about exemptions, mailing gifts, duty-free articles, as well as prohibited and restricted articles.

- *Trademark Information For Travelers* (Publication #508): deals with unauthorized importation of trademarked goods. Since you will find some copies of trademarked items in Singapore and Indonesia, this publication will alert you to potential problems with Custom inspectors prior to returning home.

- *International Mail Imports* answers many questions regarding mailing items from foreign countries back to the US. The U.S. Postal Service sends all packages to Customs for examination and assessment of duty before they are delivered to the addressee. Some items are free of duty and some are dutiable. The rules have changed on mail imports, so do check on this before you leave the U.S.

- *GSP and the Traveler* itemizes goods from particular countries that can enter the U.S. duty-free. GSP regulations, which are designed to promote the economic development of certain Third World countries, permit many products, especially arts and handicrafts, to enter the United States duty-free, but only if GSP is currently in effect. If not, U.S. citizens will need to pay duty as well as complete a form that would refund the duties once GSP goes into effect again and is made retroactive—one of the

U.S. Congresses' annual budgetary rituals that is inconvenient to travelers and costly for taxpayers. Most items purchased in Bali are allowed to enter duty-free when GSP is operating. However, many items from Singapore will be dutiable since Singapore no longer enjoys full GSP status. In addition, most of Singapore's arts and artifacts are imported from other countries. Therefore, they are not necessarily exempt from duties since you are not buying in the countries of origin—a fine distinction Customs may make when enforcing the letter of the law. However, since ASEAN (Association of Southeast Asian Nations) countries are treated as one country by U.S. Customs, many items originating in Thailand, Malaysia, Indonesia, or the Philippines but purchased in Singapore may enter the U.S. duty-free.

MANAGE YOUR MONEY WELL

It is best to carry traveler's checks, two or more major credit cards with sufficient credit limits, U.S. dollars, and a few personal checks. Our basic money rule is to take enough money and sufficient credit limits so you don't run short. How much you take is entirely up to you, but it's better to have too much than not enough when shopping in Singapore and Bali.

We increasingly find **credit cards** to be very convenient when traveling in Asia. We prefer using credit cards to pay for hotels and restaurants and for major purchases as well as for unanticipated expenses incurred when shopping. Most major hotels and stores honor American Express, MasterCard, Visa, and Diner's cards. It is a good idea to take one or two bank cards and an American Express card. You may also want to take your ATM card which is readily accepted in Singapore and to a lesser extent in Bali, although beware of transaction fees.

Take plenty of **traveler's checks** in U.S. denominations of $50 and $100. Smaller denominations may seem expensive to cash after a transaction fee is deducted. If you only need to change ten or twenty dollars, it is often cheaper to change cash than traveler's checks. Most major banks, hotels, restaurants, and shops accept traveler's checks, although some do add a small service charge. Money-changers and banks will give the best exchange rates, but at times you'll find hotels to be more convenient because of their close proximity and better hours.

Personal checks can be used to obtain traveler's checks with an American Express card or to pay for goods to be shipped later—after the check clears your bank. Consider keeping one personal check aside to pay Customs should you have dutiable goods when you return home.

Use your own judgment concerning how much **cash** you should carry with you. Contrary to some fearful ads, cash is awfully nice to have in moderate amounts to supplement your traveler's checks and credit cards. But of course you must be very careful where and how you carry cash. Consider carrying an "emergency cash reserve" primarily in $50 and $100 denominations, but also a few 20's for small exchanges.

USE CREDIT CARDS WISELY

Credit cards can be a shopper's blessing. They are your tickets to serendipity, convenience, good exchange rates, and a useful form of insurance. Widely accepted throughout Asia, they enable you to draw on credit reserves for purchasing many wonderful items you did not anticipate finding when you initially planned your adventure. In addition to being convenient, you usually will get good exchange rates once the local currency amount appearing on your credit slip is converted by the bank at the official rate into your home currency. Credit cards also allow you to float your expenses into the following month or two without paying interest charges. Most important of all, should you have a problem with a purchase—such as buying a piece of jewelry which you later discover was misrepresented or has fake stones, or electronic goods which are incompatible with your systems back home—your credit card company **may** assist you in recovering your money and returning the goods. Once you discover your problem, contact the credit card company with your complaint and refuse to pay the amount while the matter is in dispute. Businesses accepting these cards must maintain a certain standard of honesty and integrity. In this sense, credit cards may be an excellent and inexpensive form of insurance against possible fraud and damaged goods when shopping abroad. If you rely only on cash or traveler's checks, you have no such institutional recourse for recovering your money.

❑ Use credit cards to pay for hotels and restaurants and for major purchases.

❑ Carry one to two bank cards and an American Express card.

❑ Consider requesting a higher credit limit on your cards.

❑ Keep one personal check aside to pay Customs should you have dutiable goods when you return home.

❑ Carry an "emergency cash reserve" primarily in $50 and $100 denominations.

❑ Keep a good record of all charges in local currency— and at official exchange rates.

The down-side to using credit cards is that some businesses will charge you a "commission" for using your card, or simply not go as low in the bargaining process as they would for cash or traveler's checks. Commissions will range from 2 to 6 percent. This practice is discouraged by credit card companies; nonetheless, shops in both Singapore and Bali do this because they must pay a 4-5 percent commission to the credit card companies. They merely pass this charge on to you. When bargaining, keep in mind that shopkeepers usually consider a final bargained price to be a "cash only" price. If you wish to use your credit card at this point, you will probably be assessed the additional 2 to 6 percent to cover the credit card commission or lose your bargained price altogether. Frequently in the bargaining process, when you near the seller's low price, you will be asked whether you intend to pay cash. It is at this point that cash and traveler's checks come in handy to avoid a slightly higher price. However, **don't be "penny wise but pound foolish."** You may still want to use your credit card if you suspect you might have any problems with your purchase.

A few other tips on the use and abuse of credit cards may be useful in planning your trip. **Use your credit cards for the things that will cost you the same amount no matter how you pay,** such as lodging and meals in the better hotels and restaurants or purchases in most department stores. Consider requesting a higher credit limit on your bank cards if you think you may wish to charge more than your current limit allows.

Be extremely careful with your credit cards. Be sure merchants write the correct amount and indicate clearly whether this is U.S. dollars, Singapore dollars, or Indonesia rupiah on the credit card slip you sign. It is always a good practice to write the local currency symbol before the total amount so that additional figures cannot be added or the amount mistaken for your own currency. For example, 167 Singapore dollars are roughly equivalent to 100 U.S. dollars. It should appear as "S$167" on your credit card slip. And keep a good record of all charges in local currency—and at official exchange rates—so you don't have any surprises once you return home!

SECURE YOUR VALUABLES

Singapore and Bali are relatively safe places to travel if you take the normal precautions of not inviting potential trouble. We have never had a problem with thieves or pickpockets but neither have we encouraged such individuals to meet us. If you take a few basic precautions in securing your valuables, you should have a worry-free trip.

Be sure to keep your traveler's checks, credit cards, and cash in a safe place along with your travel documents and other valuables. While money belts do provide good security for valuables, the typical 4" x 8" nylon belts can be uncomfortable in Singapore's and Bali's hot and humid weather. Our best advice is for women to carry money and documents in a leather shoulder bag that can be held firmly and which should be kept with you at all times, however inconvenient, even when passing through buffet lines. Choose a purse with a strap long enough to sling around your neck bandolier style. Purse snatching is not a common occurrence in Singapore and Bali, but it is best to err on the side of caution than to leave yourself open to problems that could quickly ruin your vacation.

For men, keep your money and credit cards in your wallet, but always carry your wallet in a front pocket. If you keep it in a rear pocket, as you may do at home, you invite pickpockets to demonstrate their varied talents in relieving you of your money, and possibly venting your trousers in the process. If your front pocket is an uncomfortable location, you probably need to clean out your wallet so it will fit better.

You may also want to use the free hotel safety deposit boxes for your cash and other valuables. If one is not provided in your room, ask the cashier to assign you a private box in their vault. Remember, most hotels assume no responsibility for thefts from in-room safes. Under no circumstances should you leave your money and valuables unattended in your room, at restaurant tables, or in dressing rooms. You may want to leave expensive jewelry at home so as not to be as likely a target of theft.

If you get robbed, chances are it will be in part your own fault, because you invited someone to take advantage by not being more cautious in securing your valuables.

TAKE ALL NECESSARY SHOPPING INFORMATION

We recommend that you take more than just a copy of this book to Singapore and Bali. At the very least you should take:

- A prioritized "wish list" of items you think would make nice additions to your wardrobe, home decor, collections, and for gift giving.

- Measurements of floor space, walls, tables, and beds in your home in anticipation of purchasing some lovely home furnishings, tablecloths, bedspreads, or pictures. Both Singapore and Bali are great places to acquire both antique and reproduction furniture.

- Photographs of particular rooms that could become candidates for home decorative items. These come in handy when you find something you think—but are not sure—may fit into your colors schemes, furnishings, and decorating patterns.

- Take an inventory of your closets and identify particular colors, fabrics, and designs you wish to acquire to complement and enlarge your present wardrobe.

- If you think you will have tailoring work done, be sure to take pictures or models of garments you wish to have made. If you have a favorite blouse or suit you wish to have copied, take it with you. It is not necessary to take a commercial pattern, because Asian tailors do not use these devices for measuring, cutting, and assembling clothes.

DO COMPARATIVE SHOPPING

You should also do comparative shopping before arriving in Singapore and Bali. This is particularly important in the case of cameras, computers, and electronic goods as well as designer label clothes and accessories found in Singapore which are readily available elsewhere in the world. Based on your comparative shopping, you may discover many so-called duty-free items are actually higher than the same products available back home. You'll never know unless you have done your homework. However, items found in Bali do not easily lend themselves to international comparative shopping because of the unique nature of each item; once in Bali, the only comparisons you can make are between shops on the island.

If you are a true comparative shopper, you should first make a list of what you want to buy and then do some "window" shopping by visiting local stores, examining catalogs, checking Internet shopping sites, and telephoning for price and availability information. If, for example, your list includes cameras or electronic equipment, you should compile a list of prices for comparable items found in stores, discount houses, and Web sites back home. In the U.S., call the toll-free numbers of mail-order discount houses in New York City for phone quotes on cameras, film, computers, and electronic equipment as well as check out the many highly competitive online shopping sites (many offer products at or below cost!). Start by comparing items and prices on several major Web sites, such as *www.buy. com, www.valueamerica.com*, and *www.amazon.com*. The Sunday and Wednesday editions of The New York Times include ads from these highly competitive firms. You will quickly discover their prices may be 10-30 percent cheaper than the best price you can find in your local discount houses. Some of these New York firms, especially 47th Street Photo and Bi-Rite, will even bargain over the phone when you inform them of a competitor's better price! You also will discover that most imported camera and electronic equipment purchased through these mail-order and Internet sources are 20 to 40 percent cheaper than in Singapore; they also come with international guarantees. So be sure to do your pricing research **before** you buy such items in Singapore. There's nothing worse to deflate your shopping enthusiasm than to return home with what appeared to be a terrific Singapore buy and then discover you could have gotten the same item for much less over the Internet or through a mail-order catalog. Indeed, you'll quickly discover such items are not good buys in Singapore, despite their so-called "duty free" status. Singapore shops simply can't compete with large U.S. warehouse operations, catalog discounters, and aggressive Web sites that sell at or below cost in their pursuit of market share.

Jewelry is another item that begs comparative shopping and some minimal level of expertise in determining authenticity and quality. Read as much as you can on different qualities of jewelry and visit jewelry stores at home where you can learn a great deal by asking salespeople questions about craftsmanship, settings, quality, and discounts.

KEEP TRACK OF ALL RECEIPTS

Be sure to ask for receipts and keep them in a safe place. You will need them later for providing accurate pricing information on your Customs declaration form. Take a large envelope to be used only for depositing receipts. Organize it periodically by country and type of items purchased. List on a separate sheet of paper for each country what, where, and how much for each purchased item. When you go through Customs with your purchases organized in this manner, you should sail through more quickly since you have good records of all your transactions.

Pack Right and Light

Packing and unpacking are two great travel challenges. Trying to get everything you think you need into one or two bags can be frustrating. You either take too much with you, and thus transport unnecessary weight around the world, or you find you took too little.

We've learned over the years to err on the side of taking too little with us. If we start with less, we will have room for more. Your goal should be to avoid lugging an extensive wardrobe, cosmetics, library, and household goods around the world! Make this your guiding principle for deciding how and what to pack: *"When in doubt, leave it out."*

Above all, you want to return home loaded down with wonderful new purchases without paying extra weight charges. Hence, pack for the future rather than load yourself down with the past. To do this you need to wisely select the proper mix of colors, fabrics, styles, and accessories.

You should initially pack as lightly as possible. Remember, Singapore's and Bali's climates are hot and humid. Take only light-weight clothes made of natural fibers. Avoid any garments made of polyester or wool. Since dress in these countries is very casual—at best "smart casual"—you need not take suits and coats. The very top restaurants have dress codes, but they are very casual by Western standards: a coat and tie or a long-sleeve batik shirt for men and a dress or skirt and blouse for women. Plan to buy and wear additional clothes as you go, such as batik shirts, blouses, and skirts.

Items you are likely to pack but are also readily and inexpensively available in Singapore and Bali include clothes, suitcases, bags, maps, stationery, and CDs. Consequently, you may want to limit the number of such items you take with you since you can always buy more along the way. But do take all the shoes, specific medications, and makeup you will need on the trip. These items may be difficult to find in the brands you desire.

Since you will do a great deal of walking in Singapore and Bali, we recommend taking at least one pair of comfortable walking shoes and one pair of dress shoes. Break these shoes in before you take them on this trip. Wearing new shoes for lengthy periods of time can become quite uncomfortable.

Choose Sensible Luggage

Whatever you do, avoid being a slave to your luggage. Luggage should be both **expandable and expendable**. Flexibility is the key to making it work. Get ready to pack and re-pack, acquire new bags along the way, and replace luggage if necessary.

Your choice of luggage is very important for enjoying your shopping experience and for managing airports and airplanes. While you may normally travel with two suitcases and a carry-on, your specific choice of luggage for shopping purposes may be different. We recommend taking two large suitcases with wheels—perfect if one fits into another; one large carry-on bag; one nylon backpack; and one collapsible nylon bag.

If you decide to take hard-sided luggage, make sure it has no middle divider. With no divider you can pack some of your bulkier purchases. This type of luggage may appear safer than soft-sided luggage, but it is heavier, limited in space, and not necessarily more secure. A good soft-sided piece should be adequately reinforced.

Your **carry-on bag** should be convenient—lightweight and with separate compartments and pockets—for taking short trips outside Singapore and within Bali. For example, if you plan to make short trips to Malaysia or other parts of Indonesia, such as Lombok or Jokjakarta, you may want to leave most of your luggage at your hotel in Singapore or Bali and travel only with the carry-on bag.

We also recommend taking a small nylon **backpack** in lieu of a camera bag. This is a wonderfully convenient bag, because it can be used as a comfortable shoulder bag as well as a backpack. It can hold cameras, film, travel books, wind-breakers, umbrella, drinks and snacks and still have room for carrying small purchases. When you find your hands filled with purchases, your backpack can go on your back so your hands are free for other items.

> ❑ Take at least one pair of comfortable walking shoes.
>
> ❑ We recommend taking two large suitcases with wheels.
>
> ❑ Your carry-on bag should be convenient for taking short trips outside major cities.

A collapsible **nylon bag** also is a useful item to pack. Many of these bags fold into a small 6" x 8" zippered pouch. You may wish to keep this bag in your backpack or carry-on bag for use when shopping.

Ship With Ease

One of the worst nightmares of shopping abroad is to return home after a wonderful time to find your goods have been lost, stolen, or damaged in transit. This happens frequently to people who do not know how to ensure against such problems. Failing to pack properly or pick the right shipper, they suffer accordingly. This should not happen to you in Singapore or Bali.

On the other hand, you should not pass up buying lovely items because you feel reluctant to ship them home. Indeed, some travelers only buy items that will fit into their suitcase because they are reluctant to ship larger items home. But you can easily ship from Singapore and Bali and expect to receive your goods in excellent condition within a few weeks. We seldom let shipping considerations affect our buying decisions. We know we can always get our purchases home with little difficulty. For us, **shipping is one of those things that must be arranged**. We have numerous alternatives from which to choose, from hiring a professional shipping company to hand carrying our goods on board the plane. Shipping may or may not be costly, depending on how much you plan to ship and by which means. It is seldom a hassle in Singapore and Bali.

Before leaving home, you should identify the best point of entry for goods returning home by air or sea. Be prepared to specify the "Port of Entry." For example, in Virginia our port of entry can be Baltimore, Norfolk, or Richmond. We usually specify Baltimore. Once you are in Singapore and Bali, you generally have five alternatives for shipping goods home:

- Take everything with you.

- Do your own packing and shipping through the local post office (for small packages only).

- Have each shop ship your purchases.

- Arrange to have one shop consolidate all of your purchases into a single shipment.

- Hire a local shipper to make all shipping arrangements.

Taking everything with you is fine if you don't have much and you don't mind absorbing excess baggage charges. If you are overweight, ask about the difference between "Excess Baggage" and "Unaccompanied Baggage." Excess baggage is very expensive while unaccompanied baggage is much less expensive, although by no means cheap.

Most major shops are skilled at shipping goods for customers. They often pack the items free and only charge you for the actual postage or freight. Many of these shops use excellent shippers who are known for reasonable charges, good packing, and reliability. If you choose to have a shop ship for you, insist on a receipt specifying they will ship the item and specify that you want the shipment insured for both loss and damage—frequently called "all-risk."

If you have several large purchases—at least one cubic meter—check with local shippers since it is cheaper and safer to consolidate many separate purchases into one shipment which is well packed and insured. Choose a local company which has an excellent reputation among expatriates for shipping goods. Consult the Yellow Pages under the headings "Shipping" or "Removers." Do some quick research. If you are staying at a good hotel, ask the concierge about reliable shippers. He should be able to help you. Personnel at the local embassy, consulate, or international school know which companies are best. Call a few expatriates and ask for their best recommendations.

❏ Shipping is one of those things that must be arranged.

❏ Before leaving home, identify the best point of entry for goods arriving by air or sea.

❏ Most major shops are skilled at shipping goods for customers. They often pack items free and only charge for actual postage or freight.

❏ Be sure to insure your shipments against both loss and damage.

Sea freight charges are usually figured by volume—either by the cubic meter or a container. **Air freight** charges are based on a combination of size and weight. For a sea shipment there is a minimum charge—usually one cubic meter—you will pay even if your shipment is of less volume. There are also port fees to be paid, a broker to get the shipment through Customs, and unless your hometown is a major seaport that handles freighters, you will also pay to have your shipment trucked from the port of entry to your home. On air freight you pay for the actual amount you ship—there is no minimum charge. You can usually have it flown to the international airport nearest your home and avoid port fees altogether. However, there will be a small Customs fee.

If your items are less than three feet in length and you don't wish to hand-carry them home, consider sending them by **parcel post**. This is the cheapest way to ship and parcel post tends to be reliable, although it may take four months for final delivery. Most shops will take care of the packing and shipping for parcel post.

If you have items that are too large for parcel post, but nonetheless are small and relatively lightweight, air freight may be a viable option. Consider air freight if the package is too large to be sent parcel post, but much smaller than the minimum of one cubic meter, and does not weigh an excessive amount relative to its size. Air freight is the transportation of choice if you must have your purchase right away. Sea freight is the better choice if your purchase is large and heavy and you are willing to wait several weeks for its arrival. When using air freight, contact a well established and reliable airline. It will be most cost effective if you can select one airline, i.e., the same carrier flies between your point of shipping and your hometown airport.

We have tried each of these shipping alternatives with various results. Indeed, we tend to use these alternatives in combination. For example, we take everything we can with us until we reach the point where the inconvenience and cost of excess baggage requires some other shipping arrangements. We often consolidate shipments with shops where we know we will probably be making purchases. Such an approach requires trusting a few key shops with handling the shipping of all purchases. This approach usually works well, although it is not without potential problems, and we receive our goods with little or no problem.

When you use a shipper, be sure to examine alternative shipping arrangements and prices. The type of delivery you specify at your end can make a significant difference in the overall shipping price. If you don't specify the type of delivery you want, you may be charged the all-inclusive first-class rate. For example, if you choose door-to-door delivery, you will pay a premium to have your shipment clear Customs, moved through the port, transported to your door, and unpacked by local movers. On the other hand, it is cheaper for you to just have the shipment arrive at your door; you do your own unpacking and carting away of the trash. If you live close to the point of delivery, you can easily clear Customs and pick up the shipment yourself. By doing this, you can save US$100 to US$125 that a local broker will charge to clear Customs and move the shipment out of the port; you'll probably save another $300 to $500 in local transportation and delivery charges.

We simply cannot over-stress the importance of finding and establishing a personal relationship with a good local shipper who will provide you with services which may go beyond your immediate shipping needs. A good local shipping contact will enable you to continue shopping in Singapore and Bali even after returning home!

PART II

Acquiring Treasures With Ease

3

Shopping Rules and Bargaining Skills

S HOPPING IN SINGAPORE AND BALI IS AS MUCH
cultural experience as it is a set of buying and selling
transactions in unique commercial settings. While many
of the shops, department stores, and markets may look
similar to ones you shop in back home, they do have important
differences you should know about prior to starting your
Singapore and Bali shopping adventures. Most of these differences relate to certain shopping and pricing traditions that
constitute an important set of shopping rules and bargaining
skills you can and should learn before you begin making
purchases in these countries.

15 RULES FOR SHOPPING SUCCESS

The structure of shopping in Singapore and Bali is such that
you should make a few adjustments to the way you normally
approach shopping if you are to best enjoy your shopping
adventure. The most important adjustments constitute a set of
shopping rules that are applicable in most shopping situations.
Over the years, we have discovered these local shopping rules:

1. **The most important shopping areas are concentrated along the main commercial streets and in a
   few outlying areas of major cities.** The best products

in terms of quality, designs, and colors are found in shopping centers, hotel shopping arcades, department stores, and shophouses concentrated along one or two major streets in the central business districts of most major cities. In Singapore, Orchard Road, Scotts Road, and Bras Basah Road/Raffles Boulevard are the main shopping streets. In Bali, most major shopping is found along one or two main streets of Kuta and Ubud and in several nearby villages. Knowing these shopping patterns, it's a good idea to stay at a hotel in close proximity to the main shopping streets. In the case of Bali, you may want to chose two hotel locations—Jimbaran, Kuta, or Sanur and Ubud. Except for an occasional trip to visit factories and shops outside the central business district, expect to do 90 percent of your shopping along only a few streets.

2. **Concentrate your shopping on a few shopping areas within close proximity of each other each day.** While it is relatively easy to get around in Singapore and Bali, it's best to focus your shopping in particular shopping areas rather than continuously travel from one shop to another between areas. Compile a list of shops or areas you wish to visit, locate them on a map, and each day try to visit those close to one another. Systematically complete one shopping area before moving on to the next.

3. **Prepare to do a great deal of walking within and between shopping areas.** While most shops, shopping centers, and department stores are located along a few streets in the central business district, these are often very long streets requiring a considerable amount of walking. Take a good pair of walking shoes, slow down your walking pace, and take public transportation whenever possible.

4. **Use public transportation when going between shopping areas or even within some shopping areas.** Public transportation, such as taxis, buses, and subway, are inexpensive and convenient for shoppers in Singapore. In Bali, public transportation, especially buses, are less convenient and more trouble than they are worth, which is not much; you are well advised to hire a car and driver by the half or full day in Bali. Given the high heat and humidity as well as the long distance walking in-

volved in shopping, avoid extensive walking. Our rule of thumb: if we must walk more than one kilometer, take public transportation.

5. **Pack your rain and sun gear whenever you go out**. Unless you know for certain the weather forecast for the day, it's always a good idea to take an umbrella—a small collapsible one is perfect—sunglasses, and hat when you go out during the day and an umbrella at night. Singapore and Bali have hot and humid climates that can be unpredictable at times. The umbrella keeps both the rain and sun off our heads. When we forget to take our umbrella, invariably it rains!

6. **Expect to shop in two very different shopping cultures**. The first world is a very familiar one for most visitors—the attractive world of upscale shopping centers, department stores, and hotel shopping arcades. Shops in this culture tend to have window displays, well organized interiors, good customer service, and fixed prices which may or may not be all that fixed, depending on your ability to get discounts. The second shopping culture consists of the traditional shophouses, markets, and hawkers which tend to be somewhat disorganized, lack appealing window displays and good customer service, and involve a great deal of price uncertainty; they expect many customers will haggle over prices which are left to the discretion of the shopkeeper who may quote different prices to different types of customers (if you look rich, you get quoted a high price!) and nationalities (Japanese often pay a premium because of their reputation for being rich and naive shoppers; Italians get quoted high initial prices because they are known to bargain hard; and Americans get better initial price quotes because they are known to walk away if they don't like the first price!). You will most likely be able to directly transfer your shopping skills to the first culture, but you may have difficulty navigating the promises and pitfalls of the second shopping culture—unless you know how to bargain.

7. **The day and night markets can be fun places to shop, but only if you are open to many new sights, sounds, and smells you normally do not find in other shopping sites.** Many of the markets combine fresh fruits, vegetables, and meats with hawker food

stalls and shop stalls selling household goods. Usually clean and well organized, although seemingly chaotic, these markets can be very interesting and colorful places to visit. They tend to cater to a different class of local resident—lower to lower-middle—than the department stores and shopping centers. Many of the markets also have distinct ethnic characteristics. Locals especially love to shop in the Chinese markets because the prices appear cheap compared to their other shopping alternatives. While shopping may be limited to a few handcrafted items, it's the cultural experience and photo opportunities that make these places so interesting for visitors. Other markets primarily offer inexpensive clothes, accessories, and household goods along with exotic dishes prepared by the ubiquitous hawker food stalls. These, too, are great places to experience the more traditional buying and selling culture. While you will seldom find good quality products in these markets—the emphasis is on buying cheap goods—there are exceptions and you will find plenty of inexpensive clothes, souvenirs, and fake products to make the trip to these markets worthwhile. Bargaining, with discounts ranging from 20 to 70 percent, is the only way to buy in these markets. You will be foolish to pay the first asking price.

8. **Shopping centers tend to be crowded, noisy, and multi-level buildings filled with small shops.** Except for the indoor pedestrian mall concept incorporated in the Marina Square shopping arcade in Singapore, shopping centers in Singapore and Bali are not shopping malls where shoppers can leisurely browse. Given the high costs of urban land, most shopping centers are high density buildings occupying very little land. Instead, they arc built up with shops occupying as much interior space as possible. Levels are connected by several escalators and one or two elevators. Given the structure of such buildings, they tend to look and feel very crowded, especially on weekends when most locals do their shopping. These centers are also very noisy and many are social centers for young people who enjoy window shopping, eating, and meeting friends. If you are not used to such types of shopping centers, they may feel unfamiliar to you at first.

9. **Most shopping centers as well as department stores cater to the shopping preferences of local residents**

rather than to foreign tourists. Don't expect to find a great deal of quality local products in shopping centers and department stores. Most of these places orient their product lines to the local middle-class with numerous average quality consumer products and imported goods. However, you will find a few exceptional quality shopping centers—primarily in Singapore—that are "must visit" places for most visitors, such as the Raffles Hotel Arcade and Tanglin Shopping Centre.

10. **The best quality products are invariably found in the major hotel shopping arcades and a few shopping centers with reputations for quality.** It's not surprising to discover that the best quality shops tend to congregate near the best quality hotels which cater to the more affluent business travelers and tourists. The shops in these places will offer a mix of expensive imported products—designer label clothes, jewelry, luggage, shoes, and accessories—as well as excellent quality local products, especially antiques, artifacts, textiles, and tailored clothes. The prices in such shops may seem high, but such shops offer good quality products. The "best buys" will be on high quality local products rather than the usual mix of upscale imported goods that are available in many other cities and duty-free shops around the world.

11. **Expect to get the best prices on locally produced items that use inexpensive labor.** Imported goods will be expensive regardless of their duty-free status. But any products that use inexpensive local labor—hand crafted furniture, textiles, wood carvings, paintings, and woven handicrafts—are excellent buys because the cost of labor is going up and many of the handcrafting skills are quickly disappearing with the onslaught of inexpensive plastic materials and machine labor.

12. **Don't expect to get something for nothing.** If a price seems too good to be true, it probably is. Good quality products, especially jewelry, antiques, and artifacts, may not seem cheap in Singapore and Bali. But they are bargains compared to similar items found in the shops of Tokyo, Sydney, Paris, London, or New York City.

13. **Expect the design and color selections of many locally produced items to be different from your design and color preferences.** This is an especially

valid observation in the more traditional handicraft production areas of Bali. Take, for example, the fine filigree silver products found in the famous village of Celuk or the many traditional Balinese paintings and wood carvings. Many are best left in Bali. The designs and colors of traditional handicrafts may appeal to locals, but they have a long way to go to catch the eyes of westerners who have a very different sense of what constitutes good quality in design and color in their own cultural settings. Clothes by local designers also have their own unique styles and colors which may or may not appeal to your wardrobe tastes. At the same time, many expats have opened shops that offer excellent designs and colors. The influence of expat Italians, Australians, French, British, and Americans is clearly evident in Bali.

14. **Ask for assistance whenever you feel you need it.** While Singapore and Bali are in reality easy to get around, at times you may feel lost and have difficulty finding particular shops or products. Whenever this happens, just ask for assistance from your hotel, tourist office, shopkeepers, and people you meet on the street. Singaporians and Balinese are friendly and will assist you if they can.

15. **Don't be surprised if some shopkeepers take a great deal of your time in developing a personal and long-term relationship with you.** Especially in many traditional shopping settings, business in Singapore and Bali is still a personal set of relations, regardless of all the symbols of impersonal efficiency and effectiveness. While some merchants may initially appear distant and suspicious, most are generally inquisitive if you will initiate a conversation that involves their family, work, or country. Many merchants in Singapore and Bali, for example, are extremely friendly, enjoy learning more about visitors, are willing to share their knowledge about their country and products, and prefer cementing personal relationships with their customers. The lines between buyer and seller may quickly fade as you develop a friendship with the shopkeeper. You may even find some shopkeepers inviting you to lunch, dinner, or their home as well as giving you special gifts. You may even feel you are being adopted by the family! This is usually a genuine expression of interest, concern, and friendship rather than a sales tactic. In fact, you may find such per-

sonal encounters to be the highlights of your shopping adventure in Singapore and Bali; they may lead to lasting friendships with these individuals.

You will also learn other shopping rules as you proceed through the many shophouses, shopping centers, hotel shopping arcades, department stores, and markets in Singapore and Bali. Many of these relate to pricing policies and bargaining practices that you can and should learn if you want to become an effective shopper in Singapore and Bali.

PRICING PRACTICES AND BARGAINING

Bargaining still remains the way of shopping life in many parts of Singapore and Bali. While more and more shops in Singapore have fixed prices, bargaining is still an important part of the shopping scene. In Bali, expect to bargain for most purchases. Therefore, if you want to become an effective shopper in Singapore and Bali, you need to know something about the basics of bargaining.

Most North American and European tourists come from fixed-price cultures where prices are nicely displayed on items. Only on very large-ticket items, such as automobiles, boats, houses, furniture, carpets, and jewelry, can you expect to negotiate the price. If you want to get the best deal, you must do comparative shopping as well as wait for special discounts and sales. Bargain shopping in such a culture centers on comparative pricing of items. Shopping becomes a relatively passive activity involving the examination of printed advertisements in newspapers and catalogs as well as using price comparison search engines on the Internet.

Expert shoppers in fixed-price cultures tend to be those skilled in carefully observing and comparing prices in the print advertising media. They clip coupons and know when the best sales are being held for particular items on certain days. They need not be concerned with cultivating personal relationships with merchants or salespeople in order to get good buys.

Like a fish out of water, so-called savvy shoppers from fixed-price cultures may feel lost when shopping in Singapore and Bali. Few of their fixed-price shopping skills transfer well to the Singapore and Bali shopping environments. Except for department stores and some ads in the monthly tourist literature, as well as local newspapers announcing special sales, few shops advertise in the print media or on TV and radio.

COPING WITH PRICE UNCERTAINTY

Goods in Singapore and Bali fall into three major pricing categories: **fixed, negotiable, or discounted**. The general trend in Singapore is toward fixed prices on more and more goods. In the meantime, **price uncertainty**—negotiable or discounted prices—is the standard way to sell most goods and services in Singapore and Bali. The general pricing guideline is this: **Unless you see a sign stating otherwise, you can expect prices of most goods in small shops to be negotiable.** You can safely assume that all stated prices are the starting point from which you should receive anything from a 10 to 60 percent discount, depending upon your haggling skills and level of commitment to obtain reduced prices.

Discount percentages in Singapore and Bali will vary for different items and from one shop to another. In general, however, expect to receive at least a 10 to 20 percent discount on most items in shops willing to discount. Many will discount as much as 50 or 60 percent.

The structure of prices on certain goods and services varies. The prices on items in department stores are fixed. Prices for tailors, hairdressers, metered taxis, and medical personnel are fixed. Hotel prices are subject to a variety of discounts for different categories of travelers—VIP, business, government, weekend, tourist, and last minute arrivals.

When in doubt if a price is fixed, negotiable, or subject to discounts, **always ask for a special discount**. After the salesperson indicates the price, ask one of two questions: *"What kind of discount can you give me on this item?"* or *"What is your best price?"* Better still, ask the classic *"Is it possible?"* question: *"Is it possible to do any better on this price?"* Anything is possible in Singapore and Bali! If the person indicates a discount, you can either accept it or attempt to negotiate the price through a bargaining process.

While skilled shoppers in fixed-price cultures primarily compare prices by reading ads and listening to special announcements, the skilled shopper in bargaining cultures is primarily engaged in face-to-face encounters with sellers. To be most successful, the shopper must use various interpersonal skills to his or her advantage. Once you know these and practice bargaining, you should become a very effective shopper in Singapore and Bali.

Establish Value and Price

Not knowing the price of an item, many shoppers from fixed-price cultures face a problem. *"What is the actual value of the item? How much should I pay? At what point do I know I'm getting a fair price?"* These questions can be answered in several ways. First, you should have some idea of the value of the item, because you already did comparative shopping at home by examining catalogs and visiting discount houses, department stores, and specialty shops. If you are interested in a camera, for example, you should know what comparable quality cameras sell for back home.

Second, you have done comparative shopping among the various shops you've encountered in Singapore or Bali in order to **establish a price range** for positioning yourself in the bargaining process. You've visited a department store in Singapore to research how much a similar item is selling for at a fixed price. You've checked with a shop in your hotel and compared prices there. In your hotel, you might ask *"How much is this item?"* and then act a little surprised that it appears so expensive. Tell them that you are a hotel guest and you want their *"very best price."* At this point the price usually decreases by 10- 20 percent as you are told this is *"our very special price," "our first-customer-of-the-day price,"* or *"our special hotel guest price."*

Once you initially receive a special price from your first price inquiry, expect to get another 10 to 20 percent through further negotiation. But at this point do not negotiate any more unless it is a unique item you may not find again and don't want to risk losing. Take the shop's business card and record on the back the item, the original price, and the first discount price; thank the shopkeeper, and tell him or her that you may return. Repeat this same scenario in a few other shops. After doing three or four comparisons, you will establish a price range for particular items. This range will give you a fairly accurate idea of the going discount price. At this point you should be prepared to do some serious haggling, playing one shop off against another.

Effective shoppers in Singapore and Bali quickly learn how to do comparative shopping and negotiate the best deal. In learning to be effective, you don't need to be timid, aggressive, or obnoxious—extreme behaviors frequently exhibited by first-time practitioners of the Asian art of bargaining. Although you may feel bargaining is a defensive measure to avoid being ripped-off by unscrupulous merchants, it is an acceptable way of doing business in many Asian cultures. Merchants merely adjust their profit margins to the customer, depending on how they feel about the situation as well as their current cash flow needs. It is up to you to adapt to such a pricing culture.

One problem you may soon discover is that every situation seems to differ somewhat, and differences between items and shops can be significant. You can expect to receive larger discounts on jewelry than on shoes. For example, discounts on jewelry may be as great as 50 to 60 percent whereas discounts on home furnishings may only be 10 to 20 percent.

The one major exception to bargaining concerns tailors. Tailors normally quote you a fixed-price subject to little or no negotiation; you merely trust that you are getting a fair price and, after all, it is not a good idea to make your tailor unhappy by bargaining when he doesn't want to. He may "get even" by cheapening the quality of your clothes. Only in tailor shops do we avoid forcing the price issue by bargaining. At best ask for *"your best price,"* use a common friend's name as reference, or ask for an extra shirt, but don't risk being short-changed on quality just to save a few dollars. If you comparative shop among a few tailor shops, you will quickly identify what should be the "fair market rate" for comparable tailoring materials, skills, and services.

Our general rule on what items to bargain for is this: **bargain on ready-made items you can carry out of the shop.** If you must have an item custom-made, be very careful how you arrive at the final price. In most cases you should not bargain other than respond to the first price by asking *"Is this your best price?"* Better still, drop a few names, agree on a mutually satisfactory price, and then insist that you want top quality for that price.

Except for custom-made items, department stores, and shops displaying a "fixed prices" sign, **never accept the first price offered.** Rather, spend some time going through our bargaining scenario. Once you have accepted a price and purchased the item, be sure to **get a receipt** as well as **observe the packing process.** While few merchants will try to cheat you, some tourists have had unpleasant experiences which could have been avoided by following some simple rules of shopping in unfamiliar places.

GET THE BEST DEAL POSSIBLE

Chances are you will deal with a Chinese merchant who is a relatively seasoned businessman; he or she is a family entrepreneur who thrives on status and personal relationships. As soon as you walk through the door, most merchants will want to sell you items then and there.

The best deal you will get is when you have a personal relationship with the merchant. Contrary to what others may tell you about bargains for tourists, you often can get as good a deal—sometimes even better—than someone from the local community. It is simply a myth that tourists can't do as well on prices as the locals. Indeed, we often do better than the locals because we have done our comparative shopping and we know well the art of bargaining—something locals are often lax in doing. In addition, some merchants may give you a better price than the locals because you are *"here today and gone tomorrow"*; you won't be around to tell their regular customers about your very special price.

More often than not, the Singapore and Bali pricing systems operate like this: **If the shopkeeper likes you, or you are a friend of a friend or relative, you can expect to get a good price**. Whenever possible, drop names of individuals who referred you to the shop; the shopkeeper may think you are a friend and thus you are entitled to a special discount. But if you do not have such a relationship and you present yourself as a typical tourist who is here today and gone tomorrow, you need to bargain hard.

PRACTICE 12 BARGAINING RULES

The art of bargaining in Singapore and Bali can take several forms. In general, you want to achieve two goals in this haggling process: **establish the value of an item and get the best possible price**. The following bargaining rules work well.

1. **Do your research before initiating the process.** Compare the prices among various shops, starting with the fixed-price items in department stores. Spot-check price ranges among shops in and around your hotel. Also, refer to your research done with catalogs and discount houses back home to determine if the discount is sufficient to warrant purchasing the item abroad rather than at home.

2. **Determine the exact item you want.** Select the particular item you want and then focus your bargaining around that one item without expressing excessive interest and commitment. Even though you may be excited by the item and want it very badly, once the

merchant knows you are committed to buying this one item, you weaken your bargaining position. Express a passing interest; indicate through eye contact with other items in the shop that you are not necessarily committed to the one item. As you ask about the other items, you should get some sense concerning the willingness of the merchant to discount prices.

3. **Set a ceiling price you are willing to pay.** Before engaging in serious negotiations, set in your mind the maximum amount you are willing to pay, which may be 20 percent more than you figured the item should sell for based on your research. However, if you find something you love that is really unique, be prepared to pay whatever you must. In many situations you will find unique items not available anywhere else. Consider buying **now** since the item may be gone when you return. Bargain as hard as you can and then pay what you have to—even though it may seem painful—for the privilege of owning a unique item. Remember, it only hurts once. After you return home you will most likely enjoy your wonderful purchase and forget how painful it seemed at the time to buy it at less than your expected discount. Above all, do not pass up an item you really love just because the bargaining process does not fall in your favor. It is very easy to be *"penny wise but pound foolish"* in Singapore and Bali simply because the bargaining process is such an ego-involved activity. You may return home forever regretting that you failed to buy a lovely item just because you refused to "give" on the last $5 of haggling. In the end, put your ego aside, give in, and buy what you really want. Only you and the merchant will know who really won, and once you return home the $5 will seem to be such an insignificant amount. Chances are you still got a good bargain compared to what you would pay elsewhere if, indeed, you could find a similar item!

4. **Play a role.** Shopping in Singapore and Bali involves playing the roles of buyer and seller. Asians tend to be terrific role players, moreso than westerners. In contrast to many Western societies, where being a unique individual is emphasized, high value is not placed on individualism here. Rather, Asians learn specific sets of behaviors appropriate for the role of father, son, daughter, husband, wife, blood friend, classmate, superior, subordi-

nate, buyer, seller. They easily shift from one role to another, undergoing major personality and behavioral changes without experiencing mental conflicts. When you encounter a Chinese businessperson, you are often meeting a very refined and sophisticated role player. Therefore, it is to your advantage to play complementary roles by carefully structuring your personality and behavior to play the role of buyer. If you approach sellers by just "being yourself"—open, honest, somewhat naive, and with your own unique personality—you may be quickly walked over by a seasoned seller. Once you enter a shop, think of yourself as an actor walking on stage to play the role of a shrewd buyer, bargainer, and trader.

5. **Establish good will and a personal relationship.** A shrewd buyer also is charming, polite, personable, and friendly. You should have a sense of humor, smile, and be light-hearted during the bargaining process. But be careful about eye contact which can be threatening to Asians. Keep it to a minimum. Asian sellers prefer to establish a personal relationship so that the bargaining process can take place on a friendly, face-saving basis. In the end, both the buyer and seller should come out as winners. This can not be done if you approach the buyer in very serious and harsh terms. You should start by exchanging pleasantries concerning the weather, your trip, the city, or the nice items in the shop. After exchanging business cards or determining your status, the shopkeeper will know what roles should be played in the coming transaction.

6. **Let the seller make the first offer.** If the merchant starts by asking you *"How much do you want to pay?"*, avoid answering; immediately turn the question around: *"How much are you asking?"* Remember, many merchants try to get you to pay as much as you are willing to pay—not what the value of the item is or what he is willing to take. You should never reveal your ability or willingness to pay a certain price. Keep the seller guessing, thinking that you may lose interest or not buy the item because it appears too expensive. Always get the merchant to initiate the bargaining process. In so doing, the merchant must take the defensive as you shift to the offensive.

7. **Take your time, being deliberately slow in order to get the merchant to invest his or her time in you.** The more you indicate that you are impatient and in a hurry, the more you are likely to pay. When negotiating a price, **time** is usually in your favor. Many shopkeepers also see time as a positive force in the bargaining process. Some try to keep you in their shop by serving you tea, coffee, soft drinks, or liquor while negotiating the price. Be careful; this nice little ritual may soften you somewhat on the bargaining process as you begin establishing a more personal relationship with the merchant. The longer you stay in control prolonging the negotiation, the better the price should be. Although some merchants may deserve it, **never** insult them. Merchants need to "keep face" as much as you do in the process of giving and getting the very best price.

8. **Use odd numbers in offering the merchant at least 40 percent less than what he or she initially offers.** Avoid stating round numbers, such as 60, 70, or 100. Instead, offer $62.00, $73.50, or $81.00. Such numbers impress upon others that you may be a seasoned haggler who knows value and expects to do well in this negotiation. Your offer will probably be 15 percent less than the value you determined for the item. For example, if the merchant asks $100, offer $62.50, knowing the final price should probably be $75.00. The merchant will probably counter with only a 10 percent discount—$90. At this point you will need to go back and forth with another two or three offers and counter-offers.

9. **Appear disappointed and take your time again.** Never appear upset or angry with the seller. Keep your cool at all times by slowly sitting down and carefully examining the item. Shake your head a little and say, *"Gee, that's too bad. That's much more than I had planned to spend. I like it, but I really can't go that high."* Appear to be a sympathetic listener as the seller attempts to explain why he or she cannot budge more on the price. Make sure you do not accuse the merchant of being a thief! Use a little charm, if you can, for the way you conduct the bargaining process will affect the final price. This should be a civil negotiation in which you nicely bring the price down, the seller "saves face," and everyone goes away feeling good about the deal.

10. **Counter with a new offer at a 35 percent discount.**
Punch several keys on your calculator, which indicates
that you are doing some serious thinking. Then say
something like *"This is really the best I can do. It's a lovely
item, but $67.25 is really all I can pay."* At this point the
merchant will probably counter with a 20 percent
discount—$80.

11. **Be patient, persistent, and take your time again by
carefully examining the item.** Respond by saying
*"That's a little better, but it's still too much. I want to look
around a little more."* Then start to get up and look toward
the door. At this point the merchant has invested some
time in this exchange, and he or she is getting close to a
possible sale. The merchant will either let you walk out
the door or try to stop you with another counter-offer. If
you walk out the door, you can always return to get the
$80 price. But most likely the merchant will try to stop
you, especially if there is still some bargaining room. The
merchant is likely to say: *"You don't want to waste your time
looking elsewhere. I'll give you the best price anywhere—just for
you. Okay, $75. That's my final price."*

12. **Be creative for the final negotiation.** You could try for
$70, but chances are $75 will be the final price with this
merchant. Yet, there may still be some room for negotiating "extras." At this point get up and walk around the
shop and examine other items; try to appear as if you are
losing interest in the item you were bargaining for. While
walking around, identify a $5-10 item you like which
might make a nice gift for a friend or relative, which you
could possibly include in the final deal. Wander back to
the $75 item and look as if your interest is waning and
perhaps you need to leave. Then start to probe the pos-
sibility of including extras while agreeing on the $75:
"Okay, I might go $75, but only if you include this with it."
The "this" is the $10 item you eyed. You also might
negotiate with your credit card. Chances are the merchant is expecting cash on the $75 discounted price and
will add a 2-5 percent "commission" if you want to use
your credit card. In this case, you might respond to the
$75 by saying, *"Okay, I'll go with the $75, but only if I can
use my credit card."* You may get your price, your bank will
float you a loan in the meantime, and you may have a
form of insurance in case you later learn there is a
problem with your purchase, such as misrepresentation.

Finally, you may want to negotiate packing and delivery processes. If it is a fragile item, insist that it be packed well so you can take it with you on the airplane or have it shipped. If your purchase is large, insist that the shop deliver it to your hotel or to your shipper. If the shop is shipping it by air or sea, try to get them to agree to absorb some of the freight and insurance costs.

This slow, civil, methodical, and sometimes charming approach to bargaining works well in most cases. However, merchants do differ in how they respond to situations. In some cases, your timing may be right: the merchant is in need of cash flow that day and thus he or she is willing to give you the price you want, with little or no bargaining. Others will not give more than a 10 to 20 percent discount unless you are a friend of a friend who is then eligible for the special "family discount." And others are not good businessmen, are unpredictable, lack motivation, or are just moody; they refuse to budge on their prices even though your offer is fair compared to the going prices in other shops. In these situations it is best to leave the shop and find one which is more receptive to the traditional haggling process.

Bargaining in traditional markets requires a different approach and may result in larger discounts. In contrast to the numerous polite middle-class merchants you encounter in shops, sellers in open-air markets tend to be lower-class, earthy, expressive, pushy, persistent, and often rude as they attempt to sell you many things you cannot use or have no desire to even inspect. They may joke a great deal, shout at you—*"Hey, you mister"*—push and shove, and pester you. These markets are similar to a great big carnival.

In contrast to our previous bargaining rules, successful bargaining in open-air markets should involve **little time** and a great deal of **movement**. If you are interested in an item, ask the price, counter with a price you are willing to pay, and be relatively firm with this price. Since there is a great deal of competition in these markets, it is to your advantage to spend very little time with any one vendor. State your offer and slowly move on to the next vendor. Sellers know they will probably lose you to the competition, so they need to quickly conclude a deal before someone else gets to you; they are motivated to give you large discounts. You also can be a little more aggressive and obnoxious and less charming in these places. If, for example, an item is quoted at $10, offer $4 and move on toward the next vendor. Chances are the seller will immediately drop the price to $7. If you counter with $5 and are moving while stating your offer, the seller will probably agree to your offer. But be sure you want the item. Once your offer is accepted, you are expected to carry through with the purchase. Open-air stalls arc great places to accumulate junk while successfully practicing your bargaining skills!

BARGAIN FOR NEEDS, NOT GREED

One word of caution for those who are just starting to learn the fine art of Asian bargaining. **Be sure you really want an item before you initiate the bargaining process**. Many tourists learn to bargain effectively, and then get carried away with their new-found skill. Rather than use this skill to get what they want, they enjoy the process of bargaining so much that they buy many unnecessary items. After all, they got such "a good deal" and thus could not resist buying the item. You do not need to fill your suitcases with junk in demonstrating this ego-gratifying skill. If used properly, your new bargaining skills will lead to some excellent buys on items you really need and want.

EXAMINE YOUR GOODS CAREFULLY

Before you commence the bargaining process, carefully examine the item, being sure that you understand the quality of the item for which you are negotiating. Then, after you settle on a final price, make sure you are getting the goods you agreed upon. You should carefully observe the handling of items, including the actual packing process. If at all possible, take the items with you when you leave the shop. If you later discover you were victimized by a switch or misrepresentation, contact the national tourist association as well as your credit card company if you charged your purchase. You should be able to resolve the problem through these channels. However, the responsibility is on you, the buyer, to know what you are buying.

BEWARE OF POSSIBLE SCAMS

Although one hopes this will never happen, you may be unfortunate in encountering unscrupulous merchants who take advantage of you. This is more likely to happen if you wander away from recommended shops in discovering your own "very special" bargains or enter the *"Hey, you mister—do I ever have a deal for you"* shops. The most frequent scams to watch out for include:

1. **Switching the goods.** You negotiate for a particular item, such as a watch, camera, or blouse, but in the process of packing it, the merchant substitutes an inferior product.

2. **Misrepresenting quality goods.** Be especially cautious in jewelry stores and antique shops. Sometimes so-called expensive watches are excellent imitations and worth no more than $15—or have cheap mechanisms inside expensive cases. Precious stones, such as rubies, may not be as precious as they appear. Synthetic stones, garnets, or spinels are sometimes substituted for high quality rubies. Some substitutes are so good that experts even have difficulty identifying the difference. Accordingly, you may pay $2,000 for what appears to be a ruby worth $10,000 back home, but in fact you just bought a $25 red spinel. Pearls come in many different qualities, so know your pearls before negotiating a price. Real jade is beautiful, but many buyers unwittingly end up with green plastic or soapstone at jade prices. The antique business is relatively unregulated. Some merchants try to sell "new antiques" at "old antique" prices. Many of the fakes are outstanding reproductions, often fooling even the experts. Better still, there is a reputable business in fakes. You may want to just shop for fakes!

3. **Goods not included in the package(s) you carry with you.** You purchase several items in one shop. The seller wraps them and presents them to you, but "forgot" to include one of the items you paid for. You've become distracted in the process of paying for everything and talking with the shopkeeper to the point of forgetting to check your package(s) carefully.

4. **Goods not shipped.** The shop may agree to ship your goods home, but once you leave they, conveniently forget to do so. You wait and wait, write letters of inquiry, fax, make phone calls, and e-mail the shop; no one can give you a satisfactory response. Unless you have shipping and insurance documents, which is unlikely, and proper receipts, you may not receive the goods you paid for.

Your best line of defense against these and other possible scams is to be very careful wherever you go and whatever you do in relation to handling money. A few simple precautions will help avoid some of these problems:

1. **Do not trust anyone with your money** unless you have proper assurances they are giving you exactly what you agreed upon. Trust is something that should be earned—not automatically given to friendly strangers you may like.

2. **Do your homework** so you can determine quality and value as well as anticipate certain types of scams.

3. **Examine the goods carefully**, assuming something may be or will go wrong.

4. **Watch very carefully how the merchant handles items** from the moment they leave your hands until they get wrapped and into a bag.

5. **Request receipts** that list specific items and the prices you paid. Although most shops are willing to "give you a receipt" specifying whatever price you want them to write for purposes of deceiving Customs, be careful in doing so. While you may indeed deceive Customs, your custom-designed receipt may become a double-edge sword, especially if you later need a receipt with the real price to claim your goods or a refund. If the shop is to ship, be sure you have a shipping receipt which also includes insurance against both loss and damage.

6. **Take photos of your purchases.** We strongly recommend taking photos of your major purchases, especially anything that is being entrusted to someone else to be packed and shipped. Better still, take a photo of the seller holding the item, just in case you later need to identify the person with whom you dealt. This photo will give you a visual record of your purchase should you later have problems receiving your shipment, from being lost or damaged. You'll also have a photo to show Customs should they have any questions about the contents of your shipment.

7. **Patronize shops which are affiliated with the local tourist associations.** They are more likely to treat you honestly since the parent organization does somewhat police its members.

8. **Protect yourself against scams by using credit cards** for payment, especially for big ticket items which could present problems, even though using them may cost you a little more.

If you are victimized, all is not necessarily lost. You should report the problem immediately to the local tourist association, the police, your credit card company, or insurance company.

PART III

Surprising Singapore

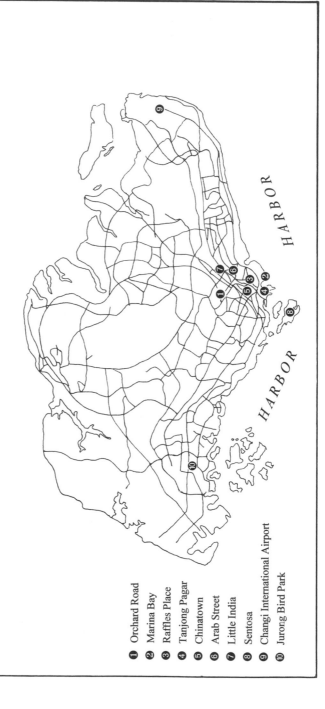

SINGAPORE

HARBOR

HARBOR

1 Orchard Road
2 Marina Bay
3 Raffles Place
4 Tanjong Pagar
5 Chinatown
6 Arab Street
7 Little India
8 Sentosa
9 Changi International Airport
10 Jurong Bird Park

Singapore

SINGAPORE IS ONE OF ASIA'S DELIGHTFUL SUR-
prises. An extremely modern and efficient city—everything seems to work remarkable well here—it's also a
shopper's paradise offering wonderful shopping opportunities not found in many other cities. If you already visited
Hong Kong, you will be tempted to compare it with Singapore.
If you've been to Thailand or Indonesia, you will notice a big
difference between shopping in less developed countries versus
clean, green, high-tech, modern, and efficient Singapore. In fact,
Singapore may give you a quick case of "reverse culture shock."

A RISING PHOENIX

Singapore is unlike any other country you will ever visit. A
small island city-state of only 646 square kilometers (248
square miles) with 150 kilometers of coastline, occupied by
nearly 3.2 million people, and visited by over 6 million travelers
each year, it is one of the world's major trading, financial, and
high-tech powerhouses. It boasts the world's busiest port, and
serves as the third largest oil refinery center in the world.

Singapore is a story of survival and determination against
numerous odds. In many respects, this small city-state defies

the logic of national survival and prosperity. A small area with no natural resources, Singapore gained independence in 1965 during a period of high unemployment and low per capita income. Within a decade, however, it rose like a phoenix as it surprised everyone—including Singapore's dynamic leader Lee Kuan Yew—with a remarkable record of economic development. Using its major resources—a hard working and relatively compliant population—Singapore's leadership helped propel this county into the status of the second most developed country in Asia, following Asia's other remarkable performer, Japan. Today, despite the collapse of many Asian economies in 1997-1998 and a continuing recession into the 21st century, Singapore still stands as a shining example of economic success far beyond its wildest dreams! It's the envy of most Asian countries that have yet to figure out the secret to Singapore's remarkable success.

Singapore is one of Asia's most westernized, comfortable, and convenient countries as well. English, one of Singapore's official languages, is spoken everywhere. The standard of living is exceptionally high. The city is ultra-modern, displaying some of the best tourist facilities found anywhere and some of the loveliest gardens in all of Asia. It's also the world's most wired city with high-speed Internet access available to over 80 percent of the population. Except for its high heat and humidity, you will feel right at home in Singapore. This country could well receive an award for being the most clean, orderly, predictable, convenient, and comfortable place in the world—ostensibly positive characteristics that surprisingly often generate criticism from many world travelers who find Singapore too westernized, hectic, orderly, and regimented—a kind of Disneyland or "LA run by the Swiss" on the equator. For many seasoned travelers, Singapore is not as much fun as their less sanitized and organized neighbors who still harbor charming Third World chaos with a smile!

Singapore is an excellent place to shop. Similar to Hong Kong, shopping seems to be everyone's favorite pastime. Singapore offers a wide variety of electronic, photo, and computer goods as well as clothes, jewelry, and accessories at duty-free prices. The emphasis here is on offering more and more upscale name-brand goods, especially designer-label clothing and accessories from the major design houses of Italy and France. But to a greater extent than Hong Kong, Singapore draws from the economies and societies of its neighboring South and Southeast Asian countries. Its multi-racial society is situated at the cross-roads of one of the world's most diverse cultural regions. As a result, Singapore presents shoppers a wide range of goods from all over the world, but with particular emphasis on the arts and crafts from all South and Southeast Asian countries. In Singapore you discover the shopping wonders of India, Pakistan, Sri Lanka, Burma, Thailand, Indonesia, the Philippines, Papua New Guinea, and Iran. No other country or city in Asia can claim such a central role in bringing together so many of the region's and world's shopping delights.

GETTING TO KNOW YOU

Singapore is a pleasant and easy country to visit. Variously dubbed the "Lion City," "Garden City," "Instant Asia," "New Asia," and the "Emporium of the East," Singapore is a mighty little wonder to behold. From the moment you step off your plane at the super efficient Changi International Airport to when you are courteously escorted to your room, you are impressed with this marvelous place called Singapore. It is so familiar, yet so unreal. If one were to invent the ideal city—neat, clean, efficient, and modern—it would probably look and feel like Singapore. In fact, many leaders from other Asian countries visit Singapore to see how they might create a little bit of Singapore back home. It is the model of what should go right in any city that claims to be civil, modern, and progressive.

We highly recommend Singapore for many reasons. First, it is one of the most **convenient and comfortable** countries to travel and shop. Singapore actively promotes itself as a travel and shopping paradise by offering some of the best transportation, hotels, restaurants, shopping centers, and travel services in Asia. Most shopping takes place in the air-conditioned comfort of shopping centers and arcades. You can easily travel to neighboring countries by making arrangements through several agents who offer a wide variety of itineraries and tours. And the Singapore Tourism Board (STB) does an outstanding job in providing self-directed materials for easily visiting this city on

❑ The shopping emphasis in Singapore is on offering more and more upscale name-brand goods, especially designer-label clothes and accessories from the major design houses of Italy and France.

❑ Singapore offers some of the best transportation, hotels, restaurants, shopping centers, and travel services in Asia.

❑ Of all cities in Asia, Singapore offers the widest variety of international foods ranging from elegant French restaurants to street stalls selling wonderful noodle dishes and *satay*.

❑ The ideal time to visit Singapore is between July and September—the period of least heat and humidity.

your own. The emphasis here is on continually offering quality products and a high standard of service.

Second, as a truly **international shopping city**, Singapore offers many items not found in other Asian cities. Here you will discover fine Persian carpets, unique designer clothes, and local paintings as well as fabulous antiques, arts, and crafts from neighboring Myanmar (Burma), Thailand, and Indonesia. If you have little time to visit these other countries, Singapore's shops will provide you with an abbreviated version of what to shop for in these other exotic places.

Third, Singapore is still **an affordable city** to visit even with the strong Singapore dollar. While hotel prices have increased substantially in recent years, hotels are less expensive than in Hong Kong and other major cities offering comparable amenities. The cost of food, transportation, and recreation appear reasonable in comparison to similar travel costs in comparable cities elsewhere. However, this price advantage is changing in response to Singapore's increasingly affluent upper middle class and the rapid increase in Asian tourists who seek quality products and services. Although shopping bargains can still be found, the emphasis in Singapore is definitely toward offering more upscale, name-brand products. This city is definitely more expensive than Kuala Lumpur. It may seem expensive to you.

Fourth, Singapore is an **extremely interesting city** in terms of its peoples, cultures, sightseeing, and entertainment. A truly multi-racial society living in remarkable harmony, you will encounter the colorful traditional cultures of the Chinese, Indians, Arabs, and Malays in the midst of modern high-rise buildings, luxury hotels, and superhighways. While Singapore is not noted for being steeped in history, nor does it honor well what history it claims, it does offer a living museum of diverse peoples and cultures. Within the past seven years, however, Singapore has begun to better preserve its past and, like good entrepreneurs, present historical and "heritage" areas as major tourist attractions.

Fifth, if you also enjoy treating your stomach to the finer things in life, Singapore is a **gastronomic delight**. Of all cities in Asia, Singapore offers the widest variety of international foods ranging from elegant French restaurants to street stalls selling wonderful noodle dishes and *satay*. All the major East Asian, Southeast Asian, and South Asian cuisines are well represented in Singapore along with the standard western fare. In addition, Singapore produces a unique Chinese-Malay cuisine called *Nonya* food. And the foods and drinks in Singapore are among the safest in the world. You can drink the tap water and consume the ice.

Sixth, Singapore is a **totally integrated travel and shopping experience**. In addition to offering shopping opportunities, it boasts fine recreational and leisure facilities, many historical and cultural sites worth visiting, good entertainment, and numerous excursions and trips to neighboring countries. The local tourist authority, the Singapore Tourism Board, is actively promoting the development of more tourist attractions to complement its many five-star hotels and shopping attractions. The emphasis here is on changing Singapore's image from that of a shopping mecca to one of a diverse, fully integrated tourist destination where quality and service are second to none. Accordingly, many new attractions relating to history, culture, sports, leisure, dining, and sightseeing are being developed to motivate the average tourist to spend more than three days in Singapore. For example, here you will discover one of the world's more interesting zoo tours—the Night Safari.

The down-side to Singapore is a comparative one of minor proportions. Compared to many other exotic Asian countries, Singapore lacks character, color, location, and reverence for the past to complement its many traveling and shopping delights. It does not, for example, have the gorgeous harbor views, breathtaking commercial skylines, towering hills and mountains, glittering neon signs, and charming ferry rides that give Hong Kong its character—unusual sights and experiences that make traveling so interesting and enjoyable. Nor does Singapore have the impressive exotic temples, palaces, and museums of Thailand and Indonesia which verify that these countries once had glorious indigenous histories. And it lacks the tranquility of Malaysia's many beautiful beaches and islands.

Singapore is a flat island in hot pursuit of the present and future. During the past decade it has begun developing an impressive skyline, using its harbor for tourism, and redeveloping important historical and cultural areas as major tourist attractions. Whatever past identity it lacks, Singapore makes up in terms of its identity with the future and new found images it hopes to create and project to the rest of the world—most recently a global high tech center with a strong "knowledge economy." The name of the game in Singapore is to be disciplined and work hard at making more money and creating more security for one's self and one's family. Except for preserving a few examples of its colonial past and ethnic heritage, or converting them into "showcase" tourist attractions, Singapore is obsessed with being modern in the present and future.

If Singapore has any character, it is to be more modern than the most modern countries in the world. Deliberately casting off its past as if it were an impediment to its future, Singapore has a very good idea where it is going. When you shop in Singapore, you contribute to its on-going character by helping to sustain the mighty money machine that is so critical to keeping this place running at such a high level of performance.

This obsession with modernity and the future initially impresses most visitors who have different expectations and images of Asian cities and societies. But after a while, many visitors find Singapore a bit boring. It is too neat, too tidy, too efficient, and too regulated—a caricature of a planner's textbook image. It's an antiseptic city where happiness is defined as orderliness, cleanliness, efficiency, air-conditioning, status, money, and materialistic pursuits and pleasures. Indeed, some have dubbed it Disneyland or a California resort run by the Mormans! If you have become captivated by the charm of Thailand's and Indonesia's living chaos, the diversity of Malaysia's culture and the mystery of its tribal peoples, the spontaneity of other Southeast Asian peoples, the serendipity of Third World travel, and the adventure of discovering unique items by digging through dusty and disorganized shops, Singapore may not be your type of city. For some people, this city is much too easy and convenient to be called an exotic place—especially if you spend most of your time confined to air-conditioned shopping centers where you constantly push and shove through crowds and are assaulted by one upscale shop after another offering the same expensive name-brand imported products that primarily appeal to status conscious and wealthy Asians. If you seek unique products, Singapore may disappoint you. Here you tend to shop for things imported from **other** exotic places.

However, if you have just come from Thailand, Malaysia, or Indonesia, you might appreciate returning to a world-according-to-Singapore for a few days. It's a wonderful place to recharge your batteries by pampering yourself with the finer things in life and literally *"shop 'til you drop."* All it takes is a comfortable pair of shoes, time, energy, and money!

Singapore is always a surprising place for visitors. It is "Instant Asia." Its diversity means that Singapore can be different things to different people. For some visitors, Singapore is a shopper's paradise and convention center. For others, it is a memorable city of the Raffles Hotel, Singapore Sling, W. Somerset Maugham, beautiful gardens, cleanliness, order, trishaws, outdoor eateries, Chinatown, ships, and sailors. The process of continuously layering more modern office buildings, hotels, shopping centers, restaurants, and subways onto Singapore's current stock of buildings and transportation arteries gives this city-state its own unique character. Only after visiting the city many times does one come away with a sense of never really knowing the "real Singapore." For the real Singapore is what is happening today and being reinvented tomorrow. If you visit one year and come back the next, you are likely to discover a new Singapore in the process of being transformed into yet another new Singapore—which will surprise you again next year!

Singapore is an exotic place, if you go beyond its exterior "Instant Asia" image and symbols of modernity. After visiting the hotels, restaurants, shopping centers, museums, and parks, be sure to walk the ethnic enclaves of Chinatown, Little India, and Little Araby—especially at night—and observe a festival or two. These areas and events have all the character of exotic places. They quickly remind you that you still are not home and there is much more to Singapore than its glitzy hotels, restaurants, and shopping centers. You will discover the other side of Singapore that remains very Asian despite its wonderful veneer of westernization which entices you and millions of others to its shores. Singapore, too, has its pockets of color, spontaneity, and chaos that give this city-state an interesting character absent along the clean green streets of Singapore's major shopping areas.

THE BASICS

LOCATION AND PEOPLE

Singapore is an island nation located just off the tip of the Malay Peninsula. It consists of the main island and 57 smaller islands. At 10° latitude and 137 kilometers (85 miles) north of the equator, Singapore looks and feels like it's on the equator. The main island is connected to Malaysia by a causeway which conveniently links Singapore by road and rail to Malaysia and eventually Thailand.

Singapore's 646 square kilometer area is constantly being enlarged due to reclamation efforts—up from 620 square kilometers in 1995. This is home to nearly 3.2 million people who primarily reside in the city proper. Singapore is one of the world's most multi-racial societies. Its population consists of Chinese (77.2%), Malay (14.1%), Indian (7.4%), and numerous other groups (1.3%). The Chinese primarily run this country but in remarkable harmony with the other groups.

Historically, Singapore developed due to its excellent location and management. Situated at the confluence of the Indian and Pacific Oceans, ships passing through the Straits of Malacca used Singapore as a convenient port and trading center. Today, Singapore continues to play a central shipping role in Asia as well as to serve as one of the world's most important trading and financial centers. Strategically located at the center of South and Southeast Asia, Singapore also is a convenient place for traveling to other Asian countries. Above all, Singapore is managed extremely well in the areas of oil refining, ship building, high-tech industries, finance, and tourism.

CLIMATE, SEASONS, WHEN TO GO

The weather in Singapore is similar to that in Kuala Lumpur and Jakarta. Being a tropical country situated almost on the equator, it is more or less hot and humid year round. The rainy season hits full force during December and January. July is the driest month. The ideal time to visit Singapore is between July and September—the period of least heat and humidity. Whenever you go, you will appreciate the fact that Singapore has moved most of its shops into air-conditioned quarters. You will not *"shop til you drop"* because of Singapore's shopping climate!

Singapore is a **walking city** with ample opportunities to escape into air-conditioned hotels, restaurants, and shopping centers. Wherever you go, you will spend a great deal of time walking. While much of this is indoor walking, much of it also is outdoors. Be sure to take it easy when outdoors. Wear lightweight cotton clothing and take comfortable shoes, an umbrella, sunglasses, a hat, and handkerchief.

GETTING THERE

Singapore is easy and convenient to get to by air, rail, road, or ship. Over 50 major **airlines** fly into Singapore from major cities around the world. Many of them, such as Northwest Airlines, United Airlines, Malaysia Air System, Japan Airlines, Singapore Airline, and China Air offer excellent round-trip airfares from major cities in North America and Europe. For example, you can fly round-trip from New York City to Singapore during much of the year for as little as $1100 as well as arrange stops in Hong Kong and Bangkok for an additional $50 per stop. Special 8-day "Asian Affair" packages go for as little as $1200 per person, including first-class hotels and round-trip airfare from the West Coast in the United States.

During our most recent trip to Singapore, we flew Northwest Airlines from Washington, DC to Singapore. We found their schedules to be the most convenient, the flights very comfortable, the service attentive, and the food well prepared.

We have often appreciated the good service we find as we travel in Asia. We found the attentive but not obtrusive service on Northwest compared very favorably with what we have experienced traveling on the most highly rated overseas airlines. The flight attendants went out of their way to make passengers comfortable and well cared for.

Best of all, we found Northwest Airlines' route—especially from East Coast and Midwest cities in the United States—to be very convenient. We flew directly from Detroit to Tokyo and then changed planes for a final direct flight from Tokyo to Singapore. In fact, Northwest flies from over 250 cities in North America.

But Northwest offers more than just a great routing to Singapore. We really enjoyed our Northwest flight and were impressed with several innovative programs that should appeal to anyone interested in ecology. Northwest has been cited for the second consecutive year as the most eco-friendly airline. Indeed, Northwest developed the first in-flight recycling program, and it pioneered a program to allow passengers to choose their food items from an a la carte service which both pleases passengers and has cut food waste by 20 percent.

If you fly frequently, consider membership in Northwest's WorldPerks^{SM} (frequent flyer) and WorldClubs^{SM} (airport lounges and special services) programs. For more information on the **WorldPerks^{SM}** frequent flyer program which also is partnered with KLM, contact Northwest by phone (1-800-447-3757) or mail: Northwest Airlines Customer Service Center, 601 Oak Street, Chisholm, MN 55719. For information on the **WorldClubs^{SM}** program, contact Northwest by phone (1-800-692-3788), fax (612-726-0988), or mail: Northwest Airlines, Inc., WorldClubs Service Center, 5101 Northwest Drive, Department A5301, St. Paul, MN 55111-3034. Also, be sure to visit Northwest Airline's Web site for detailed information on flights and services: *www.nwa.com*. You may want to make these contacts before doing your ticketing.

For most visitors from North America and Europe, the flight to Singapore is a long one. Thus, you may wish to upgrade your ticket to "Business Class" for more room and comfort. You will pay more for this upgrade but the increased comfort may be well worth it.

If you use the Internet, you can easily make reservations online by using several online ticketing groups. The four major reservation services are:

www.expedia.msn.com	*www.previewtravel.com*
www.itn.net	*www.travelocity.com*

Other popular online reservation services, with many claiming discount pricing, include:

www.air4less.com	*www.moments-notice.com*
www.airdeals.com	*www.onetravel.com*
www.airfare.co	*www.priceline.com*
www.bestfares.com	*www.smarterliving.com*
www.biztravel.com	*www.thetrip.com*
www.cheaptickets.com	*www.lowestfare.com*
www.concierge.come	*www.travelscape.com*
www.etnlinks.com	*www.travelzoo.com*
www.travelersadvantage.com	

However, while these online ticketing operations may appear to be convenient, we've found many of them can be more expensive than using a travel agent, especially one who works with consolidators. You'll get the best rates through consolidators, which may be 30 to 40 percent less than the major online ticketing operations. Consolidators often have small box ads in the Sunday travel sections of the New York Times, Washington Post, Los Angeles Times, and other major newspapers. Some of them, such as International Discount Travel, also provide price quotes on the Web: *www.idttravel.com.*

The **rail** trip into Singapore remains one of the world's most interesting. You can take a train from Bangkok, through Malaysia, and into Singapore. While the trip takes about 54 hours, it is relatively comfortable, and you will have a chance to see a great deal of urban and rural southern Thailand and Malaysia along the way.

The **roads** connecting Malaysia to Singapore are excellent. In fact, you could take buses all the way from Bangkok to Singapore. It is a grueling trip, especially through southern Thailand. The Thailand leg of the trip by bus is not recommended because of safety problems—accidents and robberies. It's also an uncomfortable trip for many travelers. Many bus seats are built for smaller bodies than that of the average American, Australian, or European. But it is an inexpensive way to go, and you will see a great deal of the colorful countryside. Better still, you can rent a car in Malaysia, drive to Singapore, and drop it with a Singapore agency.

It is easy to drive in Malaysia given the excellent road system, maps and signs in English, sane driving habits of the Malaysians, and the ease of entering Singapore. However, do not drive through Thailand into Malaysia unless you are extremely adventuresome or foolish—or both. The Thai side is even too chaotic for many Malays! It would be best to either fly or take a train into Penang/Butterworth or Kuala Lumpur in Malaysia and then rent a car to drive the rest of the way to Singapore. This is a particularly nice way of doing this leg of your shopping in exotic places adventure. Along the way—especially in Penang and Kuala Lumpur—you will find some additional shopping opportunities for Malay batiks, textiles, pewterware, pottery, silver, antiques, basketry, and woodcarvings. You may be pleasantly surprised in discovering Kuala Lumpur, a modern city with a fine museum of Malay arts and crafts, lovely parks and Moorish architecture, and modern hotels and high-rise buildings. Two to three days in Kuala Lumpur is probably plenty—it's one of Southeast Asia's least exciting major cities.

Singapore's Keppel Harbour is a major port for freighter, container, and cruise **ships**. Over 150 shipping lines regularly dock in Singapore. Several major cruise ships, such as the QE2, Pearl of Scandinavia, Royal Viking, Holland America, and Cunard Line, include Singapore on their Asian ports of call. Contact these cruise lines for information on their tours.

DOCUMENTS

Singapore encourages tourists to visit their city-state by making Immigration procedures relatively easy. Most nationalities only need to present a valid passport at the various air, sea, and land entry points to receive visa-free permission to stay for 14-90 days, depending on the specific country. Tourists from the United States and most European countries, for example, can stay up to 90 days without a visa; Canadians need a visa for stays of longer than two weeks. An international certificate documenting an appropriate vaccination is needed only if you come from a yellow fever infected area.

ARRIVAL

Singapore has cornered the market on airport efficiency. The Changi International Airport is one of the most impressive entry points into any country. Indeed, Singapore's airport usually ties with Amsterdam's airport as the best of the best in the world. Its two terminals handle over 25 million passengers a year. Normally you will pass through Immigration, pick up your bags, clear customs, change money, and be off in a comfortable taxi within 30 minutes of arrival. We've done this whole process several times in an amazing 15 minutes! It's so fast you have to think twice about whether you forgot something. Look on the wall ahead as you exit Immigration and you'll spot a sign with your flight number indicating the carousel where you can claim your luggage. Be sure you observe all the *"No"* signs awaiting you in the taxi and along the streets: *"No Smoking, No Spitting, No Stopping, No Litter, No Crossing."* Violations are punishable with stiff fines: up to S$500. Watch what you do, and get rid of any habits you may have picked up along the way in more lax Thailand or Indonesia! Welcome to the land obsessed with creating order and the culture of *"No."*

The trip by taxi into the city is even more impressive. The taxis are metered, and many drivers speak English. They may even point out some of the wonders along the way—or be so audacious as to complain that Singapore needs to be even more efficient; visitors are really perplexed when the complaint is directed toward the marvelous airport! Wide boulevards lined with trees and flowers initially greet you, and then the symbols of modernity hit you as you see hundreds of sparkling highrise apartment buildings, hotels, banks, and shopping centers. Everything looks new or freshly painted. Except for a few ethnic enclaves, there's nothing worn or makeshift about this Asian city. Here's a place that appears to have everything under control. It visually invites you to enjoy your stay. Nice streets, nice sidewalks, street lights, traffic flowing in a straight line, no litter, no beggars, no cigarette butts—just a nice clean and orderly place. Best of all, this hot and humid city looks air-conditioned!

Entry by rail, road, or ship is equally efficient. Unless you look like a hippie or druggie, with passport in hand you should be whisked through Immigration and Customs lines and on to your destination in very little time.

CUSTOMS AND IMMIGRATION

Singapore Customs allows you to bring in one liter of liquor duty-free. In line with its anti-smoking policy, it gives no concessions on cigarettes or other tobacco products. Bringing illegal drugs into the country results in long prison sentences and possible execution. Singapore also prefers granting entry to neat and tidy people. Should you have long hair or look somewhat unkempt, you may not make it through the process as quickly as others.

DEPARTURE TAX

The airport departure tax on all flights is S$15 (US$10). It's usually included in the price of your air ticket. If not, you will need to pay this tax during check-in. If you leave Singapore for Malaysia by land, you will be assessed a S$6 departure tax.

GOODS AND SERVICES TAX (GST)

Singapore now levies a Goods and Services Tax (GST) of 3 percent. Visitors who spend more than S$300 are entitled to a refund, if they complete the proper paper work and present their receipts and goods at the airport refund counter. When shopping at a place that displays a Tax Free Shopping sign, ask for a Tax Free Shopping Cheque. You can pool receipts of S$100 or more from shops displaying this sign. You must present the Shopping Cheques, along with your actual goods, at the airport departure terminal for customs inspection. You can then cash the Shopping Cheques at the Global Refund Counters in Changi Airport. You can opt to receive a bank check through the mail or have the refund credited to your credit card, less a surcharge.

❑ Singapore has cornered the market on airport efficiency—the best in the world!

❑ The taxis are metered, and many drivers speak English.

❑ A S$15 airport departure tax is either included in your airline ticket or you must pay it upon check-in.

❑ Singapore levies a Goods and Services Tax (GST) of 3 percent which is refundable at the airport.

❑ Hotels give the worst exchange rates as well as add a small service charge.

❑ Bargained prices generally are "cash only" prices.

❑ Tipping is close to being declared an official sin. The government discourages tipping.

CURRENCY AND CREDIT CARDS

At press time, the Singapore dollar was equivalent to US60¢, or S$1.67 equals US$1. The Singapore dollar comes in $1, $5, $10, $20, $50, $100, $500, $1,000, and $10,000 denominations. Each dollar is divided into 100 cents. Coins are issued in 1¢, 5¢, 10¢, 20¢ and 50¢ denominations.

You can easily exchange your money at the airport bank windows or among the numerous licensed money-changers found in the shopping complexes and Raffles Place. Most display a "Licensed Money Changer" sign. They usually give the best exchange rates. You should receive a better exchange rate on traveler's checks than on currency. As in most places, hotels in Singapore give the worst exchange rates as well as add a small service charge.

Most major credit cards are widely accepted in Singapore. Some shops, however, may try to add a surcharge to cover their costs of accepting credit card purchases. Like other Asian countries, this most often happens when you bargain for a price and then try to charge the purchase. Remember, hard bargained prices often are "cash only" prices. However, once you believe the merchant has given his final offer, you may say, *"Okay, but only if I can charge it."* Most of the time he or she will agree. If you buy expensive items which could possibly present problems later on, such as cameras or electronic goods, consider charging them even though it may cost you a bit more. Should you later have a problem—such as the VCR unit you bought is incompatible with U.S. systems, even though you specified you would be using it in the U.S.—your credit card company may help you resolve the problem.

SECURITY

Singapore is one of the world's safest cities to visit. You can walk around with little fear of having your pockets picked or getting mugged. You may occasionally encounter a tout (illegal in Singapore) in tourist shopping areas, but they are out to make a fast buck on commissions rather than physically harm you. Even women traveling alone will feel safe here. Nonetheless, take normal precautions concerning your valuables. There are a few bad people everywhere. The airport also is very safe. Singapore simply doesn't have the political and criminal problems found in many other countries.

TIPPING

Tipping in Singapore is close to being declared an official sin. The government discourages tipping. It's prohibited at the airport and discouraged at hotels and restaurants. You can help rid Singapore of this decadent practice by not tipping anyone except those from whom you ask special favors. Singapore's wages are the second highest in all of Asia, and hotels and restaurants add a 10 percent service charge and a 3 percent government tax. Taxi drivers enjoy receiving tips, and some will conveniently forget to give you change, especially if it is a small amount. Help them break this habit by requesting your change and then count it in full; they sometimes forget to give you **all** your change.

On the other hand, should you need special assistance, asking for help will eventually get help in service-oriented Singapore. However, a tip may get you even better service. Money still talks and makes people walk when it comes to getting things done quickly. If, for example, you need a taxi in a hurry but your hotel taxi queue is long, press a few small bills in the hand of the doorman or porter and you may discover how to by-pass the line altogether. Tipping may be a sin, but it's a sin many have learned to live with, and hope for.

LANGUAGE

Singapore recognizes four official languages: English, Mandarin, Malay, and Tamil. Since English is the preferred language of business, government, and tourism, you will have no problem communicating. Even many taxi drivers speak English.

BUSINESS HOURS

Banks are open from 9:30am to 3pm, Monday through Friday. They also are open from 9:30am to 11:30am on Saturday. Branches of the Development Bank of Singapore at Bukit Timah, Katong, Orchard, Thomson, and Toa Payok remain open until 3pm on Saturday. However, many banks do not exchange foreign currency on Saturdays.

Offices are normally open from 9/9:30am to 5/5:30pm, Monday through Friday. Some are open on Saturday.

Shopping hours vary. Most **department stores** and **shops** in the large shopping complexes are open every day from 10am to 9pm. Some shops stay open later. The Chinese Emporiums, for example, remain open until 10pm. While many stores in the large shopping complexes will remain open on Sunday, some open late or not at all. Many small shops are closed on Sunday.

TRANSPORTATION

Singapore offers lots of good transportation alternatives that are convenient, comfortable, and inexpensive. Although traffic at times can be very congested, especially in the major shopping areas during rush hour, you have enough transportation alternatives to get you where you want to go with relative ease. Indeed, Singapore has developed a transportation system that is the envy of most countries.

One of the easiest ways to get around in Singapore is by **taxi**. Over 15,000 air-conditioned taxis provide convenient, comfortable, and reasonably priced transportation. Operating 24 hours a day, they can be flagged down along most roads and found at well marked taxi-stands at most major shopping centers and hotels. All cabs are metered. The flag drops at S$2.40 for up to the first kilometer; each additional 240 meters, for up to the first 10 kilometers, costs 10¢. Waiting time costs 10¢ for each 30 seconds. Surcharges apply in certain restricted zone areas, at the airport, for telephone bookings, when a passenger pays by credit card (10 percent), and during different times of the day. The ride from the Singapore Changi Airport to the major hotel area along Orchard Road costs about S$20. We frequently use cabs because they are relatively inexpensive given the fact that one normally need not travel far from one shopping area to another. They also are very convenient for shopping, especially if you are carrying many items. Each cab has a list of "don'ts," fares, and additional charges clearly posted for your convenience. However, during rush hour, which can run from 4pm to 8pm, cabs can be very difficult to find, and taxi lines can be very long—taking 30 minutes or more—at the major hotels and shopping centers. If you are near Raffles City, a good alternative to the long taxi lines is to walk across the street to the entrance of the Raffles Hotel where it's much easier to find a cab.

Singapore's **subway**, the MRT (Mass Rapid Transit system), is the favored mode of transportation for local residents. More and more tourists have discovered how convenient this 67-kilometer system is for getting around Singapore. By all means learn to use it as soon as you venture into Singapore's streets—it's easy to understand and use, despite the often crowded stations. Air-conditioned underground stations are conveniently located in and around all of Singapore's major shopping areas and hotels. Fares range from 70¢ to S$1.60. You can purchase tickets from coin-operated automated machines in MRT stations. You also can purchase S$7 tourist souvenir tickets (with maps) or stored value TransitLink cards which allow you to use the MRT and buses. The MRT operates from 6am to midnight and stops at stations every three to eight minutes. Most maps and tourist literature include information and maps on how to use this convenient system.

The **buses** also are convenient, comfortable, and inexpensive. Fares range from 60¢ to S$1.20 for non air-conditioned buses and 70¢ to S$1.50 for air-conditioned buses. Carry lots of small change for using the buses. They only accept the exact fare since bus drivers do not give change. As you enter the bus, ask the bus driver for the appropriate fare for your destination. Buses 16 and 36 run between Orchard Road and Changi Airport. Over 2,800 buses operate from 6am to midnight. For details on the various routes, you can pick up a free copy of *"This Week in Singapore"* or purchase the ***Singapore Bus Guide*** which is available at most bookstores or newsstands.

One of the best transportation deals is to purchase a S$10

Tourist Day Ticket. This ticket can be used for 12 rides a day on the MRT and all basic fare bus services. You can purchase this ticket at any TransitLink Ticket Sales Office which can be found in most Mass Rapid Transit stations and bus interchanges. The ticket is only good for the date stated on the ticket and it can be purchased up to seven days in advance.

The **Singapore Trolley**, a red tram bus, operates between the Orchard Road shopping belt, the colonial district, the Singapore River, Raffles Hotel, Clarke Quay, Marina and Suntec City. A one-day ticket for unlimited rides, plus a free riverboat tour, costs S$14.90 for adults and S$9.90 for children. You can purchase tickets from hotel concierges or the Trolley driver directly. For more information, call Singapore Explorer at 339-6833.

The **SIA Hop-On** is a trolley bus service that operates in the city's major shopping, cultural, and entertainment areas. Operating from 9:30am to 9:30pm, it covers Orchard Road, Bugis Junction, Suntec City, the Colonial District, Clarke Quay, Boat Quay, Chinatown, and the Singapore Botanic Gardens. It usually stops at 30 to 45 minute intervals, depending on the traffic. A day-pass for unlimited rides costs S$5 for adults and S$3 for children. If you fly to Singapore on Singapore Airlines or SilkAir, you can use this service free of charge by presenting your boarding pass or air ticket to the driver. Tickets can be purchased from most hotels, SIA ticket offices in the city, and from the bus drivers directly.

The six-seater **Airport Shuttle** (Maxicab) operates between most hotels and the Singapore Changi Airport. You'll need to schedule this service by calling CityCab at 553-3880. It operates every 30 minutes from 9am to 6pm and every 15 minutes from 6pm to 11pm. It costs S$7 for adults and S$5 for children. You can book this service at the airport shuttle counters located in the arrival hall of Changi Airport Terminals 1 and 2. Payment is made directly to the MaxiCab driver who accepts cash and credit cards.

You also can rent **self-drive cars** from several rental agencies throughout the city. The traffic is sane, maps are excellent, signs are plentiful, parking is available, and driving can be fun. You need either a valid driver's license from your country or an international driver's license. However, if you primarily plan to confine your stay to the central part of the city, you may want to rely on public transportation since it is convenient and inexpensive. A rental car is most convenient for exploring the island as well as for venturing into neighboring Malaysia.

TOURS, TRAVEL AGENTS, INFORMATION

Travel in and around Singapore is extremely well organized and convenient for individuals and groups. The Singapore Tourism Board has developed excellent literature to assist individuals in conducting their own tours. Most of this literature is available at the airport or through the **STB Tourist Information Centre** in the Raffles Hotel Arcade (#02-34, 328 North Bridge Road, Tel. 1-800-334-1335/6, toll free in Singapore only; open 8:30am-7pm daily) and at its central office near the Traders Hotel: Tourism Court, 1 Orchard Spring Lane (Tel. 736-6622).

Numerous private tour companies, such as **Singapore Sightseeing Tour East** (Tel. 332-3755), **Gray Line Tours** (Tel. 331-8203), **Holiday Tours** (Tel. 738-2622), **SH Tours** (Tel. 734-9923), **Sentosa Discovery Tours** (Tel. 277-9654), and **RMG Tours** (Tel. 220-1661), offer several excellent and relatively inexpensive tours, both daytime and evening, of the city, islands, harbor, and southern Malaysia. Most companies have brochures of their tours at the front desks of major hotels. Their air-conditioned buses or vans with English-speaking guides will pick you up and drop you off at your hotel.

Singapore has hundreds of travel agents to help you plan your trip. Be aware that Malaysia Airlines, Singapore Airlines, Garuda, and Thai International offer special packages to Sumatra, Java, and Bali from Singapore. Other special tours to neighboring countries can be arranged through travel agents.

FOOD AND DRINK

Singapore is a true gastronomic delight where you can feast to your heart's content. The variety of cuisines is overwhelming. You will find just about every type of cuisine you might want, and then some—European, American, Mexican, Middle Eastern, Chinese, Indian, Pakistani, Indonesian, Malay, Thai, Korean, or Japanese. A local cuisine, called *Nonya* or *Peranakan*, is a special blending of Chinese and Malay cooking.

Your range of eating establishments includes elegant and expensive hotel restaurants as well as colorful and inexpensive open-air food markets and hawker stalls. The major international fast-food chains are well represented here. Several hotels offer set breakfasts and lunches as well as the ubiquitous noon buffet. Wherever you eat in Singapore, you'll eat well.

You will find plenty of popular soft drinks, excellent local beers, and the famous Singapore Sling at its place of origin—the Long Bar in the Raffles Hotel.

ELECTRICITY AND WATER

Electricity in Singapore is 220-240 volts, 50 cycle AC power. Some hotels have 110-volt outlets. Most hotels have transformers to convert your 110-120 volt, 60 cycle AC appliances. Tap water and ice are safe to consume in Singapore.

RESOURCES

A great deal of information is available on Singapore. The best source is the Singapore Tourism Board (STB). It publishes several guide books, brochures, and maps to assist you in getting around Singapore with relative ease. Their *Official Guide Singapore* and series of *Yours to Explore* guides (Little India, Chinatown, Singapore River) are excellent self-directed guides to the city. The STB also publishes a set of useful brochures on various aspects of visiting Singapore—arts, festivals and events, food and entertainment, and shopping. Most of this literature is available at Changi International Airport as well as at the STP office in the Raffles Hotel Arcade. Be sure to stop at one of the STB stands at the airport to pick up this literature.

Since Singapore is one of the major publishing centers in the world, you will find a great deal of literature on Singapore in the local bookstores. Explore the maps and books on Singapore found in the Singapore section of the city's three major bookstores: Borders, Time, and MPH.

Should you wish to do some background reading on the history, society, and politics of Singapore, try some of the following books: Noel Barber's *The Singapore Story* and *Sinister Twilight: The Fall of Singapore*; James Clavell's *King Rat*; and Alex Josey's *Singapore: Its Past, Present, and Future*. The evolution of Singapore since World War II remains a fascinating story of how a small city-state has managed to regularly transform itself into a major economic force in Asia.

THE STREETS OF SINGAPORE

We have little other than praise for the streets of Singapore. The streets are clean, orderly, and easy to navigate. There is nothing disorienting about this city other than perhaps the initial shock of seeing a place that may even look better than back home. After that, you should be able to get around easily in this city.

A few rules outlined on page 78 for navigating Singapore's streets will help you get around to shop efficiently:

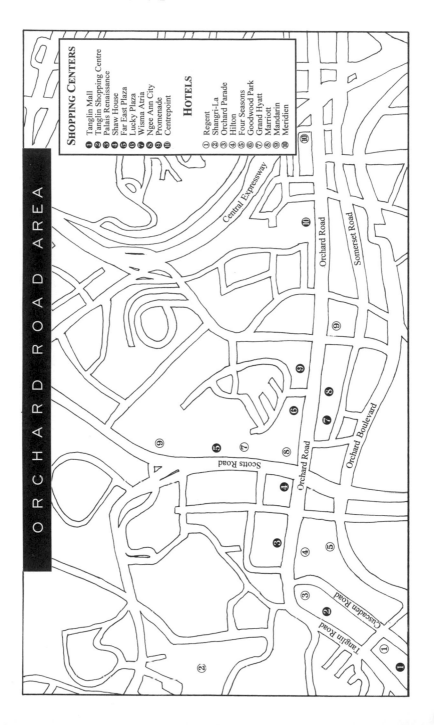

ORCHARD ROAD AREA

SHOPPING CENTERS

❶ Tanglin Mall
❷ Tanglin Shopping Centre
❸ Palais Renaissance
❹ Shaw House
❺ Far East Plaza
❻ Lucky Plaza
❼ Wisma Atria
❽ Ngee Ann City
❾ Promenade
❿ Centrepoint

HOTELS

① Regent
② Shangri-La
③ Orchard Parade
④ Hilton
⑤ Four Seasons
⑥ Goodwood Park
⑦ Grand Hyatt
⑧ Marriott
⑨ Mandarin
⑩ Meridien

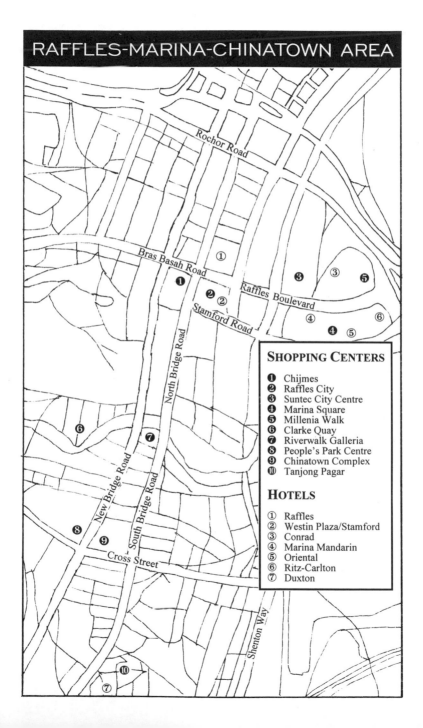

RAFFLES-MARINA-CHINATOWN AREA

SHOPPING CENTERS

❶ Chijmes
❷ Raffles City
❸ Suntec City Centre
❹ Marina Square
❺ Millenia Walk
❻ Clarke Quay
❼ Riverwalk Galleria
❽ People's Park Centre
❾ Chinatown Complex
❿ Tanjong Pagar

HOTELS

① Raffles
② Westin Plaza/Stamford
③ Conrad
④ Marina Mandarin
⑤ Oriental
⑥ Ritz-Carlton
⑦ Duxton

1. **Get ready to walk since this is a walking city.** Singapore is a compact city where the major shopping complexes are confined to stretches of road no more than one mile in length. You can easily walk from one shopping complex to another in the same area. Most of your walking, however, will be confined to the interior floors and levels of the air-conditioned shopping complexes. Take a good pair of walking shoes for Singapore.

2. **Take public transportation whenever possible.** Since Singapore is very hot and humid, do not try to walk too much outdoors. A long walk in the heat of the day can be very debilitating. Even though shopping areas, such as Chinatown and Little India, may look close to each other on a map, they are not once you start walking. Take a taxi, MRT, or a bus between areas. You can drive your own car, but it is more convenient to take taxis, the MRT, and buses. If you drive, you will need to find and pay for parking.

3. **Carry your rain and sun gear.** Umbrella, sunglasses, and a hat may come in handy, given Singapore's climate.

4. **Observe the local rules.** The Singapore government is very strict in regulating its traffic flow. This means no jay-walking, no littering, no cigarette butts, and no smoking in many public places. Cross at the street lights.

5. **Orient yourself to two distinct shopping cultures.** Singapore offers two separate styles of shopping—shopping complexes and department stores versus Third World shops. The modern shopping complexes and department stores are most heavily concentrated along Tanglin, Orchard, and Scotts roads. These are best approached like any air-conditioned shopping mall—walk in and browse. Their goods are nicely displayed, salespeople speak English and are polite, and your purchases are processed through cash registers and deposited in plastic shopping bags. The Third World shopping culture is found in the ethnic enclaves of Chinatown, Little India, and Arab Street. Lined with small row shops selling in bazaar fashion, these areas have the look, sound, and smell of similar shops found in many parts of Thailand, Malaysia, and Indonesia. Shops have a worn and cluttered look to them. You must bargain for everything. Shopkeepers may or may not speak some English.

And your purchases are likely to be calculated on an abacus or handwritten on a piece of paper. You may feel more comfortable shopping in the first culture, but the second culture is much more exotic and can be a great deal of fun.

Becoming oriented toward Singapore is relatively easy. The major destination for most visitors is the city proper, located on the southern section of Singapore Island. The city is laid out on a grid plan. Most of the hotels, restaurants, shopping complexes, and shops front on the main streets. Unlike Thailand and Indonesia, in Singapore you need not explore many back lanes or residential areas for shopping opportunities. Just go to the main streets and walk down block after block of shops and explore various levels of shopping complexes.

Take, for example, Orchard Road, which is Singapore's most famous shopping street. Lined with fine shops and shopping complexes on both sides of the street, you shop this area by walking up one side and down another. When you come to Scotts Road, which intersects Orchard Road, you'll discover even more shops and shopping complexes to explore. The same even is true for the ethnic shopping areas: Chinatown, Little India, and Arab Street. Crowded and congested, these areas, too, must be explored on foot, going from shop to shop, block after block.

To do the streets of Singapore properly, you need four things: a good map, comfortable shoes, lots of time, and persistence. You'll find lots of good maps. The shoes, time, and persistence are up to you. The major problem with Singapore is this: there is too much to do in such a small place. Like Hong Kong, you will be assaulted by shop after shop offering wonderful selections of goods. After your first day in Singapore, you wonder how in the world you will ever have time to shop this city as well as find time to see the many interesting sights! Where do I start, and when do I finish? The sheer volume of shopping complexes and shops presents you with a formidable task as you feel your way through your Singapore shopping adventure.

KNOW BEFORE YOU SHOP

SINGAPORE TOURISM BOARD

The Singapore Tourism Board (STB) plays an important role in ensuring that your Singapore shopping adventure will be most rewarding. It constantly tries to improve the image of shopping in Singapore by responding to complaints and setting standards among shops. Unfortunately, some tourists have reported a combination of rude behavior, poor workmanship, misrepresentation, and other unscrupulous practices among some merchants. Since 1985, the STB has creating various "Good Retailer" schemes to ensure quality and integrity amongst retailers. The current program recognizes shops along Orchard Road and Marina that agree to offer quality merchandise and excellent customer services. These shops display a "Singapore Gold Circle" sticker in recognition of their promise of excellence and they are listed in the back of a tear-out card in the *Singapore Official Guide*. The Singapore Tourism Board also publishes a list of blacklisted retailers.

SHOPPING COMPLAINTS

While the Singapore government has attempted to create an idyllic shopping environment for visitors—one that emphasizes quality and integrity—problems do occasionally arise and need to be dealt with as soon as possible. Many of these problems have to do with shopping touts who entice visitors to join them on a "free shopping tour" in which the touts get commissions (10-30%) on everything you buy from their recommended shops. Other problems have more to do with the behavior of the retail shop—broken promises, goods not shipped, inferior quality. Should you have a problem with a retailer or shopping tout, contact the Retail Promotion Centre at Blk 528, Ang Mo Kio Ave. 10, #02-2387, Tel. 450-2114 or Fax 458-6393. Alternatively, you can seek redress by contacting the Small Claims Tribunals at the Apollo Centre #05-00, No. 2 Havelock Road, Tel. 535-7922 or Fax 435-5994 or at Block 50 Marine Terrace, #03-265, Tel. 241-3575 or Fax 241-8938. Visitor complaints are usually heard and ruled upon within two or three days. For more information, visit the Tribunal's Web site: *www.gov.sg/judiciary/subct/courts/scat.html*.

YOUR MONEY

Most shops accept major international credit cards, such as Visa, MasterCard, and American Express. Some shops may add 3 to 5 percent to your total bill for using a credit card because they consider their prices to be "cash only" prices. While they are not supposed to engage in such a practice, and you can report them to your credit card company, this happens nonetheless. Especially if you are bargaining, the price you agree upon may be considered "cash only." Always clarify if your negotiated price is a cash or credit card price. If you pay cash, you may want to ask for a discount because the merchant does not have to pay a credit card fee.

RECEIPTS, RETURNS, "ON HOLD" REQUESTS

While most department stores and retail shops automatically give receipts, be sure you get a receipt wherever you shop. Also, check to be sure the items are correctly listed on the receipt.

Most department stores and large shops will exchange goods within three days of purchase if you present your receipt and the goods are in resalable condition. However, small shops may be less accommodating. If you are uncertain about an item, always ask about the shop's return policy. Also, you may want to ask the shop to put an item "on hold" (sometimes called "on reserve" in Asian shops) so you can think about it. Most shops will hold items for up to three days. This will at least give you some time to shop around for other items that may be more suitable for you. The wise old shopping rule that *you should buy something when you first see it or it may be gone"* can be modified by asking a shop to hold the item for a few days. Leave your name and local contact information just in case the shopkeeper needs to contact you. Putting something "on hold" may also give you some bargaining leverage should you come back later and indicate you're still not certain if you want to buy the particular item, or you saw a similar item elsewhere that cost less—but you would really like this item *"if the price were less."*

WARRANTIES AND GUARANTEES

Many items, especially cameras and electronics, should come with international guarantees. Most warranties are for one year from the date of purchase. Always ask about warranties before making a purchase. If the shop does not offer such guarantees, it's best to be suspicious and shop elsewhere. Also, check over the warranty carefully since it may have restrictions that make it useless in your country. Make sure any electronic appliances, cameras, and television sets are compatible with your electrical configuration and broadcast systems back home. Most such goods are compatible with Asian and European electronic and transmission systems but not with North American systems.

If you purchase jewelry and gems, be sure to ask for written guarantees. Many shoppers fall victim to fast talking salespeople who offer mediocre jewelry at inflated prices. If you're not a jewelry expert, safeguard your purchases with a guarantee.

DELIVERY

Most shops will arrange delivery to your hotel room or shipping to your home address; some will even deliver to the airport as you prepare to depart. Be sure to provide all details on your address as well as get a complete receipt from the shop so you can verify your purchase should you have a problem or need to present it to customs. If the item is being shipped to your home address, make sure it is insured against damage and loss by purchasing All Risk insurance. The shop can arrange for this insurance. If you need to check postal regulations on shipments from Singapore, check with the Singapore Post which is open 8:30am to 5pm on weekdays, and 8:30am to 1pm on Saturdays. Many hotels will wrap your purchases, even making a box that can be part of your checked through luggage; ask at your hotel front desk or the concierge for assistance with packing. They also may be able to recommend reliable shippers.

SHOPPING MAPS

Before venturing into the streets and subway, make sure you are armed with a good street map. You'll find several good maps of Singapore (*Map of Singapore*, *Singapore Map*, and the *Official Map of Singapore*) which are available free of charge at the airport, from your hotel front desk, and through the Singapore Tourism Board's offices at the Raffles Hotel Arcade and Tourism Court, 1 Orchard Spring Lane. Many shops and bookstores (Times, MPH, and Borders) also have copies of these and other useful maps.

WHAT TO BUY

Singapore is often compared to Hong Kong as if the two cities were in competition to attract international shoppers. This is unfortunate, because the two cities have different shopping strengths. It is true that both Hong Kong and Singapore offer similar electronics and camera equipment, but for many visitors such items are not great bargains in either city anyway. If you are from the U.S., you will be better off purchasing such items through a New York City mail-order house than buying the items in Singapore or Hong Kong.

So what does Singapore have that Hong Kong doesn't? Plenty. Singapore's most important shopping strengths are in the areas of Asian antiques, arts, crafts, carpets, fashion goods, ready-made clothes, pewterware, electronics, and imported luxury items from Europe. When comparing prices between Hong Kong and Singapore, similar goods are priced about the same. Singapore has some price advantage on cameras, watches, liquor, tobacco, household appliances, costume jewelry, toys, games, and perfume. Hong Kong has some price advantage on mens' clothing, cosmetics, and leather goods. Although some claim Singapore is cheaper than Hong Kong, whatever differences exist are minor; they don't justify the additional expense of visiting the other city just to save a little money.

ANTIQUES, CURIOS, PRIMITIVE ART

While Hong Kong serves primarily as a conduit for Chinese goods, Singapore offers a wonderful collection of antiques and curios from all over Asia as well as the South Pacific. Most shops specialize in particular types of antiques. Some, for example, specialize in antiques from China (**Kwok Gallery** in the Far East Shopping Centre) whereas others only carry local (Straits) Chinese antiques (**Petnic's** on Cuppage Road). Others only offer primitive art and textiles (**Tatiana, Tiepolo, Mata-Hari, Harvest Straits**, and **Setiawan Gallery** in Tanglin Shopping Centre). Several shops in Tanglin Shopping Centre are "must" stops if tribal art is one of your interests. These shops offer excellent quality goods often not found in their country of origin—primarily Indonesia and Malaysia. Others include a fine collection of arts and antiques from Thailand and Burma (**Exotica** in the Raffles Hotel Arcade and **Lopburi Arts & Antiques** in Tanglin Place).

Several shops have central or branch offices in Hong Kong, Bangkok, Kuala Lumpur, and Jakarta (**Tomlinson, Plum Blossoms, Setiawan Enterprise, Bin House, Royal Selangor, KenSoon Asiatic Art, Lotus Arts de Vivre, Larry Jewelry**). Linked to these other countries through an intricate web of family, professional, and friendship ties, they regularly make buying trips to neighboring countries or have their friends and relatives supply them with new items to replenish their collections. When you visit these shops, ask if they have a branch in other cities. You may want to browse in these other shops when in Hong Kong, Bangkok, Kuala Lumpur, or Jakarta.

Several shops also carry primitive art pieces from Indonesia and Papua New Guinea. Most of the Indonesian primitive art is from the nearby Batak area in Sumatra. Singapore is the only place in Southeast Asia where we have found primitive art pieces from the Sepik River area in Papua New Guinea. The art work is gorgeous and tempts one to add a Sepik River leg to one's Asian and Pacific shopping adventures!

Many shops and department stores stock Chinese, Thai, Burmese, Indonesian, and Indian antiques and curios. The Chinese antiques include the usual assortment of items: porcelain, carpets, snuff bottles, incense burners, paintings, jade carvings, and jewelry. The Thai antiques are similar to those found in Bangkok's River City Shopping Complex: Buddha images, ceramics, gilded wood carvings and gables. Burmese antiques include lacquerware, gilded panels, woodcarvings, and tapestries. Indonesian collections tend to specialize in masks, puppets, woodcarvings, and small chests. And the Indian antiques and curios are primarily oil lamps, brass and bronze figures, and jewelry.

One major advantage of buying Asian antiques in Singapore is that you can take them out of the country without special export permits. Thai Buddha images, which are illegal to export from Thailand without special permits, are plentiful in Singapore. However, be very careful about fakes. Some shops may claim the newly carved Thai "antiques" are indeed old and charge you accordingly. Many of the bronze Buddha images claimed to be from the Sukhothai and Ayuthaya periods may have similar age and price claims.

Prices for antiques, curios, and primitive art in Singapore are higher than in their countries of origin. For example, Batak house gables selling for S$350 in Parapat, Lake Toba (Northern Sumatra, Indonesia) may cost over S$2000 in Singapore. The same is true for Burmese and Thai antiques. Lacquerware selling for S$500 in Bangkok goes for S$1000 in Singapore. Nonetheless, we have found many lovely Burmese and Thai antiques as well as Indonesian ethnographic art in Singapore which we could not find in Burma, Thailand, or Indonesia. On the other hand, if you have already been to Indonesia—especially Jl. Kebon Sirih Timur Dalam in Jakarta and Kuta Beach on Bali—you may be disappointed with the limited Indonesian selections found in Singapore. Except for a few shops in Tanglin Shopping Centre (**Tatiana, Mata-Hari, Harvest Straits, Tiepolo, Setiawan Enterprise**) that specialize in ethnographic pieces and **Exotica** at the Raffles Hotel Arcade, most Indonesian items are the ubiquitous Balinese woodcarvings. You would find a wider selection and save a great deal of money by making a quick trip to Medan, Lake Toba, Jakarta, or Bali than to make your Indonesian purchases here in Singapore—this is especially true if you are interested in other than "museum quality" pieces. Special tour packages from Singapore make such trips inexpensive and worthwhile. Savings on your purchases can more than make up for the expense of such trips into Indonesia from Singapore. But if you are interested in top quality ethnographic pieces and are willing to pay for them, a serious look in Singapore is worthwhile.

Shops selling antiques, curios, and primitive art are primarily found in the shopping complexes, department stores, and hotels in and around Orchard Road. The largest concentration of good quality shops is found throughout the Tanglin Shopping Centre and in the Dempsey Road and Watten Estate areas. The Tanglin Shopping Centre shops specialize in small collectors' items, such as antique Buddhas, ethnographic pieces, and sculptures. Many shops in the Dempsey Road (**Eastern Discoveries**, **Renaissance Antique Gallery**, and **Red House Antiques**) and Watten Estate areas primarily specialize in antique furniture. Two of Singapore's best antique shops are found at the Raffles Hotel Arcade—**Tomlinson** and **Exotica**.

ART

Several art galleries are located in the major shopping areas and hotel shopping arcades. While much of the art is imported from other Asian countries, as well as Europe, many shops also offer oils, watercolors, and sculptures produced by Singapore's and Malaysia's local artists. We have been very pleased with the overall quality of this art—some of the best in all of Asia. Famous local artists such as Chen Wen Hsi, Thomas Yao, Anthony Poon, Wan Soon Kam, Teng Juay Lee, Nai Swee Leng, James Tan, Ang Ah Tee, and Gog Sing Hoi are producing everything from Chinese brush paintings to abstract landscapes. Much of this art reflects a creative blending of traditional Asian and contemporary western motifs and styles. You may find much of this art integrates nicely into your home.

Works of art are often found in the antique and curio shops. One of the largest concentration of art galleries is found on the fifth level of the Paragon Shopping Centre on Orchard Road. Here you will find several fine art galleries: **Jasmine Fine Arts**, **Sin Hua Gallery**, **Orchard Gallery**, and **Cony Art Gallery**. Another large concentration of art galleries is found at **Riverwalk Galleries** (top floor) which is adjacent to Boat Quay and Clarke Quay. Other shops offering good quality art include **HaKaren Art Gallery** and **Antiques of the Orient** in Tanglin Shopping Centre.

CARPETS

More than any other city in Asia, Singapore offers a varied selection of new and antique Chinese, Pakistani, Afghan, Persian, and Turkish carpets. Several shops specialize in such carpets. If your timing is right and you make a point to survey announcements in the local newspapers, you may have a chance to attend a carpet auction.

You will find the carpet shops in several shopping areas. On Tanglin Road and Dempsey Road is a huge shop which operates under two names: **Orientalist** (10 Tanglin Road) and **Tandis** (Dempsey Road #01-05). In the Dempsey Road area, look for **Mountain Looms**. Several shops along **Orchard Road** and **Arab Street** specialize in Persian carpets. For copies of Chinese carpets, go to the **Singapore Carpet Manufacturers** (Haw Par Centre, Clemenceau Avenue). Other places to explore are **Amir & Sons** in Lucky Plaza; **Hassan's** in Tanglin Shopping Centre; **Eastern Carpets** in Raffles City; and **Tabriz** and **Qureski's** in Centrepoint.

Wherever you shop for carpets, be sure to bargain hard. Buying carpets in Singapore is like buying carpets anywhere else in the world. Bargain, bargain, bargain. As with many of the antiques found in Singapore, if you are looking at an expensive carpet, be sure you know about carpets before buying.

JEWELRY

Singapore is a good place to buy jewelry. Workmanship is excellent, and prices are comparable to those in Hong Kong. In fact, several jewelry stores along Orchard Road are actually branches of Hong Kong shops. Family enterprises, the brothers, sisters, sons, and daughters regularly move back and forth between Hong Kong and Singapore.

The range of jewelry in Singapore is excellent. You will find Chinese gold and jade everywhere, but especially in Chinatown and the Chinese Emporiums. You can also find excellent quality pearls, diamonds, sapphires, rubies, emeralds, topaz, coral, and turquoise as well as inexpensive Indian jewelry.

Jewelry designs in Singapore range from traditional to modern. In Chinatown, for example, you will find 22-karat gold jewelry made in traditional designs. Most of these shops are concentrated in **People's Park** and along **South Bridge Road**. Several shops in the shopping complexes along **Orchard Road** offer exquisite designer jewelry using diamonds, semi-precious stones, and pearls. You also will find shops selling loose stones, jewelry in Italian designs, and antique jewelry. Many shops offer average quality necklaces, earrings, pins, and rings.

Excellent quality jewelry can be found in Singapore. Visit enough shops to get an accurate feel for the quality, designs, and prices. Like buying jewelry anywhere the world, be sure you know what you're doing rather than trust the observations and advice of salespeople in jewelry shops. Again, be sure to bargain hard in all the shops.

One of the best jewelry stores in Singapore is **Je Taime Jewellers** on the second floor of Ngee Ann City (#02-12 C/D) on 435 Orchard Road. This well established jeweler with a preference for Italian craftsmanship, creates exquisite designs in gold and diamonds. Prices start at S$2,000 and go up. The owner, Regina Wong, also has a branch shop in Reno, Nevada.

Other excellent jewelers include **Larry Jewelry** with shops at Orchard Towers, Ngee Ann City, Paragon, and Raffles City; **Minh Anh** and B. P. DeSilva in the Marina Square Shopping Mall; and **Chap Mai Jewelry** in Raffles City.

For very exclusive and exquisite jewelry, visit two shops at Raffles Hotel Arcade: **Lotus** and **Tiffany & Co**. Lotus, one of Bangkok's top jewelry designers, offers some of the most unique jewelry in all of Southeast Asia.

Most of the major upscale shopping arcades, such as Raffles Hotel Arcade, Tanglin Place, Palais Renaissance, The Paragon, and The Hilton Shopping Gallery at The Hilton Hotel, have numerous fine jewelry shops carrying the latest Italian, Swiss, and French designs in jewelry and watches: **Bvlgari** (The Hilton), **Piaget** (The Hilton and the Mandarin hotels), **Van Cleef & Arpels Jewellery** (The Paragon), **The Hour Glass** (Palais Renaissance), **Patek Philippe** (The Regent Singapore), and **Rolex Centre** (1F Tong Building, 302 Orchard Rd.).

HANDICRAFTS AND SOUVENIRS

Singapore is filled with handicrafts from all over Asia. Department stores, emporiums, and shops carry woodcarvings, basketware, rattan and cane goods, lacquered goods, copper and brass items, pewterware, batik, and all types of knickknacks. Like so many handicrafts found in other countries, many of the ones in Singapore have that distinct "Made for Tourists Only" look. Nonetheless, you may be able to find some quality handicrafts amidst the tourist junk.

If you are interested in Chinese handicrafts, the best place to shop are the **Chinese emporiums** in People's Park Complex and along Orchard Road as well as in a few suburban areas. Offering a large variety of handicrafts from China, these emporiums are similar to the ones in Hong Kong—packed with a large assortment of items, including large pieces of furniture. They are especially well stocked with inexpensive—although not fashionable—clothes from China. In **Chinatown**, explore the shops along Trengganu, Temple, and Smith streets. These three streets are full of discoveries. Just walk into the cluttered shops and look everywhere for handcrafted items. Shophouses along these streets sell a variety of baskets, kites, ceramics, dolls, costumes, pottery, and fans. You will find plenty of nice gift items amongst the many Chinese handicrafts found in these shops. If you are interested in some of the most unique Chinese folk art, look for funeral items in the shops on Sago Street.

Along **Arab Street** you will find numerous imported handicrafts. Several shops are crammed with attractive and inexpensive baskets, carpets, cloth, batik, lamps, leather goods, hats, fans, and much more. Many handicrafts are imported from Malaysia, India, the Philippines, Indonesia, and even Kenya. We especially like the selections at **Habib Handicraft, B&K Textile,** and **Jothi Palayakat Co.**

Little India, which begins at the corner of Sarangoon and Sungei roads, has several shops selling Indian handcrafted items: brass, flowers, brocades, paintings, and batik.

Many shops that used to be found in the Singapore Handicraft Centre near Tanglin Road have relocated to two new locations—**Chinatown Point** (tall blue building across from People's Park Centre and Furama Hotel) and the **Tanjong Pagar Conservation Area** (200+ restored two-storey shophouses along old Tanjang Pagar Road, next to Chinatown). Somewhat difficult to find, you must browse through numerous shops in each area to discover the handicraft shops. You also will find several handicraft shops surrounding **Boat Quay** and **Clarke Quay** (The Cannery shopping arcade). **Crafts By Design** in The Cannery at Clarke Quay has a very good selection of Indonesian handicrafts in its two large shops on the second floor.

Some of the best shops offering Asian handicrafts include **Borobudur Arts & Crafts** and **Polar Arts of Asia** in the Far Eastern Shopping Centre; **Lim's Arts & Crafts** and **Visual Dharma** at the Holland Road Shopping Centre; **Antiquity Hands of the Hills** in the Orchard Parade Hotel; and **Royal Selangor** in Delphi Orchard and Raffles City (for pewterware). For a unique collection of arts and crafts from South Africa, visit **Jjrico By The Grange** at Tanglin Place (91 Tanglin Road).

Be sure to look for handicrafts and souvenirs in **department stores, Mandarin Shopping Arcade, Lucky Plaza, Raffles City,** and **Marina Square Shopping Arcade.**

CLOTHES AND ACCESSORIES

Singapore is a good place to buy fashionable **ready-made clothes.** Many department stores and boutiques offer the latest imported European as well as locally produced fashion clothes. You will find many designer-label clothes produced in Singapore under licensing arrangements with Europe's top designers. You will also find some unique styles designed by such famous Singapore designers as Bobby Chang, Peter Kor, Kelvin Choo, Esther Tay, Arthur Yen, Rest & Relax, Tan Yoong, and Benny Ong as well as the latest Japanese fashions. Most of the department stores and small boutiques offering such clothes are found in the shopping complexes along the Tanglin-Orchard-Scotts Road shopping corridor as well as in several hotel shopping arcades.

The best place to view and buy clothes designed by local fashion designers is **Studio** designer showcase at Scotts shopping center on Scotts Road. On this one floor you will find the fashion designs of Singapore's major designers.

For the best quality imported fashion clothes, visit the numerous shops in the **Raffles Hotel Arcade** on North Bridge Road; **Millenia Walk** on Raffles Boulevard; and the **Hilton Hotel Shopping Arcade, Ngee Ann City, Mandarin Hotel Shopping Centre, Promenade, Palais Renaissance, Paragon Shopping Centre, Forum The Shopping Mall**, and **Isetan** on Orchard Road. All the major department stores and shopping centers are filled with fashionable ready-made clothes.

Palais Renaissance on Orchard Road (across from Hilton Hotel) and **Millenia Walk** are two of Singapore's most ambitious attempts to represent numerous major designer-labels (**Chanel, Cartier, Gucci, Leonard, Etro, Krizia, Genny, Dunhill, Salvatore Ferragamo, Christian Dior, Etienne Aigner, Escada**) under one roof. These are very popular shopping centers with Japanese, Taiwanese, South Korean, and other status conscious shoppers.

The Raffles Hotel Arcade houses one of the largest collections of name-brand clothing and accessory stores in Singapore. Here you will find **Etro, Gucci, Celine, Loewe, Mulberry, A. Testoni, Jim Thompson, Loewe, Louis Vuitton, Etienne Aigner, Alfred Dunhill, Prada**, and **Kenzo**. This shopping arcade also is one of the most pleasant places to shop in all of Singapore.

The Hilton Hotel Shopping Arcade at the Hilton Hotel on Orchard Road is one of Singapore's top hotel shopping arcades for imported designer goods. Here you will find numerous exclusive clothing and accessory shops offering the latest in international fashions. Look for such quality shops as **Missoni, Ferre, Fendi, L'Ultimo, Donna Karan, Moschini, Calvin Klein, Giorgio Armani, A. Testoni, Hunting World, Iceberg, Issey Miyake, Gucci**, and **Louis Vuitton**.

The **Mandarin Hotel Shopping Arcade** also has several upscale boutiques, clothing, and accessory stores. Look for **Etro, Kwanpen, Gianni Versace, A. Testoni**, and **Cellini Silk**. Most of these shops are located on the first level of this somewhat fading hotel shopping arcade.

Other shopping centers offering exclusive womenswear and menswear are **The Promenade** and the **Paragon Shopping Centre** on Orchard Road. At the Promenade look for **Ralph Lauren, Charles Jourdan, Tyan, Man & His Woman, Ayers Design, Apricot Design, Matsudu**. At the Paragon Shopping Centre you will find numerous trendy boutiques and such exclusive brand names as Emanuel Ungaro and Gucci. Next door you will also find the **Esprit** building offering the latest in European fashion clothes.

Several other shopping centers offer exclusive fashionwear. Try, for example, the shops at **Wisma Atrium, Specialists' Shopping Centre**, and **Raffles City**. Look for **Amour Silk & Batik** in the Marina Square shopping arcade and **Jin T, Designer Labels, MayeeLok**, and **St. Ives Collection** in Wisma Atrium.

Department stores, such as **Takashimaya, Tangs, John Little, Metro Far East, Metro Grand, Isetan, Sogo, Tokyu**, and **Robinson's**, also carry a full range of designer-label fashionware. Both Takashimaya and Isetan department stores offer some of the most extensive collections of designer-label clothes and accessories.

TAILORED CLOTHES

Singapore used to be a good place to buy **tailor-made clothes**. Promotional literature may still tell you that one of the great shopping treats and buys in Singapore is tailor-made clothing. Some tourists report getting excellent tailoring done in Singapore. However, more often than not, tailoring is one of the biggest shopping disappointments when traveling abroad. While you can still have good tailoring done here, it simply is no bargain compared to the quality and prices of Singapore's ready-made clothes. The cost of labor in Singapore has risen greatly during the past seven years to the point where tailors are now competing with the ready-made clothes market. And they can't compete successfully on price. Nonetheless, should you need a good tailor, one of Singapore's best is **Ed Kwan** at the Westin Stamford and Westin Plaza of Raffles City (Hotel Shop #9, Level 3, Tel. 338-0819). Several other tailors are located in Tanglin Shopping Centre and in the Specialist Centre.

The large concentration of tailors in Lucky Plaza and the Far

East Shopping Centre on Orchard Road offer inexpensive tailored garments. However, you normally get what you pay for in tailored clothes. If the price is cheap, expect your garments to look cheap. Indeed, tailored clothes are the number one shopping complaint from tourists in Singapore, and the complaints often deal with tailor shops in Lucky Plaza and the Far East Shopping Centre. The complaint is usually the same: they didn't get what they expected, workmanship was poor, or the garments weren't delivered on time. This is not surprising. These are the same problems we find in Hong Kong and Thailand. The basic problem, however, is the buyer: he or she tries to get something for nothing, does not know how to communicate with a tailor, and had little time to do the proper number of fittings. The combined results of being cheap, uninformed, and out of time result in poorly tailored garments that are largely a waste of time and money.

There are exceptions to our general tailoring observations, but our experience is that time and again tourists will make this their number one shopping mistake in Singapore and other countries where they will be tempted to purchase custom-tailored garments. Our advice: if you are determined to have tailoring work done, go to a reputable tailor, get it done right (allow enough time for 2-3 fittings), and be willing to pay for good quality. Review these tailoring tips before hiring a tailor:

1. **Don't expect to get something for nothing.** Quality fabrics and workmanship cost money anywhere in the world. Go to a good tailor and be willing to pay for quality work. The best tailors tend to be located in the arcades of the deluxe and first-class hotels.

2. **Look at fabrics and examples of finished work carefully.** Are the fabrics of good quality? Are they soft and supple so they will lay smoothly in the finished garment? Go to the racks of completed sample garments. Check the general appearance of garments including top-stitching, buttonholes, and button quality, smoothness of darts and pocket application. Hand sewing is one mark of quality custom tailoring. Turn up the collar and examine the underside for the slightly uneven hand stitches which indicate that it was partly hand sewn. Check the way hems are finished. Check women's jackets and coats to see that the chest area is not excessively form fitted with darts which create a fitted look not popular in the West—especially if you plan to wear the jacket unbuttoned and loose.

3. **Check garments waiting for first or second fittings.** Next, go to the rack where other customers' unfinished garments are waiting for first or second fittings. Examine the inside construction of several garments to see how well each is constructed. Firm interfacing should be used inside the upper part of jackets and coats and inside the lapels and collar to give support and shape to the garment. Many tailors now use fusible (iron-on) interfacing to save time instead of the more supple woven interfacing which needs to be sewn into place. Fusible interfacing is fine when used in a limited way, but the exclusive use of fusible rather than woven interfacing results in stiff garments. If fabrics have a pattern, check to see how well the pattern matches wherever seams meet.

4. **Specify the right style for you.** Be prepared with photos showing the style or combination of styles you want. (Remember, these tailors are not working from pre-packaged patterns. You can select a collar from one photo, for example, to be combined with a jacket front from another) Know what looks best on you and avoid being swayed by the salesperson to go with the "latest fashion" if it won't fit your lifestyle back home or your shape.

5. **Communicate every detail.** Don't assume your image is similar to the salesperson's image of the finished product. For example, if the fabric you've selected has stripes, specify the direction—horizontal, vertical or diagonal—for the stripes in the finished garment. The rule here is to: **assume nothing and explain everything.**

6. **Give the tailor enough time to do a quality job.** Expect to have a minimum of two fittings—three is better—for garments in which fit is critical such as suits or slacks. One fitting might be acceptable for a loosely constructed garment such as a blouse. Expect a suit to take at least four days while a blouse might be completed in one or two days. Good work is not done overnight, and usually only *"Hey, you mister"* shops will make such rash promises.

7. **Arrange to take delivery of your finished garments no later than the day before you leave.** Leave yourself a little extra time in case the tailor fails to make the scheduled deadline or time is needed to rectify problems you discover when picking up the completed garments and trying them on for the first time.

Reputable tailors are more expensive than the many *"Hey, you mister"* tailors found in Singapore's many shopping centers. They are expensive because they use the best fabrics and spend the proper amount of time on cutting, assembling, and fitting the garments. The best tailors invariably are found in the arcades of Singapore's best hotels.

A final word of advice: In most cases you will be much better off buying ready-made clothes which are less expensive and more fashionable than much of the tailoring work produced by the small tailor shops in Singapore. But most important, you can try on ready-made clothes prior to purchasing them.

If you will be wary of potential pitfalls of custom tailoring and follow these guidelines, you will be a smart shopper for tailored garments. Like many other people, you may be pleased with the outcome of having tailoring completed during your stay in Singapore. The satisfied individuals are the ones the tourist associations never hear from.

We address custom tailoring at some length, including a separate chapter on how to ensure proper tailoring, in our *Treasures and Pleasures of Hong Kong* volume. You might want to refer to this book for more detailed "how-to" information on tailoring if you believe you need more specifics than outlined here.

TEXTILES

Singapore offers a large variety of fabrics from all over Asia. You will find Chinese and Thai silks, Malay and Indonesian batiks, Malay *kain songket* (silk interwoven with gold thread from Kelantan), Filipino *jusi* or *pina* (a fine nearly transparent fabric), Indian cottons and silks, and European, American, and Japanese fabrics in all types of colors and designs.

For **Chinese** fabrics, browse through the Chinese emporiums as well as the shops along Smith Street in Chinatown.

For **European, American, Japanese**, and **Indonesian** fabrics, try department stores, People's Park Centre, North Bridge Road, Arab Street, High Street Plaza, Sultan Plaza, High Street, and Katong Shopping Centre. For one of the best selections of Indonesian textiles, be sure to visit **Bin House** in Ngee Ann City (#02-12F). Also, check out **Arcadia Tree** (#01-06, Orchard Towers), **Naga Arts and Antiques** (Tanglin Shopping Centre), and **Cahaya Gallery** (Raffles Hotel Arcade) for small collections of Indonesian textiles. **Indian** silks are found along Serangoon Road and High Street. You will find **Thai** silk in hotel shopping arcades, along Arab Street, and in several shopping complexes. The noted Bangkok-based **Jim**

Thompson can be found in the Raffles Hotel Arcade. For **Malay** *kain songket* and **Filipino** *jusi* or *pina*, visit the shops along Arab Street. One of the oldest batik shops in Singapore, offering good quality Javanese batik, is **Chop Yeo Hong Seng** at 63 Arab Street.

COMPUTERS, ELECTRONIC GOODS, CAMERAS

Many shops in Singapore are filled with the same types of computer and electronic goods and cameras as you find in Hong Kong. They overflow with cell phones; calculators; stereo equipment; CD players; VCRs; radios; televisions; 35mm, digital, and video cameras; appliances; and the latest gadgetry. Much of this is produced in Singapore as well as imported from Japan, Hong Kong, South Korea, and Taiwan.

Unless you are from a country which places high duties on imported items, you are not likely to find any great deals on electronic goods and cameras in Singapore. Similar to Hong Kong, you may be able to get better buys on such goods through direct-mail and Internet sites in the U.S. However, you may find some items not available back home. Sometimes new products are first introduced in Hong Kong and Singapore and only later appear in U.S. and European markets. These products may be the ones of greatest interest to you.

Be cautious when buying electronic goods and cameras. You should always get a receipt and an international guarantee as well as test the product. Make sure items are compatible with your systems back home. Be especially careful about televisions and video cameras. Most are designed for the Asian and European PAL systems; they will not work on NTSC systems found in the U.S. and a few other countries. While you should bargain hard for all of these goods, consider paying a little extra to use your credit card. Should you have a problem with your purchase after returning home, some credit card companies will assist you as long as you have your credit card charge slip and receipt.

Computer software is a particularly good buy in Singapore. Like electronic goods, computer hardware in Singapore is no longer the great bargain it used to be since hardware prices have fallen dramatically in the U.S. But software is still a good buy. However, be forewarned that you are entering the black market of pirated computer software which does not sit well with U.S. software companies and may present some problems when passing through U.S. Customs. The Singapore legislature passed a law to protect U.S. copyrights. Inaugurated in June, 1987, this law prohibits the sale of pirated software. The practical results of this law have been to move software purchases from a "gray market" to a "black market" and to make such purchases more inconvenient and time consuming. Rather than buy pirated software "off-the-shelf" in full public view, you must now "put-in-an-order." Within a few hours you can return to the store to pick up your purchase. Without naming names of specific shops, let's just say that most computer shops will accommodate such requests. All you need to do is walk into a shop and ask them *"Can you get me this program, including the manuals?"* In general, the quality of the software and manuals is good, but by no means guaranteed. A software package costing US$300 in the U.S. can be purchased in Singapore—complete with diskettes and manuals—for only US$50! Most of the software is for IBM or IBM compatible computers. Programs typically cost S$5 per diskette and about S$10 for each book, and the shop will often give you a discount if you ask for one.

You will find several computer shops in Chinatown at the **People's Park Centre** (Eu Tong Sen Street at Upper Cross Street) and **Fook Hai Building** (South Bridge Road and Upper Hokien Street).

FURNITURE, WICKERWARE, AND CANEWARE

Singapore offers a good selection of locally-produced and imported furniture, wickerware, and caneware. The furniture and antique shops at **Tanglin Shopping Centre, Dempsey Road** and **Watten Estates** are especially worth visiting. At Tanglin Shopping Centre, be sure to visit Lemon Grass, Plantation House, and Apsara. At the Dempsey Road complex, **Red House Carved Furniture Co.** and **Asia Passion** are well worth visiting. One of Singapore's best antique furniture shops, **Tomlinson's**, has three nice shops (Raffles Shopping Arcade, Grand Hyatt Singapore, and 460 Sims Avenue) as well as another shop at the Dempsey Road complex (shop there is called **Renaissance Antique Gallery**).

A few shops in the Holland Road area offer excellent quality Korean chests, Chinese cabinets, and wicker and cane furniture. Check out **Lim's Arts & Crafts** in the Holland Road Shopping Centre with its two floors of Korean chests and other home furnishings. Behind the Centre, look for **Excel Caneware** at 38 Lorong Mambong for cane and ratten furniture. At Cold Storage Jelita on Holland Road, you will find a shop offering nice selections of tastefully designed furniture: **Jessica**.

Wickerware in the form of baskets, hats, mats, birdcages, fans, and chests is readily available in the shops along **Arab Street**. We especially like the selections at **Habib Handicraft, Jothi Palayakat Co.**, and **B&K Textile** on Arab Street. Caneware in the form of cane and rattan furniture is best found in several shops along **Joo Chiat Road**.

SILVERWARE AND PEWTERWARE

Silverware in Singapore comes primarily from the Malaysian states of Trengganu and Kelantan where it is handmade into intricate styles. Many gift and curio shops in the shopping complexes along Orchard Road offer this silverware as well as pewterware. For simple and modern styles of silverware, visit **Georg Jensen** (shops in the Raffles Hotel Arcade, Palais Renaissance, and the Mandarin Hotel Shopping Arcade).

Pewterware is a specialty of both Malaysia and Singapore. You will find pewterware in the form of candlesticks, decorative plates, tankards, cups, bowls, and tableware. The quality is generally good, and the designs are unique to Malaysia and Singapore. Try **Royal Selangor Pewter** (shops in Delphi Orchard and Raffles City Shopping Centre for good quality pewterware.

THE MORE YOU LOOK

The longer you stay in Singapore, the more you will discover to buy. Among many other things, Singapore is well noted for its abundant supply of good quality **watches**, **sports equipment** (from fishing to golf), **carved figures** (jade, lapis, other), **furs**, **optical products**, and **reptile skin goods** (shoes, handbags, wallets, and belts made from lizard, crocodile, alligator, and snake skins). The list goes on and on. Similar to Hong Kong, but different in terms of particular shopping strengths, Singapore is indeed a shopper's paradise.

WHERE TO SHOP

Singapore is one of the easiest places in the world to shop. The maps are outstanding; the streets are convenient; most shops are found in air-conditioned shopping complexes; most people speak English; and you need not travel far from one shop to another, or from one shopping complex to another.

Singapore seems to have been designed with the international shopper in mind. The Singapore Tourism Board actively promotes an on-your-own, self-service approach to enjoying your stay. Their literature and maps make shopping easy. The MRT, Tourist Day Ticket, and Singapore Trolley make getting around Singapore both convenient and inexpensive.

SHOPPING AREAS

Singapore has over ten major shopping areas of primary interest to international shoppers: Orchard Road, Bras Basah Road/ Raffles Boulevard/Stamford Road, Shenton Way and Raffles Place, Riverside, River Valley Road, Chinatown, Little India, Kampong Glam/Arab Street, Geylang Serai, Holland Village, Dempsey Road, and the suburbs. Most of these shopping areas, which are sometimes referred to as Singapore's "Central Shopping Belt," are located within close proximity to each other in the downtown area; Holland Village, Dempsey Road, and the suburban shopping centers are located outside the city center. All of these areas are within 20 minutes of each other by taxi or the MRT. If you have limited time in Singapore, plan to concentrate most of your shopping within the "Central Shopping Belt," especially Orchard Road and Bras Basah Road/ Raffles Boulevard/Stamford Road areas

ORCHARD ROAD

Orchard Road is Singapore's fashionable "Golden Mile." Bordered on the north by Tanglin Road and intersected by the popular Scotts Road shopping extension, Orchard Road's broad tree-lined sidewalks lead to Singapore's major department stores, shopping complexes, hotels, and restaurants. Most of the better quality art, antique, fashion, and jewelry shops are located in this area alongside the more traditional shops selling electronic goods, appliances, clothes, gifts, and curios. Shopping in this area takes place in air-conditioned comfort. You only need to go outside for a few minutes on your way to the next department store, shopping complex, or hotel shopping arcade. Here amongst a dense mile of shopping centers and arcades you'll discover the shopping treasures of Tanglin Mall, Tanglin Shopping Centre, Hilton Shopping Gallery, Palais Renaissance, Shaw House, Far East Plaza, Lucky Plaza, The Promenade, Wisma Atria, Ngee Ann City/Takashimaya, Centrepoint, Specialist Shopping Centre, Orchard Plaza, and Plaza Singapura. Many visitors choose to stay at a hotel in this area because of the convenience for shopping. Excellent hotel choices in this area are the Four Seasons, Regent, Traders, ANA, Shangri-La, Marco Polo, Boulevard, Orchard Parade, and Hilton near Tanglin Road and the Goodwood Park, Marriott, and Hyatt Regency along Scotts Road.

You can easily spend two days shopping the thousands of stores on both sides of this street. For many shoppers, Orchard Road is the shopper's heaven of Asia. At times, especially on weekends, it's wall to wall people as locals head for the shopping centers and department stores to engage in their two favorite weekend pastimes—eating and shopping! This area is New York's Fifth Avenue, London's Oxford Street and Knightsbridge, and Hong Kong's Nathan Road and Queen's Road Central all rolled into one.

Bras Basah Road/Raffles Boulevard

Bras Basah Road and Raffles Boulevard are really the eastern extension of Orchard Road which leads into Bras Basah Road which, in turn, becomes Raffles Boulevard. Brass Basah Road/ Raffles Boulevard crosses Victoria Street, North Bridge Road, and Beach Road as it passes to the harbor, major hotels, shopping complexes, and convention facilities. This area has become one of the most upscale areas in Singapore with the development of the Raffles Hotel Arcade, Raffles City, Chijmes, Stamford House, Suntec City Mall, Millenia Walk, and the Marina Square shopping arcade surrounded by some of Singapore's top hotels—the Ritz-Carlton Millenia, Raffles, Conrad International, Westin Plaza, Westin Stamford, Oriental Singapore, Marina Mandarin, and Pan Pacific. This whole area has recently become Singapore's major convention center with the completion of the Singapore International Convention and Exhibition Centre which is attached to the Suntec City Mall and surrounded by major hotels, shopping complexes, and office buildings. Since more and more convention facilities, hotels, and restaurants have been built in this area during the past five years, we increasingly find ourselves spending more and more of our shopping and dining time here.

Riverside

Riverside is home to the popular Clarke Quay along the Singapore River, immediately south of River Valley Road and east of Hill Street and Boat Quay. This is a noted area for festive outdoor dining and indoor shopping with lots of entertainment and rides for kids. Its large concentration of shops is centered in and around three major buildings—The Cannery, Merchants' Court, and The Foundry. You'll find lots of shops here selling reasonably priced clothes, accessories, jewelry, and arts and crafts. Over 150 air-conditioned shops can be found in these restored godowns and shophouses. The area is especially popular for its Sunday flea markets. Shops and pushcarts offer a wide range of clothes and souvenirs. Several factory outlets also are found in this area. A very touristy area not particularly noted for its quality shopping. Adjacent to Clarke Quay is Liang Court, with its Japanese department short, boutiques, and bookstores, and Robertson Walk. Nearby Pidemco Centre is popular for its Singapore Jewellery Mart.

CHINATOWN

Chinatown, in addition to Little India and Arab Street, is one of three traditional ethnic enclaves which also functions as a distinct shopping area. Consisting of small cluttered shops and Chinese emporiums, as well as the quaint Tanjong Pagar conservation area of shops, restaurants, and pubs, this is a colorful area of traditional craftsmen and temples. Chinatown's major shopping streets are Trengganu, Temple, and Smith. It's best to start shopping this area at the **Chinatown Complex**, a large covered market bounded by New Bridge Road, Smith Street, and Sago Street where you will find several stalls selling fruits, vegetables, and meats as well as household goods and handcrafted items. A good time to come here is between 11am and noon when the commercial shops open, although the fresh market area on the lower level opens at 6:30am. Nearby the Complex you will find rows of old Chinese shophouses offering a variety of standard Chinese household goods, fresh produce, handicrafts, funeral objects, medicine, jade, silk, and bonsai trees. Bargaining in these Chinatown shops will normally get you a 10 to 20 percent discount—maybe more if you bargain hard.

Two of Singapore's largest Chinese emporiums are located just one block east of Trengganu Street on Eu Tong Sen Street near Upper Cross Street—**People's Park Complex** and **People's Park Centre**. Both of these shopping centers are packed with small shops selling everything from the latest in electronic goods to inexpensive clothes, fabrics, footwear, and luggage. Other popular shopping areas include **Yue Hwa**, **Chinatown Complex**, and **Chinatown Point** (tall blue building) which houses many arts and crafts shops. Nearby is the **Tanjong Pagar Conservation Area** with nearly 220 shophouses which function as art galleries, craft shops, restaurants, and tea houses, a major effort on the part of Singapore to convert an important historical area into a vibrant cultural and shopping center.

Riverwalk Galleria, which is located between Boat Quay and Clarke Quay, is a center for fine arts and furniture. Many of the art shops that used to be located at Orchard Plaza on Orchard Road have moved here.

Other streets in Chinatown tend to be noted for particular

items. South Bridge Road, for example, is Chinatown's goldsmith street. Sago Street is Chinatown's street for funeral objects.

Many visitors may find Chinatown more interesting as a cultural experience than as a worthwhile shopping adventure. Most products found in Chinatown are foods, medicines, clothes, and household goods for the local Chinese community. Except for the Rising Arts and Crafts shop and a few handicraft shops along Trengganu, Temple, and Smith streets, the most interesting international shopping is found in the **People's Park Complex, People's Park Centre, Chinatown Point**, and **Tanjong Pagar Conservation Area**. Each emporium (People's Park) is filled with small shops and stalls selling textiles, clothes, luggage, watches, footwear, jewelry, appliances, cameras, and computerware. Just behind People's Park Complex is the **Old People's Park Complex**. Filled with textiles, this is good place to buy lengths of fabric by the meter. **Fook Hai Building** on the corner of South Bridge Road and Upper Hokien Street is a good place to purchase computerware, modeling kits, and remote control equipment for cars, planes, and boats.

ARAB STREET

The Arab Street section, which begins just north of Beach Road, across the street from the Plaza Hotel, is filled with many shopping surprises. Shops along the streets are especially noted for offering Malay and Indonesia batiks, textiles, dress trimmings, braids, batik, basketware, luggage, jewelry, loose stones, lace, carpets, prayer rugs, brassware, and leather goods.

It's best to begin your Arab Street shopping adventure at the corner of **Arab Street** and **Beach Road**. Walk northwest on Arab Street and turn right onto **Baghdad Street**. You will find all types of interesting little shops selling traditional items in this area. When you come to the corner of **Bussorah Street**, take a left; you will see the famous Sultan Mosque in the distance. If you are interested in Malay crafts, stop at **Haija Asfiah** (#43 Bussorah Street). At the end of Bussorah Street, take a left or right onto **Muscat Street**. While most of the shops are concentrated along the Arab-Baghdad-Bussorah —Muscat streets area, you will find numerous shops selling other items on nearby streets. Of particular note are the inexpensive clothes and junk shops supposedly selling antiques in **The Golden Mile Food Centre**—not our idea of a good shopping time. The **Textile Centre** and **Sultan Plaza** on Jalan Sultan have a good selection of traditional Arab, Indonesian, Malay, and Indian textiles, including batik.

LITTLE INDIA

Little India is an ethnic area beginning at the corner of Serangoon and Sungei roads. Another cultural experience, complete with aromas from Indian spices, this is an area of goldsmiths, textile merchants, money-changers, fortune tellers, and food stores. The major shopping streets in this area are Serangoon Road, Campbell Lane, Clive Street, Dunlop Street, and Buffalo Road. Little India is noted for its **Zhu Jiao Centre** (also called the Kandang Kerbau Market) and **Thieves' Market** at the corner of Serangoon and Buffalo roads. This area is filled with *sari* shops and stores selling inexpensive clothes, musical instruments, antiques, copy watches, electronic goods, brassware, porcelain, and an assortment of knickknacks. Several shops along Serangoon Road and the adjacent side streets specialize in textiles, porcelain, antiques, Vietnamese vases, Filipino shirts, jade, carvings, brassware, Indian gold jewelry, luggage, joss sticks, birds and birdcages, medicines, and food stuffs.

Your best approach to exploring the Little India area is to walk the streets and poke into the various shops. Start just north of the juncture of Serangoon Road and Buket Timah Road (adjacent to Rochor Canal Bridge), near Buffalo Road and Campbell Lane. If you walk north along both sides of Serangoon Road for about 700 feet, you will be in the midst of the major shopping area.

HOLLAND VILLAGE

Holland Village has long been a favorite shopping area for Singapore's expatriate community. Located to the west within a 15-minute taxi ride from downtown Singapore and along Holland Road, this area offers a wide selection of antiques, gifts, souvenirs, and curios from China, Japan, Korea, the Philippines, Sri Lanka, and India, clothes from the Philippines, and ceramics, porcelain, caneware, basketry, and earthenware. As more and more ethnic restaurants have moved into this area over past few years, many unique neighborhood shops have closed, especially along Lorong Mambong Road. Be sure to visit the shops in **Holland Road Shopping Centre**, especially **Lim's Arts and Crafts**, **Jim Art**, and **Simply Divine** for good quality antiques, arts, crafts, furniture, and home decorative items.

DEMPSEY ROAD

Dempsey Road, which is approximately 10 minutes west of Holland Village by taxi and opposite the Botanic Garden, is a major center for furniture, arts, antiques, carpets, and home decorative items. It's especially popular with expatriates who go here in search of good buys on Chinese and Indonesian furniture and carpets. Housed in the old Dempsey army barracks, the shops in this expansive compound offer a wide range of shopping options. You can easily spend a couple of hours browsing through the more than 30 shops and warehouses found in this complex. On a hot day of walking around this compound, you'll most likely yearn for the air-conditioned comfort of shops along Orchard Road! You'll need to be patient in browsing through all the shops for unique treasures. After awhile, especially on a hot day, the shops begin looking the same. We especially like the following shops: **Red House Antiques**, **Eastern Discovers**, **Mountain Looms**, **Renaissance Antique Gallery**, **Heritage Gallery**, **Asia Passion**, **Journey East**, and **Vintage Palace**.

KATONG

Katong is a suburb located on the East Coast. If you take the expressway, you can get to Katong in about 20 minutes from downtown Singapore. Katong is a Chinese and Malay area. The major shopping area—**Geylang Road**—is also reputed to be the center for the Chinese Mafia. Here, as well as on **Sims Avenue**, **Changi Road**, and **Joo Chiat Road**, you will find clothes, antiques, leather goods, furniture, toys, baskets, lanterns, Chinese and Malay style jewelry, Malay costumes and bridal accessories, and the usual assortment of household goods, medicines, spices, and fresh produce. You will need a good half-day to explore the streets and shops of Katong.

SHOPPING CENTERS

Singapore's large number of air-conditioned shopping centers makes shopping both comfortable and convenient. Most of the shopping centers are located within close proximity of each other in and around Orchard Road. This is where you will find the major department stores, shops, hotel shopping arcades, hotels, cafes, and restaurants.

ORCHARD ROAD AREA

There is more shopping per meter along densely settled Orchard Road than anywhere else in Southeast Asia. You can easily spend a couple of days trying to walk from one shopping center to another. This street literally has thousands of shops, many of which offer the same goods, housed in several three to five-story shopping centers. Indeed, one wonders how they all do a profitable business given their close proximity to one another as well as their similarity of goods. The highlights of this area for quality shopping include Tanglin Shopping Centre, Hilton Shopping Gallery, Palais Renaissance, Ngee Ann City, The Promenade, and Centrepoint. The mammoth **Ngee Ann City**, with its adjacent Takashimaya Department Store, is a shopper's paradise for just about everything you need and want!

One of the best ways to shop these centers is to begin on Tanglin Road which is located just off the western end of Orchard Road. Start near the Traders Hotel. From there you can walk north along Tanglin Road visiting Tanglin Mall, Tanglin Place, Tudor Court, and Tanglin Shopping Centre and then enter Orchard Road. Continue east on Orchard Road covering both sides of this long street and also walk north a few hundred feet along Scotts Road.

As you walk north and east along this Tanglin-Orchard-Scotts Roads shopping corridor you will come to the following shopping centers:

❑ **Tanglin Mall:** *163 Tanglin Road, Orchard MRT.* Located across the street from the main headquarters of the Singapore Tourism Broad and behind the Traders and Regent Hotels. This three-storey shopping mall is a wonderful oasis from the sidewalks of Tanglin Road. Filled with a combination of small shops, restaurants, fast-food outlets, and a supermarket. Especially popular with locals in search of clothes, shoes, jewelry, and home decorative items.

❑ **Tudor Court Shopping Gallery:** *131 Tanglin Road, Orchard MRT.* Once one of Singapore's most upscale shopping centers for designer labels. Now includes primarily home decorative shops. **Gournitai Antiques**, for example, includes a good selection of Indian and Indonesian furniture and home decorative items.

❑ **Tanglin Place:** *91 Tanglin Road, Orchard MRT.* Next to Tudor Court Shopping Gallery and the Regent Hotel, this small but upscale shopping center has two very nice shops offering unique collections of arts, crafts, antiques and furniture. Visit **Lopburi Arts and Antiques** for a fine collection of Thai and Burmese antiques and Tibetan chests and **Jjrico by the Grange** for South African arts, crafts, and furniture.

❑ **Tanglin Shopping Centre:** *19 Tanglin Road, Orchard MRT.* Located within a two-minute walk and just north of Tudor Court where Tanglin Road meets Orchard Road. This is one of the best places in Singapore to shop for antiques, primitive art, furniture, porcelain, carpets, curios, and paintings. Be sure to explore the many shops lining all levels of this shopping center. Our favorite shops here include **Tiepolo, Tatiana, Mata-Hari, Naga Arts and Antiques, Lana Treasures, Plantation House, Renee Hoy Galleries, Kensoon Asiatic Art, Apsara, Alinta Art, Setiawan Gallery,** and **Harvest Straits** for excellent quality arts, antiques, furniture, and home decorative items.

❑ **Delfi Orchard:** *402 Orchard Road, Orchard MRT.* On the north side of Orchard Road, this small upscale shopping center includes household items, such as Waterford crystal and Wedgwood china, as well as a few clothing and accessory stores, such as **Ken Done's** "art to wear" from Australia. **Royal Selangor** has a shop here offering its distinctive Malaysian pewterware.

❑ **Orchard Towers:** *600 Orchard Road, Orchard MRT.* Next to Delfi, this large shopping center includes several shops selling antiques, curios, jewelry, fabrics, ready-made clothes, and food. You will find such quality shops as **Larry Jewelry,** one of Singapore's best jewelers.

❑ **Forum The Shopping Mall:** *583 Orchard Road, Orchard MRT.* Located on the south side of Orchard Road, between the Orchard Parade and Hilton hotels, this shopping center is filled with good quality boutiques, jewelry, electronic, and clothing stores. Has one of the largest **Toys 'R' Us** shops in all of Asia. Includes one floor of food outlets—Rasa Forum.

❑ **Hilton Hotel Shopping Arcade:** *Hilton Hotel, 581 Orchard Road, Orchard MRT.* See next section on hotel shopping arcades for details on this upscale shopping

center which houses some of Singapore's most exclusive
designer label shops.

❑ **Far East Shopping Centre:** *545 Orchard Road, Orchard
MRT.* Located next to the Hilton Hotel, this older and
somewhat run down shopping center has four floors filled
with jewelry, tailor, antique, electronic, photo, and souvenir shops. Don't be turned off by initial impres-
sions—you'll find a few good shops here. Look for
Borobudur Arts & Crafts for Balinese, Javanese, and
Sumatran carvings and souvenirs; **Polar Arts of Asia** for
carvings from Papua New Guinea; and **Kwok Gallery** for
top quality Chinese arts and antiques.

❑ **Liat Tower:** *541 Orchard Road, Orchard MRT.* This popular center houses the distinctive Planet Hollywood
restaurant, the exclusive Hermes boutique, Esprit, Burger
King, and Starbucks coffee house. Adjacent to Wheelock
House, this is a popular gathering place for Singapore's
growing sidewalk café and dining culture.

❑ **Wheelock House:** *501 Orchard Road, Orchard MRT.*
Located at the corner of Orchard Road and Scotts Road,
this distinctive glass building is now the center for Singapore's American-imported book superstore and coffee
culture—**Borders**. Open until 11pm weekdays and until
midnight on weekends, this user-friendly bookstore is the
place for book browsing, people watching, and making
new friends (some say it's the best "pick up place" in
town!). If you can't find a book at Borders, chances are
it isn't available through Singapore's other major bookstores, Times Books and MPH. Has a good section of
books on local history and literature. **Marks and Spencer** clothing store occupies the two lower levels along
with a restaurant (Olio Dome) and German microbrewery
restaurant (Paulaner Bräuhaus).

❑ **Palais Renaissance:** *390 Orchard Road, Orchard MRT.*
Next to the Embassy of Thailand, this represents one of
Singapore's most ambitious attempts to offer upscale
designer boutiques and name-brand shops under one
roof. Here you will find the ultimate in expensive luxury
goods. Look for such names as Lancome, Clarins, Rochas,
Estee Lauder, Guerlain, Aramis, Elizabeth Arden, Helena
Rubinstein, La Prairie, Revlon, Orlane, Plentitude,
Ultima, Mary Quant, Cartier, Hermes, Van Cleef &

Arpels, Gucci, Paloma Piccaso, Nike de St Phalle, Dunhill, Salvatore Ferragamo, Christian Dior, Etienne Aigner, and Chanel for fragrances, cosmetics, jewelry, accessories, fashionwear, and gifts.

❑ **International House:** *360 Orchard Road, Orchard MRT.* Located across the street from Liat Towers, this shopping center includes several nice boutiques, tailor shops, and restaurants.

❑ **Shaw House:** *350 Orchard Road, Orchard MRT.* Anchored by the four-storey Japanese department store, Isetan, this shopping center includes several designer shops such as Max & Co, Bally, and Trussardi, and one of Singapore's most popular cineplexes, Lido.

❑ **Shaw Centre:** *1 Scotts Road, Orchard MRT.* Just off Orchard Road on the west side of Scotts Road. A good place for Chinese rosewood furniture, clothes, jewelry, lamps, and curios. Also houses one of Singapore's best French restaurants, Les Amis.

❑ **Pacific Plaza:** *9 Scotts Road, Orchard MRT.* A popular place for young designers. Includes many popular Australian clothing lines, such as Stussy, Billabong, and Quiksilver, as well as Tower Records. The Village Place offers an interesting selection of used designer clothing.

❑ **Far East Plaza:** *14 Scotts Road, Orchard MRT.* On the east side of Scotts Road, between the Goodwood Park and Grand Hyatt hotels. A very crowded center with over 800 shops selling a wide assortment of average quality goods, especially clothes, footwear, music, eyeware, sound equipment, electronic goods, and computerware. Includes many fast-food restaurants. A favorite place for young people and bargain-seekers. Metro department store is found at the lower level.

❑ **Scotts Shopping Centre:** *6 Scotts Road, Orchard MRT.* On the east side of Scotts Road between the Grand Hyatt and Marriott Hotels. A good quality shopping center with nice boutiques, camera shops, and electronic shops. Includes some of Singapore's local fashion designers, such as Esther Tay. The trendy Coffee Bean & Tea Leaf café is found on the ground floor.

❑ **Lucky Plaza:** *304 Orchard Road, Orchard MRT.* On the north side of Orchard Road next to the Tangs department store. Filled with tourist shops selling cameras, stereos, radios, clothes, jewelry, watches, carpets, and all types of curios. Once a good place to bargain for goods as well as get a bargain in the process, this shopping center seems to be in a perpetual state of decline and revival. Watch your wallet here! Lucky Plaza tends to be overrun by touts and *"Hey, you mister"* shops. Be careful in buying cameras and electronic goods—you may not be very lucky, especially when you discover they are not guaranteed, don't work with your system back home, or are overpriced. A very crowded and noisy place.

❑ **Wisma Atria:** *435 Orchard Road, Orchard MRT.* Across the street from Lucky Plaza. Anchored by Isetan Department Store, Wisma Atria includes five floors of good quality shops selling clothes, sporting goods, jewelry, leather goods, souvenirs, toys, cameras, and electronic goods. Includes a popular Warner Bros. Studio Store, a Chanel boutique, and famous name brands such as Chopard, Ferre, and Coach. A pleasant area to both shop and eat.

❑ **The Promenade:** *300 Orchard Road, Orchard MRT.* This is one of Singapore's most elegant shopping centers. Go here if you want top quality. Great place for designer wear, jewelry, and luxurious lingerie (Glamourette shops). Look for Charles Jordan for shoes and bags.

❑ **Paragon Shopping Centre:** *290 Orchard Road, Orchard MRT.* Located next to The Promenade, this upscale shopping center includes numerous shops offering jewelry, handicrafts, optical goods, fabrics, sportswear, designer clothes, leather goods, and more. Includes two department stores—Metro and Marks & Spencer. Some of the best quality shops here include **Gucci, Lanvin, Aigner, Prada, Ferragamo, Fendi, Larry Jewelry,** and the **Metropolitan Museum of Art Store.** The fifth level is devoted to art shops and galleries (Sin Hua Gallery, Jun Hong Gallery, Orchard Gallery, Jasmine Fine Arts, New Ideal Art, Loong Hua Arts), many of which used to housed at Orchard Point.

❑ **Ngee Ann City/Takashimaya S.C.:** *391 Orchard Road, Orchard MRT.* Attached to the huge upscale Takashimaya

Department Store. Filled with name-brand jewelry, clothing, and accessory shops, such as **Celine, Chanel, Loewe, Louis Vuitton, Hugo Boss, Tiffany & Co., Ermenegildo Zegna, Alfred Dunhill, Piaget, Cartier, Burberry, Mont Blanc, Philippe Charriol, Christofle,** and the **Hour Glass**. Unique stand-out shops include **Bin House** for fine quality Indonesian fabrics, shawls, and shirts and **Je Taime** for top quality jewelry. One of Singapore's largest and most upscale shopping centers. You can literally spend much of the day shopping this huge complex which also includes many good restaurants, food outlets, and a nice supermarket. Be sure to pick up a copy of a directory map at the information desk near the entrance. It will become your passport to exploring this very popular and interesting shopping complex.

❑ **OG Building:** *228 Orchard Road, Somerset MRT.* Houses the **OG Department Store** which is popular with locals for affordable clothing and footwear.

❑ **Midpoint Orchard:** *220 Orchard Road, Somerset MRT.* Another popular center for locals. Filled with outlets offering hobby crafts, sports goods, outer wear, gold jewelry, and bridal gowns.

❑ **Orchard Emerald:** *218 Orchard Road, Somerset MRT.* This small green building is home for several shops offering watches, electronics, and sportswear.

❑ **Specialists' Shopping Centre:** *277 Orchard Road, Somerset MRT.* Across the street from Orchard Point and Orchard Plaza. Includes good quality boutiques, hobby craft shops, and the popular **John Little** department store.

❑ **The Heeren Shops:** *260 Orchard Road, Somerset MRT.* Popular with young people, this shopping center houses the HMV mega music store, Japanese One.99, and a wide range of restaurants on the fifth floor.

❑ **Centrepoint:** *176 Orchard Road, Somerset MRT* One of Singapore's most popular shopping centers. Home to **Robinson's** department store as well as numerous shops offering arts and crafts, clothes, carpets, jewelry, silverware, Korean chests, and Filipino bamboo furniture. Includes several trendy fashion boutiques and upscale shops as well as branches of Singapore's two largest bookstores—**Times** and **MPH**.

❑ **Orchard Point**: *160 Orchard Road, Somerset MRT* Until recently one of Singapore's major centers for art galleries (many have now moved to the fifth level of The Paragon), this shopping center now includes a wide range of popular clothing, cosmetics, home furnishings, furniture and linen shops. Look for such designer shops as **Episode** and **Jessica**. For new Indonesian furniture, visit **Art Decor**.

❑ **Orchard Plaza**: *150 Orchard Road, Somerset MRT.* Includes several footwear, tailor, hair salon, and make-up shops.

❑ **Park Mall**: *9 Park Mall, Dhoby Ghaut MRT.* Includes over 45 shops offering a wide range of furniture and home decorative items.

❑ **Plaza Singapura**: *Dhoby Ghaut MRT.* Located east of the Meridian Hotel at the corner of Orchard Road and Oldham Lane. Contains a Japanese department store and several specialty shops offering clothes, leather goods, electronics, handicrafts, and home furnishings. Popular shopping center for locals.

BRAS BASAH ROAD AND RAFFLES BOULEVARD

These two adjacent shopping areas flow directly from Orchard Road. Indeed, it's the eastern extension of Orchard Road. The shopping centers and hotels along these streets constitute a distinct shopping area.

❑ **Chijmes**: *30 Victoria Street, City Hall MRT.* This attractive national heritage site includes numerous shops, restaurants, and cafes. Look for several shops offering unique arts and crafts, clothes, jewelry, gourmet food, and wedding dresses. A popular gathering place in the evening for dining and shopping.

❑ **Raffles City Complex**: Located across the street from the historic Raffles Hotel on Bras Basah Road, North Bridge Road, and Beach Road, this is one of Singapore's largest and most ambitious hotel, office, and shopping complexes. Includes the Westin Plaza Hotel and the 73-

story Westin Stamford Hotel—the tallest hotel in the world. The shopping complex consists of three floors anchored by the **Sogo** department store. Includes some excellent arts, crafts, jewelry, and clothing stores. Look for **Larry Jewelry** and **Chap Mai Jewelry** for good quality jewelry; **Selangor Pewter, Gifts & Souvenirs, Chinese Embroidery House**, and **Elsee's Place** for souvenirs; **Chinese Cloisonne Ware** and **Centuries Arts & Crafts** for Chinese handcrafted items; and **The Collector's Gallery** for paintings by local artists. **Ed Kwan**, in the adjacent Westin Stamford Hotel shopping area, is one of the best tailors in Singapore.

❑ **Raffles Hotel Arcade:** See hotel shopping arcade section, page 114.

❑ **Marina Square Shopping Mall:** Located at the end of Stamford Road, one block from the Raffles Hotel and the Raffles City Complex. Consists of three deluxe hotels— The Oriental, Marina Mandarin, and Pan Pacific—joined together by a large shopping arcade with over 250 specialty shops. A mixed shopping area of average to excellent shops. Filled with trendy boutiques, footwear, tailors, home furnishings, handicraft, souvenir, antique, music, jewelry, and book stores. Unlike other shopping centers, this one is laid out as an indoor pedestrian mall complete with street signs and benches. Anchored by the **Metro** and **Tokyu** department stores, you will find several nice shops in this shopping center: **Minh Anh** for nicely designed jewelry; **B. P. De Silva** for excellent quality jewelry, silver, and pearls; and **Bonia** for Italian leather bags and shoes. You will also find a **Times** bookstore and a Starbucks, McDonald's, and KFC in this shopping arcade. Several nice shops are found in the adjacent Marina Mandarin Hotel Shopping Arcade.

❑ **Suntec City Mall:** 3 *Temasek Boulevard, City Hall MRT.* Attached to the Singapore International Convention and Exhibition Centre and accented with the world's largest fountain, The Fountain of Wealth, this is Singapore's newest and largest shopping complex. This 78,000 square meter shopping mall is divided into four thematic zones: Galleria, Tropics, Entertainment Centre, and Fountain Terrace. The Galleria includes numerous name brand (Bally, Ferragamo, Boss, Esprit) and souvenir shops. The Tropics zone houses numerous home furnishings, casual ware, lingerie, and leisure products shops. Look for a wide range of clothing, accessory, footwear, leather goods, optical, sports, jewelry, beauty, and gift shops. **Tower Records**, **Warner Brothers**, and **Polo Ralph Lauren** have huge shops here.

❑ **Millenia Walk:** *9 Raffles Boulevard, City Hall MRT.* Connected to the Ritz-Carlton Millenia Hotel and Marina Square with overhead walkways, Millenia Walk's 190 shops are found in an indoor two-level shopping center offering a variety of goods, from toys, clothes, and accessories to carpets and sports goods. It also encompasses several upscale shops along an adjacent court area called Millenia Walk of Fame, such as Cartier, Escada, Fendi, and Lalique. Singapore's largest Duty Free Shop (DFS), which is especially popular with Japanese tourists, also is located here. Despite efforts to turn this into Singapore's "Rodeo Drive" with exclusive name brand shops, this is a relatively quiet shopping area largely eclipsed by nearby Suntec City Mall and the exclusive shops found at the Raffles City Shopping Centre.

❑ **Shaw Leisure Gallery:** *100 Beach Road, City Hall MRT.* Located just northwest of the Suntec City Mall and a five minute walk from Raffles City, this shopping center is part of Shaw Towers. It includes several well known boutiques for casual wear as well as unique shops offering collector comics and computer games.

NORTH BRIDGE ROAD AND STAMFORD ROAD

Located just south of Bras Basah Road and Raffles Boulevard, this area extends south into Riverwalk and Chinatown.

❑ **Funan Centre:** *109 North Bridge Road, City Hall MRT.* Anchored by Tokyu Department Store, this is one of Singapore's major centers for computer hardware, software, and accessories.

❑ **Capitol Building:** *109 North Bridge Road, City Hall MRT.* This restored historical site is now a center for fashion boutiques, music stores, and food outlets.

❑ **Stamford House:** *39 Stamford Road, City Hall MRT.* Located on the corner of Stamford Road and Victoria Street, this restored Victorian-style building is a center for home furnishings and decorative items. Look for nice wicker furniture at **Home Ideas Furnishings** and American country furniture at **Pennsylvania House**.

❑ **Stamford Court:** *61 Stamford Road, City Hall MRT*. This small center includes a mixture of home furnishings and book and CD shops.

❑ **MPH House:** *71 Stamford Road, City Hall MRT*. One of Singapore's largest bookstores that offers four floors of books, videos, CDs, cassettes, and records. It's not quite user-friendly superstore Borders, but it's trying to emulate.

SHENTON WAY AND RAFFLES PLACE

Located south of Raffles Boulevard and the Singapore River and southeast of North Bridge Road, this is the heart of Singapore's financial district. You'll find lots of high-rise commercial buildings, restaurants, and shops in this and adjacent areas.

❑ **Clifford Centre and The Arcade:** *24 Raffles Place and 11 Collyer Quay, Raffles Place MRT*. Caters to the many office workers in this area. Look for **Marks & Spencer** and **B&N** as well as numerous speciality and souvenir shops. Includes a pedestrian mall and outdoor entertainment.

❑ **OUB Centre:** *1 Raffles Place, Raffles Place MRT*. Centered in the banking district, this shopping center is very popular with office workers and tourists. Includes a variety of shops offering clothes, footware, jewelry, and CDs.

❑ **Pidemco Centre:** *95 South Bridge Road, Raffles Place MRT*. A popular center with locals for gold jewelry. Includes many jewelry shops.

RIVERSIDE AND RIVER VALLEY ROAD

This shopping area is located southwest of North Bridge Road and north of Chinatown. Most of the shopping centers and shops are found near the Singapore River.

❑ **Clarke Quay:** *3 River Valley Road, Raffles Place MRT*. A popular place for shopping and dining alongside the Singapore River. Includes more than 150 air-conditioned shops housed in restored godowns and shophouses and numerous sidewalk pushcarts offering everything from clothes and jewelry to arts, crafts, and souvenirs. Bargain shoppers come here to shop in several factory outlets. The Sunday flea markets are especially popular. Family-friendly atmosphere with lots of entertainment, games, and rides for kids.

❑ **Liang Court:** *177 River Valley Road, Raffles Place MRT and SBS bus 54 from Orchard Road.* Located one block north of Clarke Quay, this center houses the popular Japanese department store, Daimaru, as well as several Japanese label boutiques and bookstores.

❑ **Riverwalk Galleria:** *Boat Quay, Raffles Place MRT.* Located between Clark Quay and Boat Quay, on the south banks of the Singapore River, this large six-storey complex is a center for fine arts, furniture, and jewelry.

❑ **Great World City:** *Kim Seng Promenade, SBS bus 16 from Orchard Road and on the Singapore Explorer route.* Located west of Clarke Quay, on the way to Orchard Road, this huge shopping "city" includes **OG**, **Tops** supermarket and the American furniture store, **Ethan Allen**, along with numerous other shops.

❑ **Riverside Point:** *30 Merchant Road, Raffles Place MRT.* Located along the Singapore River, this attractive shopping mall with its central atrium and interactive water fountain includes numerous jewelry, fashion, and lighting shops as well as restaurants offering both indoor and outdoor dining.

You'll find numerous other shopping centers throughout the different ethnic enclaves, such as Chinatown, Little India, Kampong Glam (Arab Street), and Geyland Serai (Malay), as well as in the suburbs, especially along Holland Road, Bishan, Tampines, and Changi Village. However, most shopping centers of interest to visitors are found in the areas outlined above as well as in several major hotel shopping arcades.

HOTEL SHOPPING ARCADES

Most major hotels will have a small to medium-sized shopping arcade located on the bottom floor or in a separate attached building. The quality of shops in these arcades is often excellent to outstanding. They offer everything from top European and Japanese designer clothes to local antiques and handicrafts. Singapore's major hotel shopping arcades include the following:

❑ **Raffles Hotel Arcade:** *252 North Bridge Road, City Hall MRT.* This is Singapore's most upscale hotel shopping arcade which is attached to the famous Raffles Hotel. It's one of our top three places to shop in Singapore. Designed by world renowned architect I. M. Pei and exuding great ambience, its two levels of shops are tastefully set in a beautifully reconstructed and expansive white stucco and pillared colonial building which is part of the Raffles Hotel complex. Here you will find major name-brand clothing, accessory, jewelry, and home furnishing shops offering the latest in quality products from around the world: **Kenzo, Georg Jensen, Lladro, Alfred Dunhill, Aigner, A. Testoni, Celine, Coach, Etro, Gucci, Loewe, Louis Vuitton, Mulberry, Prada, Tiffany & Co.,** and **Waterford Wedgwood.** Some of the most unique high quality shops include **Lotus** (Tel. 334-2085) for jewelry; **Tomlinson** (Tel. 334-0242) for antique Chinese furniture; **Cahaya Gallery** (Tel. 336-5686) for Indonesia textiles and ethnic and avant garde Asian jewelry; **Exotica** (Tel. 334-6166) for Chinese and Southeast Asian furniture and sculptures; **Plum Blossom** for art and Tibetan chests; and **Evolution** (Tel. 334-4970) for rare prehistoric natural art and museum pieces. The shopping arcade also includes a helpful Singapore Tourism Board office, a theater playhouse (Jubilee Hall), a fascinating hotel museum, a hotel signature shop, two outstanding restaurants (Doc Cheng's and Express Room), the Empress Café, and the famous Raffles Long Bar. A great place to enjoy a leisurely afternoon of shopping, dining, drinking, and sightseeing. Best of all, the Raffles Hotel is attached to this shopping center. Consider doing lunch at either the famous Tiffin Room or the Bar and Billiard Room. Combining shopping with dining doesn't get much better than at the Raffles!

❑ **The Hilton Hotel Shopping Arcade:** Located on the first and second floors of the Hilton Hotel on upper Orchard Road, this is one of Singapore's most upscale shopping arcades. Here you'll find several exquisite jewelry, fashion, accessory, and tableware shops, such as **Missoni, Gucci, Prada, Fendi, Lalique, Moschini, Calvin Klein, Ferre, Issey Miyake, Christofle, L'Ul-**

timo, Iceberg, A. Testoni, Bvlgari, Cartier, Donna Karan, Giorgio Armani, Hunting World, and Louis Vuitton.

❑ **Mandarin Hotel Shopping Arcade:** Located at the Mandarin Hotel on Orchard Road, this once high quality shopping arcade has settled for more mid-range shops offering jewelry, arts, crafts, carpets, curios, clothes, footwear, and leather goods. Some of the best shops here are located at the entrance and include **Etro, Cellini Silk, Kwanpen, Georg Jensen, A. Testoni,** and **Gianni Versace.** The second level, which tends to be very quiet, includes mostly mid-range jewelry, arts, crafts, leather goods, and clothing shops.

❑ **Four Seasons Hotel:** Located just behind the Hilton Hotel, the Four Seasons has a few nice clothing shops in its shopping arcade, which is connected to the Hilton Hotel Shopping Arcade.

❑ **Meridian Hotel:** Located on Orchard Road, this hotel shopping arcade always seems to be under renovation and shop turnover seems to be high. Look for clothing, accessories, souvenir, jewelry, and furniture shops.

Many other hotels, such as the **Ritz-Carlton Millenia, Shangri-La, Orchard Parade, Goodwood Park, Grand Hyatt,** and **Marriott,** have small shopping arcades with nice shops. The **Westin Stamford Hotel** and **Westin Plaza Hotel** —both located in the new Raffles City convention center—have small shopping arcades.

DEPARTMENT STORES

Department stores tend to be very popular with local shoppers because of prices and selections. Given the highly competitive nature of these businesses, Singapore has seen the demise of two major department stores over the past three years: Galeries Lafayette and Yaohan. Most major department stores are concentrated in and around the Tanglin-Orchard-Scotts -Raffles roads area. All of them are air-conditioned, and most are found within the shopping centers. They offer a wide selection of goods from all over the world: cosmetics, jewelry, clothes, accessories, furniture, appliances, household items, toys, CDs, cassettes, radios, and televisions. The quality of goods varies from one department store to another. Some are crowded and congested, offering inexpensive clothes and electronic goods for young people, whereas others offer upscale products for more discerning shoppers.

The department stores have different ownerships which, in turn, have different product orientations. Locally owned department stores, such as **Metro**, **Metro Grand**, **Tangs**, and **Klasse**, offer excellent quality products produced in Singapore—especially locally designed and produced fashion clothes. The Japanese are well represented with their **Takashimaya**, **Isetan**, **Daimaru**, **Le Classique**, **Sogo**, **Tokyu**, and **Mitsukoski** department stores. These stores are well stocked with Japanese goods. The English have **Robinson's** and **Marks & Spencer**, and the French have **Carrefour**, both of which offer excellent quality products and good prices

The major department stores in the Tanglin-Orchard-Scotts Roads-Raffles Boulevard area include:

❑ **Takashimaya S.C.:** Orchard Road, attached to Ngee Ann City. Singapore's largest and finest quality department store. Always crowded. Has everything from clothes and jewelry to home decorative items, gifts, and food. Includes numerous name brand shops and boutiques. If you only visit one department store in Singapore, make sure it's Takashimaya S.C.

❑ **Sogo:** The Paragon on Orchard Road and Raffles City Shopping Centre at Stamford, North Bridge, Bras Basah, and Beach roads.

❑ **Isetan:** Liat Towers and Wisma Atria on Orchard Road. Good selections. Very upscale. Popular with tourists and locals alike.

❑ **Robinson's:** Centrepoint and Specialists' Shopping Centre on Orchard Road. Very popular with locals. Famous for its outstanding service.

❑ **Tangs:** 320 Orchard Road, next to Marriott Hotel. One of Singapore's best and most popular department stores.

❑ **Daimaru:** Liang Court at 177 River Valley Road, next to Clarke Quay. Popular department store offering many Japanese label boutiques and bookstores.

❑ **John Little:** Specialists' Shopping Centre on Orchard Road. An institution. Very popular with locals.

❑ **Carrefour:** Suntec City Mall. A very popular French hypermart boasting the lowest prices in Singapore.

❑ **Metro Far East:** Far East Shopping Centre on Scotts Road. Excellent quality locally designed fashions appropriate for western tastes.

❑ **Metro Grand:** Lucky Plaza on Orchard Road, Scotts Shopping Centre on Scotts Road, and the Marina Square Shopping Mall.

❑ **Tokyu:** Marina Square shopping arcade.

❑ **OG Elite:** Plaza Singapura on Orchard Road.

❑ **OG:** OG Building on Orchard Road and Great World City at Kim Seng Promenade.

❑ **Marks & Spencer:** Wheelock Place and Paragon on Orchard Road and Clifford Centre at Raffles Place.

❑ **Duty Free Shop (DFS):** Millenia Walk shopping center. Stocks designer-label clothes, accessories, and food items. Busloads of Japanese tourists come here to do all of their shopping at special (high) "Japanese tourist" prices.

You will also find department stores in other areas of the city. Many are branches of the above stores.

EMPORIUMS

Emporiums in Singapore are structured similarly to department stores. The Chinese emporiums are basically department stores offering imported goods from China, such as inexpensive clothes, silks, and brocades. Other emporiums offer a cross-section of goods from all over Asia.

The **Chinese Emporium** is located in the International Building on Orchard Road. An **Oriental Emporium** is located in People's Park Centre and an **Overseas Emporium** is found in the People's Park Complex—both near each other along New Bridge Road in Chinatown. Other emporiums are found in **Katong** (City Plaza on Tanjong Katong and Joo Chiat Complex on Joo Chiat Road) **and Holland Village** (Holland Road Shopping Centre) as well as on **Balestier Road** (Shaw Plaza), **Mountbatten Road** (Katong Shopping Centre), **Queensway/ Alexandra Road** (Queensway Shopping Centre), **Rochor Road**

(Rochor Centre), **Bukit Timah Road** (Buket Timah Plaza), **Kitchener Road** (President Emporium in the Hotel Merlin), and **Commonwealth Avenue** (Tah Chung Emporium).

MARKETS

The traditional open-air markets which sell inexpensive goods have all but faded from Singapore. Most of the remaining markets are the traditional neighborhood "wet" markets primarily selling meats, vegetables, and fruits. Other than the cultural experience, these markets offer little of interest to international shoppers.

Most of the street bazaars have moved indoors or disappeared altogether. However, many of the traditional shops in Chinatown, Little India, and Arab Street have a bazaar-quality about them. Many of these shops spill over onto the sidewalks, and in certain areas you still find street peddlers displaying their goods on the sidewalk. You can still get a glimpse of such markets by visiting the old **Thieves' Market** area on Sungei Road, the **Kreta Ayer** complex in Chinatown, and the street peddlers along **Temple Street** in Chinatown. Colorful and festive flea markets operate on Sunday at **Clarke Quay**, although they lack the atmosphere of traditional markets.

DISCOUNT SHOPS

While Singapore does not have the factory outlets like those found in Hong Kong, it does have some discount shopping where you can expect to save up to 50 percent on popular products such as branded clothes, shoes, accessories, fragrances, and cosmetics. Especially popular with local shoppers, the major discount shops and outlets include:

❑ **B&N Cosmetics:** Offers up to 40 percent discount on such popular brands as Christian Dior, Estee Lauder, Chanel, and Calvin Klein. The B&N outlets in the Promenade on Orchard Road and Finlayson Green in Raffles Place also offer designer label clothes and accessories, such as Gucci, Lanvin, and Moschino, at discounted prices. The B&N outlet at Finlayson Green also offers discounted golf equipment.

❑ **Sasa:** Located in Wisma Atria on Orchard Road and in Marina Square, these stores offer a large assortment of discounted cosmetics, fragrances, and toiletries.

❑ **The Outerwear Shop:** Located on the third level of Pacific Plaza on Orchard Road, this shop offers a good selection of winter coats and parkas at 30 percent discount. Stocks major brands such as Façonnable and Polo Ralph Lauren.

❑ **The Shoe Warehouse:** Located on the second level of Pacific Plaza on Orchard Road (#02-99 Pacific Plaza, 9 Scotts Road, Tel. 735-3569), the Shoe Warehouse offers good buys on Norma Kamali and Alberto Gozzi shoes at 50 percent discount. However, choices are very limited if you have large feet. If you wear a size 36 or 37, you'll have numerous choices here.

❑ **Export Fashion:** Located in Holland Village, Peninsula Plaza, Forum The Shopping Mall, and Suntec City. Offers Hong Kong made casual and office wear for men and women and designer clothes from the U.S. at a 50 percent discount.

❑ **Factory Outlet:** Has several shops along Orchard Road and in Holland Village and suburban shopping malls. Operated by the Metro chain of stores, these discount outlets are popular with locals for their casual and sportswear.

❑ **Famous Brands:** Located at Capitol Centre in North Bridge Road, Scotts Shopping Centre, and Suntec City. Offers 30 percent discounts on popular brand name products, such as Timberland, Nike, Reebok, and Puma shorts shoes and Calvin Klein T-shirts and sportswear.

❑ **Esprit:** Located on the third floor of Centrepoint on Orchard Road, here you'll find casual Esprit clothes and accessories at 40 to 70 percent discount.

Other discount shops to look for include **One.99** at The Heeren and Great World City for Japanese goods; **Under S\$2 Shop** at Coleman Street and Chinatown; **Tangs' Budget Corner** at CK Tangs; **Why Pay More**, a discount sports chain store with 12 branches; and several discount outlets, such as the **Fifth Avenue Factory Store**, at Clarke Quay. Also, look for huge warehouse sales which are usually announced in the Thursday, Friday, and Saturday editions of local newspapers.

SHOPPING BY PRODUCT CATEGORIES

If you are interested in shopping for particular types of products, you may want to concentrate your shopping in these places:

Antiques
Dempsey Road
Holland Village
Raffles Hotel Arcade
River Valley Road
Tanglin Shopping Centre
Tudor Court

Art Galleries
Delfi Orchard
Orchard Towers
Paragon
Raffles Hotel Arcade
Riverwalk Galleria
Stamford House

Basketry
Arab Street
Holland Village
Kampong Glam

Books & Comics
Centrepoint
Marina Square
MPH House
OUB Shopping Centre
Pacific Plaza
Raffles City
Raffles Hotel Arcade
Shaw Leisure Gallery
Tanglin Mall
Tanglin Shopping Centre
Wheelock Place

Carpets
Centrepoint
Dempsey Road
Far East Plaza
Marina Square
Raffles Hotel Arcade
Tanglin Road (#10)
Tanglin Shopping Centre

Children's Apparel
Forum The Shopping Mall
Marina Square

Ngee Ann City
Suntec City Mall
Tanglin Mall
Wisma Atria

Computers

Funan Centre
Fook Hai Building
People's Park Centre
Sim Lim Square

Crystalware

Delfi Orchard
Paragon

Electronics
(cameras, stereos,
videos cameras,
cell phones, ete.)

Parco Bugis Junction
Centrepoint
Chinatown
Far East Plaza
Forum The Shopping Mall
Funan Centre
Ngee Ann City
Orchard Emerald
Orchard Plaza
Orchard Towers
Raffles City Shopping Centre
Scotts Shopping Centre
Shaw Leisure Gallery
Sim Lim Square
Tangs
Wisma Atria

Fashion
(designer)

Capitol Building
Delfi Orchard
Forum The Shopping Mall
Meridien Shopping Centre
Ngee Ann City
Pacific Plaza
Palais Renaissance
Raffles Hotel Arcade
Scotts Shopping Centre
Shaw House
Shaw Leisure Gallery
Suntec City Mall
The Paragon
The Promenade
Wisma Atria

Fashion	Parco Bugis Junction
(mid-range)	Centrepoint
	Clarke Quay
	Far East Plaza
	Funan Centre
	Great World City
	Hilton Shopping Arcade
	International Building
	Liang Court
	Lucky Plaza
	Marina Square
	Midpoint Orchard
	Millenia Walk
	Ngee Ann City
	OG Building
	Orchard Point
	Raffles City Shopping Centre
	Scotts Shopping Centre
	Shaw Centre
	Specialists' Shopping Centre
	Suntec City Mall
	Tangs
	The Heeren Shops
	Wheelock Place
Furniture	Dempsey Road
	Raffles Hotel Arcade
	Stamford House
	Tanglin Shopping Centre
	Wattan Estates
Golf Equipment	Specialists' Shopping Centre
	Tanglin Shopping Centre
	Wheelock Place
Herbs & Spices	Arab Street
	Chinese medical shops
	Kampong Glam
	Little India
	Geyland Serai
	Ngee Ann City
	Raffles Hotel Arcade
	Supermarkets and sundry shops
	Yue Hwa Chinese Products

Home Entertainment (Music, CDs, VCDs, LDs, etc.)	Capitol Building Centrepoint Far East Plaza MPH House Pacific Plaza Raffles City Shopping Centre The Heeren Shops
Home Furnishings	Centrepoint Great World City Marina Square Ngee Ann City Orchard Point Park Mall Stamford House Tanglin Mall The Promenade
Jewelry	Centrepoint Chinatown Clarke Quay Far East Plaza Far East Shopping Centre Forum The Shopping Mall Kampong Glam Little India Lucky Plaza Midpoint Orchard Ngee Ann City/Takashimaya S.C. Orchard Towers Pidemco Centre Raffles City Shopping Centre Raffles Hotel Arcade Shaw Centre Tanglin Shopping Centre Wisma Atria
Souvenirs & Gifts	Arab Street Chinatown Clifford Centre Far East Plaza Holland Plaza Holland Village Liang Court Little India Millenia Walk

	Ngee Ann City
	Orchard Towers
	Raffles Hotel Arcade
	Tanglin Shopping Centre
	Tangs
	Wisma Atria

Sports Equipment and Sports Wear	Centrepoint
	Ngee Ann City
	Shaw Centre
	Scotts Shopping Centre
	Pacific Plaza
	Tangs
	Tanglin Place
	Wisma Atria

Textiles	Arab Street
	Chinatown
	Little India
	Ngee Ann City
	Raffles Hotel Arcade
	Tangs
	Tanglin Shopping Centre

Watches	Bras Basah Complex
	Lucky Plaza
	Ngee Ann City/Takashimaya S.C.
	Raffles City Shopping Centre
	Raffles Hotel Arcade
	Scotts Shopping Centre
	Suntec City Mall
	Tangs
	Tanglin Shopping Centre
	The Heeren Shops
	Wisma Atria

All major department stores and many shops in the main shopping areas also carry a wide range of **cosmetics**, **perfumes**, **toys**, and **household goods**.

BEST OF THE BEST

It's easy to become overwhelmed with all the shopping choices available in Singapore. Trying to sort out the "best of the best" can be a daunting task. Nonetheless, during our numerous visits to Singapore, we've found some terrific shops which we consider to be the best of the best in Singapore for uniqueness and quality. We have not included the many name-brand imported jewelry, clothing, accessories, and tableware shops, such as Gucci, Bvlgari, A. Testoni, Fendi, Chopard, Chanel, Cartier, Loewe, Celine, Burberry, Louis Vuitton, Piaget, Tiffany, Mont Blanc, Boss, Ermenegildo Zegna, Etro, Kwanpen, George Jensen, Gianni Versace, Escada, Lalique, Celine, Alfred Dunhill, Aigner, Coach, The Hour Glass, Waterford Wedgwood, Prada, Kenzo, Bally, Ralph Lauren, Esprit, Giorgio Armani, Hunting World, Issey Miyake, Calvin Klein, Moschini, Missoni, L'Ultimo, Iceberg, and Donna Karan. These shops offer similar quality goods anywhere in the world. Many shoppers might rightfully argue that these are Singapore's best of the best shops, but they are not particularly unique to Singapore; you can shop for these same name brand products in most major cities around the world. The easiest ways to find these shops is to go to seven upscale shopping centers where these shops tend to be concentrated:

- Raffles Hotel Arcade
- Hilton Shopping Arcade
- Ngee Ann City/Takashimaya S.C.
- Palais Renaissance
- The Paragon
- The Promenade
- Millenia Walk

We also have not included many clothing and footwear stores that primarily cater to local shoppers. Sizes, styles, and selections found in these shops tend to appeal mostly to Singapore residents; unless you wear very small sizes, few clothes and shoes are appropriate for many visitors. We also have not made any particular recommendations concerning the purchase of electronic goods. While cameras, videos, VCRs, televisions, cell phones, and computers are abundantly displayed throughout Singapore, we have yet to find a good buy on such items; they often are more expensive in Singapore than if purchased through discount houses in the United States. Because of problems with pricing, guarantees, and system compatibility (PAL versus NTSC), we are reluctant to make any recommendations in these product categories. Shops like **Parisilk** (*www.parisilk.com*) and **Cathay Photo** (Marina Square and Centrepoint) are reputed to offer excellent selections and service on audio, computer, office, communication, photographic, TV, video, and other equipment. If you know what you are doing (have compared prices, know quality, and understand system differences), you can make your own determination by shopping in the major electronics centers, such as Lucky Plaza (be very careful here), Funan Centre, Sim Lim Square, Ngee Ann City, Centrepoint, Chinatown, Far East Plaza, Pacific Plaza, Orchard Plaza, Raffles City Shopping Centre, and Wisma Atria.

Our final selections reflect items that we see as being particularly unique and outstanding. As such, our selections tend to be more in the arts, antiques, furniture, and local jewelry categories rather than in clothing, accessories, electronics, and imported jewelry categories.

JEWELRY

Singapore abounds with excellent jewelers. Many can be found in the Far East Shopping Centre, Lucky Plaza, Orchard Towers, Pidemco Centre, Ngee Ann City, Raffles City Shopping Centre, Raffles Hotel Arcade, and Wisma Atria. Four very special jewelry shops include:

❑ **Larry Jewelry:** *#01-10 Orchard Towers, 400 Orchard Road, Tel. 832-3222; #01-17 Ngee Ann City, 391 Orchard Road, Tel. 235-5848; and #01-38 Raffles City, 252 North Bridge Road, Tel. 336-9648.* One of Singapore's oldest, most respected, and dependable jewelers. Offers outstanding quality jewelry and excellent service. Good selection of nicely designed diamond and ruby necklaces, bracelets, rings, and ear rings. Excellent selection of quality pearls.

❑ **Je Taime Jewellers:** *#02-12 C/D Ngee Ann City, Tel. 734-8211; and 120 Oxley Rise Je Taime Building, Tel. 737-5642.* One of Singapore's most talented and successful jewelers. Gorgeous designs and very special pieces.

❑ **Lotus Arts de Vivre:** *#01-28 Raffles Hotel Arcade, Tel. 334-3876.* Exquisitely designed and crafted one-of-a-kind pieces using Chinese, Indian, and Thai antique jewelry and objets d'art. Very expensive but very gorgeous. A branch shop of one of Thailand's top German-Thai jewelry and design teams.

❑ **Cahaya Gallery:** *#02-06 Raffles Hotel Arcade, Tel. 336-5686.* Offers a unique collection of Indonesia gold jewelry, silver, necklaces, textiles, and kris. Strong ethnic and tribal themes.

ARTS AND ANTIQUES

Many of these shops combine the arts, antiques, and furniture of East and Southeast Asia, especially China, Indonesia, Burma, Thailand, and East Malaysia (Sabah and Sarawak).

❑ **Tatiana:** *#03-29/03-30 Tanglin Shopping Centre, 19 Tanglin Road, Tel. 235-3560.* This long established shop specializes in top quality Southeast Asia arts, antiques, and textiles. Offers a treasure-trove of items from Indonesia and Malaysia, especially tribal areas, personally selected by the owner, Georgia Kan.

❑ **Tiepolo:** *#02-23 Tanglin Shopping Centre, 19 Tanglin Road, Tel. 732-7924.* Offers top quality antique Chinese porcelain, Vietnamese ceramics, Chinese furniture, and tribal art from Indonesia collected by the engaging owner David Mun. Very expensive but very exclusive collection.

❑ **Harvest Straits:** *#03-31 Tanglin Shopping Centre, 19 Tanglin Road, Tel. 836-3178.* This relatively new shop offers one of the best collections of ethnic and tribal art and antiques from Indonesia. Great collection of top quality carvings, shields, porcelain, textiles, and ceremonial staffs.

❑ **Kwok Gallery:** *#03-01 Far East Shopping Centre, 545 Orchard Road, Tel. 235-2516.* A real shopping gem in an otherwise nondescript shopping center. One of Singapore's oldest (since 1918) and most established Chinese arts and antiques galleries offering an exquisite collection of porcelains, jade carvings, sculptures, bronzes, paintings, ivory carvings, cloisonne, and snuff bottles. Popular with serious collectors.

❑ **Exotica:** *#02-32/33 Raffles Hotel Arcade, 328 North Bridge Road, Tel. 334-6166.* Offers top quality Burmese Buddhas, Chinese furniture, and Cambodian sandstone sculptures.

❑ **KenSoon Asiatic Art:** *#02-58 Tanglin Shopping Centre, 19 Tanglin Road, Tel. 732-7380.* Includes a small but very exclusive collection of Chinese ceramics and stone and alabaster Buddhas. Also has a shop in Hong Kong (K & Soon Ltd., 54 Hollywood Road).

❑ **Eastern Discoveries:** *Blk 26 Dempsey Road #01-04, Tel. 475-1814.* Includes two floors jam-packed with Burmese and Thai carvings, Buddhas, and lacquerware.

❑ **Mata-Hari:** *#02-26 Tanglin Shoping Centre, 19 Tanglin Road, Tel. 737-6068.* A small but very fine shop for silver, jewelry, lacquer pieces, boxes, and other objets d'art from Burma, Thailand, and Indonesia.

❑ **Lopburi Arts & Antiques:** *#01-03/04 Tanglin Place, 91 Tanglin Road, Tel. 738-3834.* This beautifully displayed upscale shop offers Tibetan chests, pottery, and stone and bronze Buddhas.

❑ **Antiques of the Orient:** *#02-40 Tanglin Shopping Centre, 19 Tanglin Road, Tel. 734-9351.* Offers Singapore's largest collection of antiquarian maps, prints, and rare books. Also offers Chinese ceramics and paintings.

FURNITURE

❑ **Tomlinson:** *#02-35/36 Raffles Hotel Arcade, Tel. 334-0242; 460 Sims Avenue, Tel. 744-3551; and Grand Hyatt Singapore, 10-12 Scotts Road, Tel. 235-8860.* It doesn't get much better for quality furniture than at Tomlinson. Offers excellent quality antique Chinese furniture and accessories. Beautifully restored pieces. Also, look for Tibetan chests and Buddhas. Main shop for furniture is at Sims. The Grand Hyatt shop includes many small pieces. Also has comparable shops in Thailand, Malaysia, and the Philippines.

❑ **Red House Carved Furniture Co.:** *Blk 26 Dempsey Road #01-03, Tel. 474-6980.* This large warehouse is chucked full of furniture and baskets. Includes Chinese chests, panels, doors, and chairs.

❑ **Lemon Grass:** *#01-33 Tanglin Shopping Centre, 19 Tanglin Road, Tel. 737-7198.* Includes a good collection of furniture, Tibetan chests, Cambodian silver, lamps, Thai cabinets, and carved animals. Affiliated with two other nearby furniture shops—Apsara and Plantation.

❑ **Plantation House:** *#01-32 Tanglin Shopping Centre, 19 Tanglin Road, Tel. 734-8938.* Offers a nice collection of Southeast Asia furniture, Tibetan chests, baskets, and lamps. Try out the plantation chairs. Affiliated with two other nearby furniture shops—Apsara and Lemon Grass.

❑ **Apsara:** *#02-30 Tanglin Shopping Centre, 19 Tanglin Road, Tel. 735-5018.* Great shop for home decorators in search of quality accent pieces. Look for Chinese furniture, Burmese bibles, lacquerware, Buddhas, lamps, silver, and paintings. Affiliated with two other nearby furniture shops—Apsara and Lemon Grass.

❑ **Tiara Gallery:** *#02-01 Kim Seng Plaza, 100 Kim Seng Road (near Concorde Hotel and opposite the Great Wall City), Tel. 239-427.* Offers classic Chinese furniture and antique works of art.

❑ **Renaissance Antique Gallery:** *Blk 15 Dempsey Road #01-06, Tel. 474-0338.* Includes a large collection of excellent quality Chinese furniture, especially chests, tables, and chairs. Affiliated with Tomlinson.

❑ **Asia Passion:** *Blk 13 Dempsey Road #01-02, Tel. 473-1339.* This large warehouse includes an excellent collection of Dutch colonial and primitive Indonesian furniture (tables, chests, chairs) and collectibles.

❑ **Art Decor:** *Orchard Point.* Offers a good selection of new furniture made in Indonesia.

ART

❑ **Evolution:** *#02-15 Raffles Hotel Arcade, 328 North Bridge Road, Tel. 334-4970.* One of the most unique shops you'll ever encounter! Offers a wide range of prehistoric art pieces embedded in slabs of stone. Includes small to huge pieces requiring a forklift to transport! Very expensive but very unique. Includes a small but exclusive collection of unique jewelry.

❑ **Plum Blossoms:** *#02-37 Raffles Hotel Arcade, 328 North Bridge Road, Tel. 334-1198.* This is a branch of one of Hong Kong's best fine arts galleries. Includes Chinese oil paintings and a few top quality Tibetan chests. Hosts regular exhibits of major artists.

❑ **Orchard Gallery:** *#05-11 Paragon, 290 Orchard Road, Tel. 732-7032.* Established in 1984, this gallery includes oils, watercolors, ink paintings, and sculptures of Chinese artists, many of whom are established masters, national award-winning artists, and distinguished faculty from China's famous art academies.

❑ **Jasmine Fine Arts:** *#05-13A Paragon, 290 Orchard Road, Tel. 734-5688.* Operated by Jasmine Tay, this fine arts gallery offers an excellent collection of oil paintings by noted artists from China, Russia, Australia, Myanmar, Vietnam, and Thailand.

❑ **Cony Art Gallery:** *#05-15 Paragon, 290 Orchard Road, Tel. 738-6672.* Offers a fine collection of antique ceramics. Includes an extensive collection of Han, Tang, Song, Yuan, Ming, and Qing Dynasty porcelain as well as ancient ceramics of Annamese, Sawankhalok, and Sukhothai.

❑ **HaKaren Art Gallery:** *#02-43 Tanglin Shopping Centre, 19 Tanglin Road, Tel. 733-3382.* Offers a nice selection of attractive Chinese oil paintings.

ARTS AND CRAFTS

❑ **Singapore Handicraft Centre:** *China Point, New Bridge Road, Chinatown.* Includes over 60 shops under one roof. Includes everything from arts, crafts, and jewelry to antiques, lamps, gifts, and fine art.

❑ **Royal Selangor:** *#02-38 Raffles City Shopping Centre, 252 North Bridge Road, Tel. 339-3958.* Offers an excellent collection of Malaysian produced pewterware.

❑ **Jjrico By The Grange:** *#01-01 Tanglin Place, 91 Tanglin Road, Tel. 738-9995.* You won't find anything Asian here at this interesting South African arts, crafts, and furniture shop. One of the most surprising shops in Singapore with its wide range of unique items, from carved giraffes and hippos to finely crafted railwood furniture.

❑ **Antiquity Hands of the Hills:** *#01-06 Orchard Parade Hotel, 1 Tanglin Road, Tel. 836-3923.* Offers a unique collection of textiles, jewelry, and gift items from Tibet, Bhutan, Thailand, Indonesia, and other exotic areas of Asia.

❑ **Setiawan Enterprise:** *#03-07 Tanglin Shopping Centre, 19 Tanglin Road, Tel. 235-6601.* This relatively new shop represents one of Indonesia's best arts, crafts, textile, and antique shops in Jakarta—Djody. Includes lots of tribal crafts, textiles, Batak carvings, wayang puppets, carved doors, masks, and baby carriers. Top quality.

❑ **Polar Arts of Asia:** *#02-16 Far East Shopping Centre, 545 Orchard Road, Tel. 734-2311.* What a crazy shop! It may be more of a cultural experience than a place to do serious buying. One of the most cramped, crowded, and dusty shops in Singapore. Jam-packed with carvings from Papua New Guinea, puppets from Burma, and masks from China. Watch where you step.

CLOTHES/TEXTILES

❑ **Bin House:** *#02-12F Ngee Ann City, Takashimaya S. C., Tel. 733-6789.* Represents one of Indonesia's finest textile and clothing shops as well as the genius of Josephine Komara, one of Indonesia's pioneers in reviving traditional Indonesia weaving skills. Offers a wonderful collection of finely woven one-of-a-kind shawls, fabrics, shirts, and other garments.

CARPETS

❑ **Orientalist/Tandis:** *10 Tanglin Road #01-01, Tel. 235-3343; and Blk 26 Dempsey Road #01-05, Tel. 475-7220. Web site: www.orientalist.com.sg.* These two locations offer a huge selection of hand knotted carpets from Persia, the Caucasus, Pakistan, India, Turkey, Afghanistan, Kashmir, Nepal, Central Asia, and East Turkestan.

❑ **Mountain Looms:** *Blk 16, #01-03 Dempsey Road, Tel. 476-7629.* A small two-storey shop, but it offers a very fine collection of carpets personally selected by the owner, B. J. Fernandes, one of Singapore's noted collectors of oriental carpets and textiles. Excellent service and attention to detail.

SHOPPING RIGHT, SHOPPING WELL

Your shopping in Singapore should go well as long as you observe certain basic shopping rules.

1. **Avoid touts**. You will occasionally encounter individuals on the street who want to show you where to shop, especially around Orchard Towers, Far East Shopping Centre, and Lucky Plaza. While it is illegal for them to solicit in this manner, it still goes on. Avoid these people. They will take you to a shop that gives them a commission which, in turn, is added to your tab!

2. **Bargain where appropriate**. Singapore has fast become a fixed-priced city which offers discounts through periodic sales. The Singapore Tourism Board does not encourage bargaining, but bargaining remains alive and well in many parts of Singapore. While you cannot bargain in fixed-price department stores and many exclusive shops (except on high-ticket items), you should try bargaining elsewhere. Expect some jewelry stores, for example, to give you up to a 50 percent discount off the marked price; exclusive jewelry stores may only give a 10-20 percent discount. Discounts on other items may average 20 to 30 percent with some as much as 40 to 50 percent. Even stores you may think will not give you a discount often do if you just ask *"What is the best discount you could give me?* or *"Is it possible to do better on this price?"* Anything is possible in Singapore. This question may result in a 10 percent discount.

3. **Compare prices**. In addition to doing your comparative pricing research at home prior to arriving in Singapore, the many shops in Singapore also offer numerous opportunities to compare prices on similar items. Shops tend to be very competitive and are willing to bargain to get your business. A good starting point is to visit the fixed-price department stores (try Tangs on Orchard Road) to get an overview of Singapore's products and prices. Keep in mind that the shops along Orchard Road pay the highest rents in all of Singapore and thus they must add this overhead cost to their prices. You can often do better on prices in shops elsewhere in Singapore, especially in the suburbs, but those shops may not have the same quality goods as found along Orchard Road; they also are less convenient to shop. Consequently, less is not always better.

4. **Ask for receipts**. All shops are supposed to give receipts. However, in many cases you will have to ask for one. Always collect receipts for both customs officials and any

potential problems you may have with your purchase. Consider using your credit card to purchase big ticket items which might later pose problems due to misrepresentation. Ask the seller to specify gold content such as "18k" on jewelry or "cultured pearls" on your receipt. If the seller indicates the video camera you are purchasing is compatible with your NTSC system, ask him to note this on your receipt. If he won't, be wary. If he does, you have greater leverage later if you have a problem.

5. **Get international guarantees**. When buying electronic goods, check to see if the item works properly and is covered under an international guarantee. The warranty card should be included with the item. If it does not come with such a guarantee, you will be taking a chance.

6. **Report any problems to the Retail Promotion Centre**. The STB is committed to promoting Singapore as a reputable place to shop. Should you have a problem with a merchant, register your complaint with the Retail Promotion Centre at Blk 528, Ang Mo Kio Avenue 10, #02-2387, Tel. 450-2114 or Fax 458-6393.

SHIPPING

You should have no problem shipping your goods from Singapore as long as you shop in reliable shops. Shops catering to international shoppers are experienced in packing and shipping purchases abroad. Most will use good packing materials—bubble wrap is widely used—and take care of all shipping arrangements. Make sure you have a receipt for your shipment in case you later have a problem in receiving it.

Keep in mind that you only need to make one shipment from Singapore since most shops will consolidate all of your purchases into a single shipment—but only if you ask them to do so. Most major hotels also can assist you in making contact with reliable local shippers who will consolidate your shipments. Make sure you fully insure the shipment against both loss and breakage as well as get a receipt for your shipment in case you later have a problem in receiving it.

ACCOMMODATIONS

A population of 3.2 million hosting over 6 million guests a year is very experienced in the hotel business. Singapore offers a wide range of excellent accommodations and services for travelers. While once offering some of the best hotel bargains in Asia, during the past five years hotel prices increased significantly until they were nearly comparable to Jakarta, Bangkok, and Hong Kong.

Most major hotels are conveniently located near the major shopping areas along Tanglin Road, Orchard Road, Scotts Road, Bras Basah Road, and Raffles Boulevard. Many visitors with a sense of history stay at the grand old **Raffles Hotel**. Extensive reconstructed in the early 1990s, the deluxe Raffles Hotel still has the character of the by-gone British colonial era combined with modern amenities and one of Singapore's top shopping arcades. This remains one of Asia's most fabulous hotels. But for pure luxury and outstanding service, it's hard to beat the **Four Seasons** and **Ritz-Carlton Millenia** hotels. These are two of the world's top hotels.

Singapore has numerous first-class and deluxe hotels that rank as some of the world's finest. The hotels along Orchard and Scotts roads are the most convenient for walking to the numerous shopping complexes along this street. You can choose from many fine hotels, such as the **Four Seasons, Ritz-Carlton Millenia, Shangri-La, Goodwood Park Hotel, Duxton, Regent, Hilton International, Grand Hyatt, Marriott Hotel, Marco Polo, Oriental**, and the **Mandarin Hotel**. Just as convenient to Orchard Road is the **Boulevard Hotel**. The **Shangri-La** (one of the world's best) is located nearby as is the **ANA Hotel**.

The Four Seasons, Regent, Shangri-La, Goodwood Park, Marco Polo, Boulevard, Mandarin, Hilton, and ANA are especially convenient locations in relation to the shopping centers along Tanglin, Orchard, and Scotts roads. The Raffles, Oriental, Mandarin, and Ritz-Carlton are close to the shopping centers along Bras Basah Road and Raffles Boulevard.

Among Singapore's many fine hotels, we've found the following properties to be the best:

❑ **Four Seasons Hotel:** *190 Orchard Boulevard, Singapore 248646, Tel. (65) 734-1110, Fax (65) 733-0682 or toll-free from U.S. 800-332-3442, from Canada 800-268-6282. Web: www.fourseasons.com.* A personal favorite, The Four Seasons Hotel Singapore is located on tree-lined Orchard Boulevard. Although only a few steps away from the business, shopping and entertainment belt of Orchard Road via an air-conditioned skywalk and a five minute walk to the MRT, the hotel is in a tranquil residential setting shared by several embassies. The rare art and antiques that decorate the hotel create the ambiance of a fine private residence. A book centering on the art and artists represented at The Four Seasons provides a lasting reminder of one's visit. An elegant and huge fresh floral arrangement graces the center of the entrance rotunda. Beyond the rotunda a promenade and an imposing staircase lead to the Business Center, a residents' lounge, the Chinese restaurant, and ballrooms. Tucked into the rear of the rotunda is a small gift shop that offers an exquisite selection of local decorative products—some old, perhaps antique, others new—of excellent quality. Although offering all the amenities of a large hotel, it has the feel of a boutique hotel and the staff offers unparalleled service. Four Seasons has garnered awards in polls conducted by *Travel and Leisure, Business Traveller* and *Conde' Nast*. The Singapore Tourist Promotion Board has named it "hotel of the year." The 257 guestrooms and 43 suites are spacious and beautifully appointed as are the generous sized marble baths which offer a separate soaking tub and shower, as well as bidet and toilet in separate enclosed area with phone. The large double vanity with double sinks and lighted make-up/shaving mirror, make the baths both functional and luxurious. Each room provides two-line speaker phones on the desk and at the bedside console, additional phone outlets for in-room fax or modem hook-ups and voice mail. A multidisc player in each guestroom hidden in a beautiful amoire along with the television and well-stocked minibar, add to each guest's comfort and in-room safes provide a sense of security. Seasons Restaurant specializes in contemporary American cuisine. Jiang-Nan Chun offers fine Cantonese cuisine and is renowned for its lunchtime dim sum. Seasons Café offers informal dining with a selection of Asian and Western dishes. The Terrace Lounge offers afternoon tea. Spanning two floors, the club at Four Seasons offers full recreational and fitness facilities. In the spacious open foyer leading to the fitness center, the figure of a Padi God from Borneo, called Nunpatong, graces the informal area adding both charm and a sense of place—Singapore's location on the trading routes of Southeast Asia. A flotation tank provides ultra-deep relaxation and some claim it can help travelers recover from jet-lag. A lap pool located in the fitness center and a sunning pool on the 20th floor, two indoor air-conditioned tennis courts, two outdoor courts, an opti-golf simulator which transports the player to exotic golf locations, a gymnasium, a dance/aerobic studio and five therapeutic massage and treatment rooms provide options for the health and fitness conscious traveler. Business Center and Conference Facilities.

❑ **The Ritz-Carlton Millenia Singapore:** *7 Raffles Avenue, Singapore 039799, Tel. (65) 337-8888 or Fax (65) 338-0001. Web: www.ritzcarlton.com.* The 32-storey hotel is the centerpiece of Marina Centre, Singapore's designated new downtown core—the fastest growing business and commercial center. The 610 guestrooms include 22 suites. All guestrooms and bathrooms offer views of either Marina Bay or Kallang Bay and the city skyline. The bathrooms are positioned on the outside walls and provide panoramic views from large octagonal windows. Guestrooms are spacious—claimed to be 25 percent larger than any other luxury hotel in Singapore. Modern style decor is softened by the use of light timber finishes and Tibetan-style woven floor covering. Bathrooms have separate shower stalls. The Ritz-Carlton is a five minute walk from the MRT (public transportation), a few steps from Singapore International Convention and Exhibition Centre (Suntec City), and a 20-minute drive from Changi International Airport. The Ritz-Carlton Club, comprised of 52 guestrooms and 6 suites, is located on the top three levels of the hotel. Five complimentary food and beverage presentations are served daily. Continental breakfast is offered each morning, followed by salads and sandwiches in the late morning and early afternoon. Afternoon tea is served mid-afternoon, followed by cocktails and hors d'oeuvres in the early evening; later Club guests can enjoy cordials and chocolates before retiring for the evening. Indeed a Club guest could dine all day and hardly leave the Club lounge. However, one might select fine Cantonese cuisine in the Summer Pavilion—the signature restaurant at the Ritz-Carlton in a distinctive glass pavilion set in a picturesque garden. An innovative mixture of traditional and contemporary, Eastern and Western flavors await those who dine in the Greenhouse. Snappers is an al fresco dining venue specializing in seafood and set against lush tropical greenery and a tranquil Greco-Roman pool. Or enjoy tea, evening cocktails, or late night beverages in the Lobby Lounge while listening to classical tunes or Broadway favorites by the Diamond Strings Quartet. As dusk settles over the bay, strategically placed lights illuminate world-famous glass artist Dale Chihuly's wall sculpture

"Sunrise." The hotel also offers a fully equipped Health Club and Business Centre.

❑ **Duxton Hotel**: 83 Duxton Road, Singapore 089540, Tel. (65) 227-7678 or Fax (65) 227-1232. or toll-free from U.S. and Canada 800-552-6844. Web: *www.inta gra.fr/ relaiscchateaux/duxton*. With a facade reminiscent of the Straits Chinese trading houses that once dominated the Tanjong Pagar area of Singapore, this boutique hotel has a thoroughly modern interior. Located on a quiet street, nearby attractions include Boat Quay and Clarke Quay, Chinatown and the central business district. Each of the 50 guestrooms have been individually designed for the guests' comfort while retaining the architectural details inherent in the building. 9 duplex suites provide a living room separated from the bed and bath area by a spiral staircase. These suites are ideal for people who will be conducting business in their suite as it does not feel like you are having a conference in a bedroom. However, the only television is in an amoire on the living room level, so there is no watching television from bed. There are 2 garden suites with French doors which open onto a beautifully landscaped courtyard. Tea and coffee making facilities, mini-bar, hairdryer, personal in-room safe, and complimentary fruit basket are provided. Fax machines, cordless telephones, personal computer, iron and ironing board available upon request. L'Aigle d'Or serves a fine breakfast as well as French cuisine. No pool. Facilities for small meetings and private car transfers in the mornings to the major business and financial districts.

❑ **Goodwood Park Hotel**: *22 Scotts Road, Singapore 228221, Tel. (65) 737-7411 or Fax (65) 732-8558. Web: www.good woodparkhotel.com.sq* A national landmark of Singapore, The Goodwood Park Hotel combines a charming restored historic building with contemporary amenities. A frequent award winner for service, the Goodwood Park has also been the recipient of the Singapore award for the best decorated building at Christmas. It is the only low rise building in the hub of the Orchard Road entertainment and shopping complexes and sits on 14 acres of land-scaped gardens. A true oasis only steps away from the Orchard/Scotts Road shopping and entertainment venues. The hotel's 235 guestrooms offer a great variety from spacious rooms, 1 to 3 bedroom suites, split-level suites, poolside suites, or if you have the means and really want to splurge there is the Brunei suite–truly fit for a Sultan! Rooms in various wings have different decor, but all are spacious and elegantly decorated and house the amenities business and leisure travelers expect: 2 IDD telephones by the bedside or on the writing desk and in the bathroom, one phone has dual lines and data port facility, voice mail, 24 hour in-house movies on television, a well-stocked mini-bar as well as coffee/tea making facilities, hairdryers, and in-room safe. The Gordon Grill offers a continental menu, Chang Jiang Shanghai Restaurant serves authentic Shanghainese cuisine, Min Jiang serves spicy Sichuan specialities, along with Garden Seafood Restaurant, Bice Ristorante Italaino, Shima Japanese Restaurant and the Café L'Espresso assure that the guest has a variety of dining choices without leaving the hotel. Fitness center and three swimming pools of which one is a children's pool. Business Center/Conference Facilities.

❑ **Shangri-La Hotel**: *Orange Grove Road, Singapore 258350, Tel. (65) 737-3644 or Fax (65) 737-3257 or toll-free from U.S. & Canada 800-942-5050. Web: www.shangri-la.com.* Set in 15 acres of lush tropical foliage, the Shangri-La Singapore is a frequent award winner which consistently ranks at or near the top of the reader survey lists for *Conde Nast Traveler* and *Travel & Leisure*. Be it European refinement at the Valley Wing, tropical living at the Garden Wing, or the elegant newly renovated (1999) Tower Wing, the Shangri-La offers luxury with a personal touch. The three wings offer a choice of 750 spacious guestrooms and 60 suites. The Garden Wing with its bougainvillea filled balconies makes the guest forget that he is only a few steps away from the shopping on Orchard Road. Guests at the Valley Wing appreciate its private driveway and check-in area as well as complimentary continental breakfast and beverages and snacks in the lobby throughout the day. The top floors of the Tower Wing house the Horizon Club which offers private reception, the business center for club floor guests, meeting rooms and breakfast room–all featuring panoramic views of the city. On the level below, Horizon Club guests can access their very own private health club with state-of-the-art exercise equipment. All rooms feature a well-stocked mini-bar, tea and coffee making facilities, and in-room safe. A shopping arcade provides guests a choice of last-minute gifts. The Latour for fine continental dining, Shang Palace Chinese restaurant, and Nadaman Japanese restaurant have reputations for serving exquisite food in plush surroundings. Take afternoon tea in the Rose Veranda. Private dining rooms are available. Fully equipped health club, indoor and outdoor swimming pools plus spa pools, tennis and squash courts, three hole pitch-and-putt course. 24-hour Business Center. Extensive conference and corporate meeting facilities.

❏ **The Oriental**: *5 Raffles Avenue, Marina Square, Singapore 039797, Tel. (65) 338-0066 or Fax (65) 339-9537.* With panoramic views of Singapore's picturesque harbor, The Oriental is close to the financial district and linked to Marina Square Shopping Centre and Suntec City Convention and Exhibition Centre. Its 518 guestrooms and suites are built around an 18-story atrium lobby with natural skylight and six chandeliered glass elevators. A consistent winner of awards from international travel magazines as well as the Singapore Tourism Board, The Oriental is known for providing both luxury accommodation and top service. The elegant guestrooms are complimented by marble bathrooms with separate shower enclosure and tub. Three IDD telephones, coffee and tea making facilities, mini-bar, and in-room personal safe are in all rooms. 100 luxurious suites including deluxe theme suites are truly spectacular—some of the largest comprise two levels. The two club floors offer a fax line in all rooms, a boardroom for private meetings, and complimentary breakfast, hors d'oeuvres, and cocktails to Oriental Club guests. Liana's offers contemporary cuisine, Cherry Garden features Sichuan and Hunan specialities, Café Palm for all day buffet and casual dining, Captain's Bar serves traditional roast beef buffet luncheon, or try Pronto for Italian cuisine al fresco by the pool, or the Atrium Lounge for English afternoon tea. A state-of-the-art health center features a fully equipped gym, tennis and squash courts, massage rooms, saunas, and hot and cold spa pools and steam bath. Step out on the verandah that surrounds one of the best hotel pools in Singapore and you are greeted by one of the best harbor views in the city. Business Center /Conference and meeting facilities.

❏ **Raffles Hotel**: *1 Beach Road, Singapore 189673, Tel. (65) 337-1886 or Fax (65) 339-7650 or toll-free from U.S. & Canada 800-232-1886.* The Raffles Hotel is one of Singapore's historic landmarks and visitor attractions. From the romantic images evoked by mention of the "Long Bar" to the wonderful shopping opportunities provided by the 70 upscale shops and boutiques that line the Raffles Hotel Arcade, the Raffles attracts Singapore visitors whether or not they are hotel guests. Winner of frequent awards, the restored all-suite hotel has 104 suites. The original 14-foot high ceilings with their grand arches and ceiling fans maintain the spacious, airy feeling. Each of the typical suites is divided into four rooms: a parlor and dining area leads to the bedroom and beyond is a dressing room and bathroom. Sunlight filters in through the verandah windows. Elegant period furnishings—including oriental carpets on the teak, marble and tile floors—ensure that each suite exudes warmth and character. The eight Grand Hotel Suites are even more spacious and luxurious. Deluxe amenities and service, including valets who attend to each suite, are of the highest international standard. The Raffles Grill offers fine continental dining, the Tiffin Room specializes in tiffin curry, and the Bar & Billiard Room serves a wonderful lunch buffet. The Raffles has several other restaurants including the Courtyard outdoor café for dinner or Doc Cheng's for fusion cuisine in a setting juxtaposing antiques with red leather upholstered seating. Pool and Health Club facilities. Business Center and Conference facilities.

❑ **The Regent**: *1 Cuscaden Road, Singapore 249715, Tel. (65) 733-8888 or Fax (65) 732-8838 or toll-free from U.S. 800-332-3442, from Canada 800-268-6282.* Located close to the shops on Orchard Road, and a frequent award winner, The Regent is built around a large central atrium with skylights and fountains. Guests are welcomed at the entrance and escorted via a glass enclosed elevator to their rooms for registration. With the registration completed, a tea tray with fruit and cookies arrives. All 441 spacious guestrooms, including 48 suites which have private balconies, feature unique interior decor reflecting Southeast Asia's rich heritage. The high ceilings and Asian designed fabrics and art lend warmth to the decor. All rooms have IDD phones located at the bedside, desk, and bathroom as well as a mini-bar and in-room safes. Bathrooms feature hairdryers and a full range of Regent toiletries. You may request coffee or tea making facilities for your room or you may choose to have complimentary service in the tea lounge which also serves a high tea on a silver tray service. If you are in Singapore at Thanksgiving or Christmas, The Regent serves a wonderful holiday buffet with the traditional trimmings plus extras Grandma never thought of! Home to what may be Singapore's best French restaurant, the award winning Maxim's de Paris duplicates the aura of the original with its art deco furnishings and combines this with superb food and outstanding service. The Summer Palace offers Cantonese cuisine in an elegant setting. Capers, an all-day café, serves an eclectic mix of Asian and Western favorites. Fitness Center, a small outdoor pool, Business Center and Conference Facilities.

❑ **The Westin Stamford & Westin Plaza:** *2 Stamford Road, Singapore 178882, Tel. (65) 338-8585 or Fax (65) 338-2862.* The two Westin hotels stand only a few hundred feet from one another. Both have entrances directly into Raffles City which includes Raffles City Convention Centre and Raffles City Shopping Mall, home to over 100 specialty shops including the Sogo Department Store. Their location above the MRT provides easy access to public transportation. Just 20 minutes from Singapore Changi Airport, the hotels are set in one of the oldest historical districts of Singapore which has been designated as a prime area of conservation and development. The Westin Stamford claims the distinction as the world's tallest hotel and its famous Compass Rose restaurant, with it breath-taking views and fine food, occupies the 70th floor. The Stamford has 1,263 guestrooms including 63 suites decorated in a variety of motifs from 18th century French and modern Italian to contemporary and traditional Asian themes. Perched on the 64th to 66th floors of the Westin Stamford are 29 luxurious new suites named "The Stamford Crest." Offering a television in the bathroom and spectacular views of the island—from the bathtub as well as from the guestroom, the suites include a Bose hi-fi system and remote control that works through the walls, providing a sound quality very much like a live performance. The Plaza has 764 rooms, 29 suites. In addition to the Compass Rose, there are 11 other restaurants and lounges featuring Continental, Italian, Japanese, Cantonese, Szechuan, and local cuisines. Both Westin properties offer the amenities expected by business and pleasure travelers alike. The swimming pool is the largest in a Singapore hotel; an extensive fitness center and business center are available for guests. Given its excellent location and facilities, these two hotels are especially popular with tour and convention groups.

❑ **Mandarin Singapore**: *333 Orchard Road, Singapore 238867, Tel. (65) 737-4111 or Fax (65) 235-6688 or toll-free from U.S. & Canada 800-380-9957. Web: www. commerceasia.com/mandarin.* Centrally located in the midst of Orchard Road's shopping and with a shopping arcade attached to the hotel, this two tower complex has recently gone through a complete renovation. The lobby is decorated with strong Chinese influences. Guestrooms are comfortable with greater than average closet space. Bathrooms are equipped with expected amenities. The revolving restaurant, Top of the M, serves continental cuisine. Fitness Center, outdoor pool, tennis court, squash court. Business Center/ Conference Facilities.

❑ **Marina Mandarin**: *6 Raffles Boulevard, Marina Square, Singapore 039594, Tel. (65) 338-3388 or Fax (65) 339-4977. Web: www.marina-mandarin.com.sq.* Linked to Marina Square Shopping Mall, the Marina Mandarin's soaring light-filled atrium lobby with hanging plants lining the corridor balconies welcomes each guest. Guestrooms are spacious; bathrooms have double sinks, separate shower and tub. Fitness center, large outdoor pool, two outdoor tennis courts and putting green. Business Center. Conveniently located within easy walking distance of Suntec, Millenia Walk, Raffles City, and the Raffles Hotel.

❑ **Marco Polo**: *247 Tanglin Road, Singapore 247935, Tel. (65) 474-7141 or Fax (65) 471-0521.* The Marco Polo is a ten minute walk from Orchard Road set on 4 acres of tropical landscaped grounds. Room decor varies with some rooms decorated in Chinese decor and others decorated in continental style. Fitness Center, large swimming pool, Business Center/Conference Facilities.

❑ **Hilton International**: *581 Orchard Road, Singapore 238883, Tel. (65) 737-2233 or Fax (65) 732-2917 or toll-free U.S. & Canada 800-445-8667. Web: www.travel web.com/thisco/hiltnint/common/search/html.* Not only are you in the midst of Orchard Road shopping opportunities, the Hilton's own two level shopping arcade is upscale and elegant. The lobby is attractive and rooms deliver what guests expect from Hilton. Floor-to-ceiling windows provide views either of the Thai Embassy across Orchard Road or greenery in the rear. The award winning Harbour Grill restaurant serves continental cuisine. Fitness Center, outdoor pool. Business Center/Conference Facilities.

❑ **Traders Hotel**: *1A Cuscaden Road, Singapore 249716, Tel. (65) 738-2222 or Fax (65) 831-4314*. Adjacent to Orchard Road, Traders is the mid-priced hotel chain from the Shangri-La Group with the goal of providing excellent accommodations at very affordable rates by foregoing some of the facilities expected in the 5-star hotels. However, it may be difficult to identify what is missing. The rooms are attractive and comfortable. There is a Club Floor available, Fitness Center, swimming pool, and Health Club. Business Center.

During low occupancy periods, many hotels are willing to extend discounts or they offer special weekend prices. For best rates, contact the hotels directly or through a travel agent.

You will also find numerous middle-range and inexpensive hotels in Singapore. Try, for example, **Hotel Asia, Dai-Ichi Hotel, Hotel Equatorial, Hotel Miramar, Peninsula Hotel, President Merlin Singapore** for moderate accommodations. **Hotel Bencoolen, Metropole Hotel, New Seventh Storey Hotel,** and **Hotel Royal** are relatively inexpensive. Some of the inexpensive hotels are small family-run homey hotels that give one a glimpse of local culture.

RESTAURANTS

Dining and shopping are close competitors for the best things to do in Singapore. To give both equal time is to experience the ultimate in travel treasures and pleasures—and in the process experience a weight gain!

Visiting Singapore without indulging in one of its favorite pastimes—eating—is like going to Italy and not sampling the pasta and wine. Like Hong Kong, Singapore is a gastronomic's delight; its range of cuisines is truly international and inventive. Reflecting its crossroads location in Southeast Asia and its rich multi-ethnic makeup, Singapore's thousands of restaurants offer a bewildering array of cuisines and dishes, from Chinese, Indian, Malay, Thai, Indonesian, and Japanese to Continental, American, French, Italian, Mexican, Middle Eastern, and Russian. Its homegrown Straits Chinese or Nonya dishes top off what is unquestionably one of the world's great dining experiences. Be it standard food fare or inventive fusion cuisine with strong influences from California, London, and Paris, food and fun are synonymous in gastronomic Singapore. Here you'll find the usual assortment of Western fast-food outlets alongside local food courts and hawker stalls. You can dine alfresco by the ocean or in cafes lining the major boulevards or enjoy the air conditioned comfort of spectacular restaurants with a view of the city's ever changing skyline. Yes, Singapore has it all in the dining department!

The dining scene in Singapore is constantly changing due to the highly competitive nature of restaurants and food outlets and the trendy nature of international dining. Don't be surprised to find a little bit of Paris, New York, and California in your Singapore dining experience, from the content of the menu and the view of the kitchen to the ambience of the dining experience. Upon arriving in Singapore, be sure to pick up a copy of the Singapore Tourism Board's booklet on food, *Food and Entertainment Singapore*, as well as the "Food and Entertainment" section of the Singapore Tourism Board's Web site: *www.newasia-singapore.com*. Also, the monthly tourist magazine *Where Singapore* includes an extensive list of Singapore's best restaurants which is usually fairly reliable. Most major bookstores have copies of *Singapore's Best Restaurants*, an annual book based on a survey of the Singapore Tatler magazine's readers. You also should check out this Web site which offers candid reviews of Singapore's best restaurants, including many hawker stalls: *www.makansutra.com*.

Highlights of, and recent trends in, Singapore's dining scene include:

1. **Dining alfresco:** Despite Singapore's legendary heat and humidity, dining alfresco remains very popular. Forget the crowded and noisy outdoor hawker stalls. Now it's Starbucks, Burger King, and Border's Books along with many upscale cafés and restaurants. Be it the trendy outdoor dining along the river at Clarke Quay and Boat Quay, traditional open air ocean front seafood dining, or the tables and chairs that line the shopping mecca of Orchard Road, to see and be seen sipping a cool drink, eating a croissant, drinking a capuccino, or having lunch or dinner in the outdoors is definitely the "in" thing to do. Try the beautiful Grill on Devonshire (6 Devonshire Road, just off Orchard Road) for one of the best alfresco dining experiences in Singapore.

2. **Fusion cuisine:** Straits Chinese or Nonya food used to be Singapore's unique contribution to fusion cuisine—a delightful marriage of Chinese and Malay dishes. While Nonya food remains popular, especially is such places as Blue Ginger, look for more international fusions. Following the trends of other major international cities, Singapore's chefs are introducing more and more inventive

menus. Be it the East meets West fusion cuisines of Doc Cheng's at the Raffles Hotel or Shrooms at Chijmes, such restaurants draw a popular following of diners interested in unusual dishes. Also, try Club Chinois (Orchard Parade Hotel) and Qhue (242 Pasir Panjang Road).

3. **Open kitchens:** The open kitchen concept, where diners literally see the drama of cooking from their table, has become very popular as more and more restaurants add an open area or window to the their kitchens. Recent converts include: Nadaman and Coffee Garden (Shangri-La Hotel), Tandoor Restaurant (Holiday Inn Park View), Club Chinois (Orchard Parade Hotel), Movenpick Marche Restaurant (260 Orchard Road), Michelangelos (Chip Bee Garden), The Fig Leaf (Central Mall), Doc Cheng's (Raffles Hotel), Mezza9 (Grand Hyatt Singapore), Pronto (Oriental Singapore), Imagiku (Westin Plaza), and the Harbour Grill and Oyster Bar (Hilton Singapore).

4. **Pubs, karaoke, and pick-up music bars:** Pub hopping, karaoke bars, and pick-up music bars remain popular with young people who are looking for loud music, dancing, and new faces to share the evening with. Two of the largest concentrations of such establishments are found in the trendy Tanjong Pagar Road, just south of the central financial district and adjacent to Chinatown, and the Boat Quay and Clarke Quay areas, especially nearby Robertson Walk and River Valley Road. And then there is always the venerable institution at the Raffles Hotel, the Long Bar. Fabric's World Music Bar at the Marriott Hotel (320 Orchard Road) bills itself as the best pick-up place in Singapore. Most music bars have cover charges ($15 - $25) and food that varies from bar snacks to light meals.

5. **New dining concepts:** More and more restaurants like to experiment with new dining concepts and trendy settings. The latest popular addition is Mezza9 at the Grand Hyatt which can accommodate 450 diners who sit at a variety of open kitchen food stations. Try the House of Mao for the latest in kitsch surroundings, including Mao portraits and propaganda.

6. **Unique ethnic dining experiences:** Ethnic dining is everywhere in Singapore. You'll find lots of Chinese, Japanese, and Thai restaurants that have become standard

fare in most large cities around the world. But for something really unique, try the popular Indian restaurants that scoop your dishes out on banana leaves and where patrons eat with dripping hands. It doesn't get much better, or the show more interesting, than at Muthu's Curry and Banana Leaf Apollo. Try their fish head curry. At the same time, be sure to try Singapore's popular 24-hour hawker stalls, especially Newton Circus, and its many food courts, such as Lau Pa Sat which was once Singapore's Victorian wet market. The rijsttafel, with its twelve maidens serving, at the Alkaff Mansion (10 Telok Blangah Green) is always a hit with those who have not experienced this popular Dutch-Indonesia adaptation of the buffet.

7. **Afternoon English teas:** It's one of those delightful afternoon traditions, usually from 2 to 5pm or 3 to 5:30pm, left over from the British colonial tradition. Afternoon tea means assorted teas, sandwiches, pastries, and long conversations in a delightful hotel lobby or restaurant setting. Try afternoon tea at the Four Seasons, Regent, and Goodwood Park hotels.

8. **Fast food, chains, and coffee houses:** McDonald's, Burger King, KFC, and Pizza Hut have been around for several years and they remain very popular with both locals and tourists. A branch of the famous upscale American steakhouse, Morton's of Chicago (The Oriental Singapore), has recently made its debut in Singapore. Coffee houses, such as Starbucks and local imitators, now occupy prominent places in shopping centers and along major shopping streets. Even the ubiquitous superstore bookstore café, introduced by the American bookstore retailing giant Borders Books, has found its way into Singapore's changing book buying culture.

9. **Good value restaurants:** Given the highly competitive nature of Singapore's food business, coupled with a greater sensitivity to the overall cost of eating in a less than stellar economy, more and more restaurants are offering luncheon specials which are nearly half the regular menu price. Good restaurant values can be had for less than US$10 per person for lunch. Be sure to look for such specials when selecting a restaurant for lunch, especially at restaurants in or near shopping centers.

10. **Theme restaurants:** Yes, they are taking over the world and most come from America. The ubiquitous Hard Rock Café and Planet Hollywood serve up standard American fare as well as operate signature shops where you can purchase T-shirts and other memorabilia of these popular theme restaurants. Family-friendly Snoopy Place with its giant screen filled with animated versions of Charles Schulz's famous comic strip and booths and bar stools shaped to represent Peanuts themes distinguish this restaurant as truly unique.

11. **Something very special:** If you're only in Singapore for a short time, you should try some of Singapore's very special dining experiences. Start with the noon buffet or a romantic dinner at the top of the world's tallest hotel—the Westin's signature Compass Rose restaurant. The view is spectacular and the food surprisingly good. Or try the popular Tiffin Room, if you can get in, at the Raffles Hotel for the traditional curry buffet. Or try the Alkaff Mansion for its popular Indonesian buffet or its traditional Dutch-Indonesian rijsttafel set in a romantic house filled with history and old world charm overlooking lush hillsides. All three of these restaurants are very special dining experiences you should not miss while in Singapore.

CHINESE

Being primarily a Chinese city-state, Singapore abounds with good quality Chinese restaurants. For some of the very best, try the following:

❑ **Jiang-Nan Chun:** *Four Seasons Hotel, 190 Orchard Boulevard, Tel. 734-1110. Open daily 11:30am-2pm and 6pm-10pm.* This elegant yet chic gourmet Chinese restaurant exudes a contemporary ambience (art deco look with art nouveau furnishings) while still offering excellent Cantonese cuisine with a modern twist. The affable Master Chef Sam Leong runs a busy and talented kitchen serving outstanding and inventive dim sum for lunch. A la carte menu features Chinese delicacies such as bird's-nest soup, shark's fin, and abalone Good selection of fresh seafood and seasonal creations. Try the pan-fried beef fillet in continental guise, fried prawns with sesame seeds and mayonnaise, and steamed soon hook fish. For dessert, try the Shanghai pancake.

❑ **Summer Pavilion:** *The Ritz-Carlton Millenia Singapore, 7 Raffles Avenue, Tel. 336-8888. Open daily 11:30am-2:30pm and 6:30pm-10pm.* This is The Ritz-Carlton's elegant signature restaurant. Built as a glass pavilion nestled amidst a picturesque garden. Serves outstanding Cantonese cuisine. Try its braised shark's fin soup with crab meat and crab roe and braised lobster with minced garlic.

❑ **Empress Room:** *Raffles Hotel, 328 North Bridge Road, #03-09, Tel. 331-1738 or 337-1886. Open 12pm-2:30pm (Sunday 11am-2:30pm) and 6:30pm-10:30pm.* This could be the good ole days of fine dining in decadent Shanghai. This truly elegant and spacious Cantonese restaurant, complete with lanterns, wood panels, and rosewood furniture, serves outstanding dim sum and a la carte selections. Be sure to try the barbecued Peking duck, braised supreme shark's fin with brown sauce, and deep-fried prawns with walnut and mayonnaise.

❑ **Grand Pavilion:** *Chinese Swimming Club, 21 Amber Road, Tel. 440-2222. Open daily 11:30am-2:30pm and 6:30pm-10:30 pm.* Located outside the city in the Katong district, this landmark restaurant is noted for serving outstanding and moderately-priced Cantonese cuisine. The restaurant overlooks a large swimming pool. Try the Peking duck, beef with black pepper sauce, sautéed spicy prawns with melted cheese, lobster salad, barbecue chicken, and suckling pig. Efficient service.

❑ **Li Bai:** *Sheraton Towers, 39 Scotts Road, Tel. 737-6888, ext. 3490. Open daily 12noon-3pm and 6:30pm-11:30pm.* This attractive restaurant with its marbled walls and beautiful paintings is a culinary delight. Try the fabulous signature dish—"monk jumps over the wall"—but call ahead to make sure it's available for your dining date. Also try the roast pork, pan-fried beef, barbecued duck, and a variety of seafood dishes, especially the abalone and king prawns.

❑ **House of Blossoms:** *Marina Mandarin Singapore, 6 Raffles Boulevard, Marina Square, Tel. 331-8540 or 338-3388. Open daily 12pm-3pm and 6:30pm-11pm.* Decorated in a rich and elegant Chinese style, including murals, lanterns, and rosewood furniture, this attractive dining room offers a wonderful range of fine Chinese dishes. Try the Peking duck, dim sum, fried egg white with crab and conpoy.

❑ **Kelong Thomson:** *Thomson Plaza, 301 Upper Thomson Road #01-85/88, Tel. 454-9036. Open 11am-3pm (Saturday and Sunday 10am-3pm) and 6:30pm-10:30pm.* This long established Cantonese restaurant continues to draw a loyal clientele that appreciates its good food and reasonable prices. Popular with families and professionals alike. Try the buttered prawns with kaffir leaves, and shark's fin in earthen pot. Also serves excellent dim sum.

❑ **Lei Garden Restaurant:** *Three locations: Chijmes, 30 Victoria Street #01-24, Tel. 339-3822; Orchard Plaza, 150 Orchard Road #09-01/02, Tel. 738-2448; and Orchard Shopping Centre, 321 Orchard Road, Tel. 734-3988. Open daily 11am-2:30pm and 6pm-10:30pm.* The Chijmes branch is reputed to be the *"best of the best"* as well as the most popular—reservations for both lunch and dinner are essential! One of Singapore's most popular restaurants serving outstanding seafood dishes. Try the Peking duck, pork spare ribs, lobster soup, and most seafood dishes. Consistently excellent food espccially popular with Singaporeans "in the know."

❑ **Min Jiang:** *Goodwood Park Hotel, 22 Scotts Road, Tel. 730-1704 or 737-7411. Open daily 12noon-2:30pm and 6:30pm-10:30pm.* Unquestionably Singapore's best and most authentic Sichuan restaurant. Long established and popular with local lovers of Sichuan cuisine, the restaurant offers an expansive menu of over 100 dishes. Try the hot and sour soup, fillet of smoked duck, shredded beef "Min Jiang" style, and stewed aubergine with minced meat and chilli. Also serves excellent seafood dishes.

❑ **New Kirin Court:** *Devonshire Building, 20 Devonshire Road #01-01, Tel. 732-1188. Open daily 11:30am-2:30pm and 6:30pm-10:30pm.* This outstanding restaurant consistently delivers top quality Cantonese cuisine. Especially noted for its shark's fin with crab roe, double-boiled superior shark's fin with chicken, cold crabs, lobster sashimi, and braised sliced fresh abalone with goose web.

❑ **Shang Palace:** *Shangri-La Hotel, 22 Orange Grove Road, Tel. 730-2473 or 737-3644. Open daily 11:30am-2:30pm and 6:30pm-10:30pm.* This grand and elegant dining hall is the perfect setting for fine dining. Try the stewed duck with plum sauce, stir-fried beef with macadamia nuts, yellow chives poached with century eggs and salted eggs, stir-fried black peppered beef, and stir-fried local clams with XO sauce. For dessert, try the thousand-layer cake.

❑ **Summer Palace:** *Regent Hotel, 1 Cuscaden Road, Tel. 733-8888. Open daily 11:30am-2:30pm and 6:30pm-10:30pm.* This popular Cantonese restaurant is great for dim sum. New menu selections each month. Excellent service.

❑ **Crystal Jade Palace:** *#04-19 Takashimaya Shoppping Centre, 391 Orchard Road, Tel. 735-2388. Open daily 11:30am-3pm and 6pm-11pm.* One of Singapore's best. Part of the popular Crystal Jade group of restaurants. Famous for dim sum, fresh seafood, and barbecue dishes. Tasteful contemporary decor and excellent service.

SEAFOOD

Almost every restaurant in Singapore offers some seafood selections. For hotel dining, try Snappers:

❑ **Snappers:** *The Ritz-Carlton Millenia Singapore, 7 Raffles Avenue, Tel. 336-8888. Open 6pm-11pm.* Al fresco dining surrounded by lush tropical greenery. Its international seafood menu includes everything from Maine lobsters to Belon oysters and Australian yabbies. Try the barbecued stingray wrapped in banana leaves and the popular Singaporean chilli crab. Includes a fresh catch of the day and the lively sounds of a three-piece Cuban band.

If you are in the mood for doing strictly seafood in a festive atmosphere, try these two large seafood emporiums:

❑ **Long Beach:** *1018 East Coast Parkway (next to the Singapore Tennis Centre), Tel. 445-8833. Open daily 11am-3pm and 5pm-12:15am (Saturday 5pm-1:15am).* This is one of nearly a dozen similar seafood restaurants that are located close to one another along East Coast Parkway in an area called the "UDMC Seafood Centre." As you enter this area, you'll see a sign pointing you to this and other restaurants. You can't go wrong trying one of these places for excellent seafood dishes. However, Long Beach is considered by many seafood lovers as the *"best of the best."* Try the popular black pepper crab, crispy baby squid, and crullers stuffed with minced cuttlefish. The fresh prawns and fish, cooked to your specifications, are always hits. Also try the deep-fried crispy duck.

❑ **Jumbo Seafood:** *Blok 1206, #01-08 East Coast Parkway, Tel. 442-3435; 22 Kensington Park Road, Tel. 383-3435; and #01-01 Juronng Reptile Park, Tel. 266-3435.* Famous for Sri Lankan black pepper crabs. Very popular, reasonably priced, and casual.

PERANAKAN (STRAITS CHINESE)

Some of Singapore's best cuisine is peranakan, nonya, or Straits Chinese cuisine. Representing a unique blend of Chinese and Malay cooking,

❑ **Blue Ginger:** *97 Tanjong Ragar Road, Tel. 222-3928, and #05-02C The Heeren Shops, 260 Orchard Road, Tel. 835-3928. Open daily 11:30am-3pm and 6:30-11pm.* Excellent Paranakan cuisine including such signature dishes as beef rendang, ayam panggang, ikan chili, and ngoh heong. Try the recommended dishes. Reasonably priced, excellent service, and charming atmosphere.

❑ **Nonya & Baba:** *River Road (halfway up the hill). Open daily 11am-3pm and 6-10pm.* This out of the way restaurant remains one of Singapore's most popular dining spots. Try the otak otak and the clear crab- and prawn-ball soup.

❑ **House of Peranakan Cuisine:** *Meritus Negara, 10 Claymore Road, Tel. 733-4411. Open daily 11:30am - 3pm and 6-10:30pm.* Atmosphere is a little tacky but the food is excellent. Try the chef's recommendations, especially chili promfret and Nonya duck. Generous portions.

SOUTHEAST ASIA

❑ **Alkaff Mansion:** *10 Telok Blangah Green, Tel. 278-6979. Open 12noon-2:30pm and 7pm-10:30pm.* Convert an old mansion (Alkaff family) into a charming colonial-style restaurant, situate it on a hill overlooking the island, and serve fine Indonesian dishes and French pastries and you have a perfect recipe for a great dining experience that is also a cultural experience. Since opening more than five years ago, the historical Alkaff Mansion has continued to draw crowds to experience its unique ambience and grand dining away from the hustle and bustle of the city. One of Singapore's most romantic restaurants where ambience is its greatest strength. Serves a wonderful noon buffet and a grand high tea. For dinner, try the Indonesian Rijsttafel where the show is as delightful as the food itself—each of 10 dishes you are served by young ladies are ceremonially announced with a bang of a gong. Colonialism never had it so good as this delightful recreation!

❑ **The Tiffin Room:** *Raffles Hotel, 1 Beach Road, Tel. 337-1886. Open 7:30am-10am (breakfast); 12noon-2pm (lunch); 3:30pm-5pm (high tea); 7pm-10pm (dinner).* The Raffles Hotel remains one of Singapore's major tourist attractions, and the Tiffin Room is partly responsible for this honor. This is probably the busiest hotel dining room in Singapore, operating from 7am to 10pm, and always packed for lunch and dinner. Indeed, this restaurant is a Singapore institution—you really can't claim to have "been in Singapore" without trying the Tiffin Room. It serves the traditional curry tiffin buffet for lunch and dinner which is a combination of curried South and Southeast Asian dishes. Such curried dishes have been served at this hotel since 1899. Be sure to make reservations. This restaurant seems to be on every Japanese tourist's "must see and do" list!

❑ **Aziza's:** *Albert Court, 180 Albert Street #02-15, Tel. 235-1130. Open 11:30am-3pm (closed Sunday) and 6:30pm-11pm.* If you've never tried Malay food, here's the perfect introduction. This charming restaurant offers terrific Malay cuisine and service. Everything here is excellent and has the personal attention of Aziza, the owner and charming hostess. Try the fried fish with chilli and coriander sauce, beef rendang, sambal prawns, rojak, and grilled chicken with black shallot, lemon grass, kasturi lime and tamarind sauce (ayam panggang kasturi).

❑ **Sanur:** *Centrepoint, 176 Orchard Road #04-17/18, Tel. 734-2192; Takashimaya Shopping Centre, 391 Orchard Road #004-16, Tel. 734-3434; 2 Alexandria Road #08-00, Tel. 275-2622; Chinatown Point, Tel. 534-5152; Northpoint, 930 Yishun Avenue 2 #B2-03, Tel. 754-7541; and Suntec City, 3 Temasek Blvd. #B1-010, Tel. 338-2777. Open daily 11:45am-2:30pm (except Saturday and Sunday) and 5:45pm-10pm.* If you're looking for good Indonesian food as well as good value, Sanur is the perfect choice. This small family restaurant consistently produces excellent Indonesian dishes. Try their award-winning signature dish, tahu telur (fried bean curd and eggs topped with sweet sauce), kepala ikan (fish head cooked in hot and sour gravy), beef rendang, ayam goreng kampong (fried spring chicken "kampong style", gado-gado, satay, ikan pepes (grilled fish fillet in banana leaves), and coconut rice.

❑ **Thanying**: *Clarke Quay, 3 River Valley Road, Block D #01-14, Tel. 336-1821; Amara Hotel, 165 Tanjong Pagar Road #02-00, Tel. 222-4688. Open daily 11am-3pm and 6:30pm-11pm.* This long established restaurant offers authentic and superb Thai cuisine in a stately setting. Try the khao tang na tang (rice crackers with minced chicken and shrimp dip), pomelo salad, spicy and sour fish soup, and deep fried boneless garoupa.

INTERNATIONAL

❑ **Bar and Billiard Room**: *Raffles Hotel, 1 Beach Road, Tel. 331-1746. Four choices here: seafood lunch buffet Mon.-Sat. 11:30am - 2:30pm; high tea daily 3:30-5pm; Sunday brunch 11:30 - 3pm; bar open daily from 6pm to 12:30 am.* Classy operation with real character. Great place to wile away your afternoon. Everything is excellent, as you would expect from another Raffles food outlet.

❑ **Mezza9**: *Grand Hyatt Hotel, 10-12 Scotts Road, Tel. 738-1234. Open daily noon-2:30pm and 6-10:30pm.* This huge 450-seat dining extravaganza has been fully booked since it opened in late 1998. Consists of separate food stations from which you can order Chinese, Japanese, Italian, and other cuisines. An interesting and lively dining experience.

❑ **Shrooms**: *#02-01 Chijmes, Victoria Street, Tel. 336-6909. Open daily 11:30am-2:30pm and 6:30-10:30pm; Sunday brunch, 11:30am-3pm.* This beautifully elegant yet casual restaurant offers excellent international and inventive fusion cuisine. Try the interesting appetizers as well as the tandoor lamb and grilled rib eye steak with garlic mashed potatoes. Dine al fresca on the first level or in air conditioned comfort on the second level. Good service. A popular meeting place in one of Singapore's most interesting shopping and dining complexes.

JAPANESE

❑ **Unkai**: *ANA Hotel, 16 Nassim Hill, Tel. 839-1555. Open daily 12pm-2:30pm and 6:30pm-10:30pm.* One of Singapore's most popular high quality restaurants with the

Japanese community. Especially noted for its fresh sashimi. Be sure to try the maguro (tuna), shake (salmon), unagi kabayaki (broiled eel with Unkai sauce), and teppanyaki dishes. Also try the Bento boxes or teppanyaki set lunches for a quick lunch. A comfortable and attractive setting with four tatami rooms.

❑ **Shima:** *Goodwood Park Hotel, 22 Scotts Road, Tel. 734-6281. Open daily 12noon-2:30pm and 6:30pm-10pm.* One of Singapore's finest quality Japanese restaurants popular with locals and Japanese alike. The ground floor includes a sushi bar. The first floor offers teppanyaki, shabu shabu, sukiyaki buffet, yakiniku buffet, and steamboat buffet. Everything here is first class, including the sea urchin.

❑ **Suntory:** *Delphi Orchard, 402 Orchard Road #06-01/02. Tel. 732-5111. Open daily 12noon-2pm and 6:30pm-10pm.* One of the most popular and highly regarded Japanese restaurants in Singapore.

❑ **Nadaman:** *Shangri-La Hotel, 22 Orange Grove Road, Tel. 734-4805. Open 12pm-2:30pm and 6:30pm-10:30pm.* This chic restaurant is a culinary delight with its 'magic' tables producing outstanding shabu-shabu (beef steamboat) and kaisen kaminabe (seafood steamboat in a paper pot). Offers a good selection of traditional Japanese cuisine, complete with sushi, sashimi, tempura bars, and teppanyaki grills. Good service, great ambience, and a terrific view to complement the fine food served in this restaurant.

FUSION OR NEW AGE

❑ **Doc Cheng's:** *Raffles Hotel Arcade, 328 North Bridge Road, #02-02 Level 2, Tel. 331-1612 or 337-1886. Open daily 12noon-2:30pm and 7pm-10:30pm.* Part of the Raffles Hotel, this innovative restaurant offers restorative "Trans-Ethnic" food. Honored by *Hotels*, a global publication from the US, as one of the 10 Great Hotel Restaurants in the World, a first for a restaurant in Singapore. An attractive restaurant divided into three sections surrounding an exhibition kitchen and decorated with huge chandeliers, art deco leaded glass, and antique colonial pieces. Try the innovative tempura ahi in English mustard sauce, red spotted garoupa seviche, and lemongrass and tamarind beef fillet. Has own gift shop offering signature

"Doc Cheng" items, from porcelain napkin rings to coffee mugs.

☐ **Club Chinois:** *#02-18 Orchard Parade Hotel, 1 Tanglin Road, Tel. 834-0660. Open daily 11:30am-2:30pm and 6:30pm-10:30pm.* Offers a unique blend of classical Chinese and Western cuisines. Try the unusual treatment of Peking duck with foie gras. Offers set lunches and dinners.

☐ **House of Mao:** *#01-09/10 Orchard Hotel Shopping Arcade, 442 Orchard Road, Tel. 733-7667 and #03-02 China Square Food Centre, 51 Telok Ayer Street, Tel. 533-0660. Open Sunday-Thursday, 11:30am-3pm and 6:30pm-11pm; Friday-Saturday, 11:30am-11pm.* The ultimate kitsch restaurant decorated with Mao portraits and paraphernalia. Everything is good. Try the green curry linguine, mushroom and vegetable pizza, pork ribs, and cabbage dumplings.

WESTERN

☐ **Compass Rose:** *The Westin Stamford, 2 Stamford Road, 70th Floor, Tel. 431-6156. Open daily 12noon-2:30pm and 7pm-10:30pm.* This is one of our favorites we return to again and again. It never disappoints. Singapore's tallest restaurant perched atop the world's tallest hotel. Offers a terrific view of Singapore and an excellent menu to match. Great for intimate romantic evening dining or for a sumptuous noon buffet with a panoramic view of Singapore. Try the deepfried soft shell crab, lobster bisque, peppered lobster tail and sea scallops, Dutch veal tenderloin and grilled gooseliver, and sweet temptation for dessert. Offers a seafood luncheon buffet, Monday through Saturday, and a popular international luncheon buffet on Sunday. If you try only one buffet in Singapore, make sure it's this one. Reservations essential since this restaurant fills up quickly and the lines for the elevator get very long in the lobby of the Westin Stamford. Also open for drinks only, just in case you only want to sample the view. Attentive service.

☐ **Liana's:** *The Oriental Singapore Hotel, 5 Raffles Avenue Marina Square, Tel. 338-0066, Ext. 3447. Open daily 12noon-2:30pm and 6:30pm-10pm.* Chef Liana Doyle brings her inventive California and Continental cuisine together into one of Singapore's finest restaurants. Try the lobster ravioli with lemon grass butter, fallow-deer rack with cherry compote, and several excellent vegetarian dishes. Leave room for her specialty dessert—chocolate cake.

❑ **Harbour Grill:** *Hilton International Singapore, 581 Orchard Road, Tel. 730-3393 or 737-2233. Open daily 12noon-2:30pm (Monday-Friday) and 7pm-10:30pm (Monday-Saturday); closed Sundays.* Long a favorite for fine Continental dining, this attractive restaurant is noted for its dependable menu, fine service, and loyal clientele. Try the spiced salmon steak wrapped in crispy bacon with braised chicory for lunch, veal sweetbread and morel mushroom ravioli with Sauternes wine butter sauce, and grilled John Dory with white clams on a leek fondue.

❑ **Seasons:** *Four Seasons Hotel, 190 Orchard Boulevard, Tel. 831-7250 or 734-1110. Open daily 6:30am-10:30am, 11:30am-2pm, and 6pm-10pm.* This elegant and fashionable restaurant draws crowds all day long with its varied and appealing menu. Try the mushroom ravioli with tomato and basil broth, duck terrine, smoked trout and sturgeon, and medallions of veal. Serves buffet appetizers and decadent desserts.

❑ **Raffles Grill:** *Raffles Hotel, 1 Beach Road, Tel. 331-01611 or 337-1886. Open daily 12noon-2pm and 7pm-10pm; closed Saturday and Sunday.* This elegant restaurant exudes classic colonial ambience. Fine chefs and impeccable service add to its reputation as one of Singapore's best restaurants. Try the freshly smoked salmon with Oscietra caviar cream, oven-roasted fillet of John Dory with parmesan risotto, and pan-fried tenderloin of black angus beef with tarragon sabayon and balsamic sauce. Be sure to save room for the decadent desserts.

❑ **Nutmegs:** *Grand Hyatt Singapore, 10 Scotts Road, Tel. 730-7112 or 738-1234. Open daily 12noon-2:30pm and 7pm-11pm.* This classy restaurant offers both good food and chic atmosphere. Famous for its Caesar salad and rotisserie duckling. Also try the flower crab bisque with cognac cream. Round it all off with a trip to the dessert buffet table.

❑ **Morton's of Chicago:** *5 Raffles Avenue, The Oriental Hotel, Tel. 339-3740. Open Monday-Saturday, 5:30-11pm; Sunday 5-10pm.* This famous American steakhouse is especially popular with the well-heeled business crowd. Serves large juicy prime aged beef as well as fresh fish and seafood. Excellent service. Somewhat pricey.

❏ **Top of the M:** *Mandarin Hotel, 333 Orchard Road, 39th Floor, Tel. 737-4411. Open daily 12 noon-2:30pm and 6-10:30pm.* This long established revolving restaurant still brings in the crowds for lunch and dinner. Offers appetizer buffets and a set dinner.

ITALIAN

❏ **Bice:** *Goodwood Park Hotel, 22 Scotts Road, Tel. 735-3711. Open daily 12noon-2:30pm and 6pm-10:30pm.* For many dining experts, this is Singapore's best Italian restaurant. Related to the Milan-based restaurant family, Bice Singapore is renowned for its exacting standards of excellence that have made Bice a welcome addition to the international fine dining scene. Primarily offers Milanese Italian dishes. Try the salmon carpaccio with sambucca and marinated tuna salad with avocado focaccia for antipasti as well as the gnocchi in lobster sauce, veal with bacon in truffle sauce, and the various pasta dishes. Save room for a delectable dessert, especially the gianduja meringue topped with hand-made ice cream.

❏ **Domus:** *Sheraton Towers Singapore, 30 Scotts Road, Tel. 737-6888. Open daily 6:30pm-11:30pm.* Fine Italian dining in a lovely setting accompanied by excellent service. Try the wonderful antipasti, especially the smoked salmon with mustard and herbs, and snails in herb butter and baked potato. Also try the rack of lamb with garlic puree and the grilled T-bone steak. For dessert, go for the tiramisu and hot coffee pudding with rum sabayon.

❏ **Paladino di Firenze:** *7 Muhammad Sultan Road (off River Valley Road), Tel. 738-0917. Open daily 12noon-3pm and 7pm-11pm.* This small and charming restaurant is located in a newly renovated shophouse in the reconstructed Mohammad Sultan Road area near Boat Quay. Try the osso bucco (veal shank) and arrabiata, linguine with mussels, and homemade semifreddo.

❏ **Ristorante Bologna:** *Marina Mandarin Singapore, 6 Raffles Boulevard, Marina Square, Tel. 331-8470. Open daily 12noon-2:30pm (closed Saturday) and 7pm-10:30pm.* Specializing in Northern Italian cuisine, this fine dining establishment continues to serve some of Singapore's best Italian food. Try the scallops with black truffle and pigeon served in a pot. For dessert, select "grandmother's" traditional cake with apricot sauce.

❑ **Prego**: *The Westin Plaza, 2 Stamford Road, 1st floor, Tel. 431-5156. Open daily 11:30am-12:30am. Deli open daily 10:30am-12:30am.* This once popular restaurant now gets mixed reviews. This lively and cheerful eatery, with semi-circular windows, faces the busy streets and sidewalks as you watch the bustling traffic go by. Serves its own special blended coffees from a cappuccino bar and excellent pastas from the pasta counter. Expansive menu includes such stand-out dishes as sliced veal with tuna sauce and capers, sauteed duck breast on eggplant puree, breaded pork chop with vegetables, and poached fillets of sole with pimento sauce. Watch how many dishes you order since portions tend to be rather hardy. If you still have room for dessert, try the popular tiramisu or creme brulée.

❑ **Michelangelo's**: *Chip Bee Gardens, Block 44 Jalan Merah Saga #01-60, Tel. 475-9069. Open daily 11:30am-2:30pm (Monday-Friday) and 6:30pm-11pm.* One of Singapore's annual award winning restaurants. Located in the popular Holland Village area and especially popular with locals who have discovered this small but outstanding Italian restaurant. The pastas and main dishes are all winners. Try the mozzarella bocconchini; Marisa's eggplant beauty; char-grilled rack of lamb in white wine, rosemary, and garlic; and lobster with squid-ink pasta.

FRENCH

❑ **Maxim's de Paris**: *The Regent Singapore, 1 Cuscaden Road, Tel. 739-3091 or 733-8888. Open daily 12noon-2:30pm and 7:30pm-10:30pm.* This luxurious dining room with its stained glass lighting panels and art nouveau style provides the perfect setting for its fine cuisine. Try the charlotte of green asparagus with truffle sauce, salmon parfait with chive sauce, cream of winter truffle soup, fillet of tenderloin, and sauteed lamb with herb olive crust and thyme sauce.

❑ **Latour**: *Shangri-La Hotel, 22 Orange Grove Road, Tel. 730-2471 or 737-3644. Open daily 12noon-2:30pm and 6:30pm-*

10:30pm. This elegant and cosy restaurant is the perfect choice for a romantic evening. While the menu frequently changes, the inventive kitchen continues to deliver the very best in gourmet dining. Try the truffle soup, parfait of goose liver, medallion of Dutch milk-fed veal, and Latour salad with flower petals. Tempting desserts include a selection of hot soufflés. Offers a set lunch and a popular Sunday buffet.

❑ **L'Aigle d'Ore:** *Duxton Hotel, 83 Duxton Road, Tel. 227-7678. Open daily 12noon-2pm and 7pm-10pm.* This chic and innovative restaurant serves some of Singapore's best French cuisine. Try the fresh pan-fried duck liver with sweet baked figs, French turbot with black truffles, and loin of French veal. Offers an excellent selection of desserts. The daily set menu is usually a good choice.

❑ **Les Amis:** *Shaw Centre, 1 Scotts Road #02-16, Tel. 733-2225. Open daily 12noon-2pm and 7pm-10pm; closed Sunday.* This elegant yet contemporary restaurant serves excellent French dishes without the traditional heavy sauces and creams normally associated with French cooking. Try the charcoal grilled rib-eye, quail, sea scallops, or veal. Select the hot souffle for dessert. Expansive wine list. Exceptional service.

❑ **Chez Georges:** *Le Meridian Singapore, 100 Orchard Road, Tel. 733-8855. Open daily 12noon-2:30pm and 7pm-10.30pm.* This surprising restaurant, located along the lower end of Orchard Road, offers excellent French food at moderate prices and in an attractive setting. We especially enjoy stopping here for the appealing noon buffet after a hectic morning prowling Orchard Road. Popular restaurant with French expatriates. Try the marinated fresh salmon in olive oil and fennel, sauteed snails in garlic and parsley butter sauce with bacon, and hake fish with garlic sauce and trompette mushrooms. Save room for the créme brulée.

INDIAN

❑ **Muthu's Curry Restaurant:** *76/78 Race Course Road, Tel. 293-2389 or 293-7029. Open daily 10am-10pm and even on holidays.* Get ready to literally dig in with your hands at this popular neighborhood restaurant that has become a Singapore institution for its fish head curry. Truly an adventure in eating for those not used to dining in such an Indian restaurant. If you don't mind having a bed of rice and condiments ladled onto a banana leaf and then eating off of the leaf with your hands (spoons and forks are provided for the uninitiated), this is a great place to sample some terrific Indian cuisine. In addition to its signature fish head curry dish, try the crab masahla, fried prawn, chicken biryani, mutton biryani, and mutton curry. Everything here is good and it may even taste better when eating with your hands. A crowded and casual cultural experience you won't forget. Moderately priced.

❑ **Banana Leaf Apollo:** *54-58 Race Course Road, Tel. 293-8682.* Owned by the brother of Muthu's Curry Restaurant. One of Singapore's most popular Indian restaurants, a "must visit" for many visitors who want a unique dining experience complete with a banana leaf "plate" and eating with your fingers. If you don't get to Muthu's Curry restaurant for a similar experience, be sure to try Banana Leaf Apollo. Good place to visit for lunch.

❑ **Hazara:** *Holland Village, 24 Lorong Mambong, Tel. 467-4101. Open daily 12noon-2:30pm and 6:30pm-10:30pm.* This quaint and attractive restaurant exudes Indian ambience both inside and out (you may find yourself dining al fresco). Try the tandoor leg of baby lamb in rum and spices, lentil curry, boneless chicken, murgh malai or crab curry with garlic naan and Kashmiri pilau. Also has a branch restaurant (Kinara)at 57 Boat Quay (Tel. 533-0412).

HAWKER FOOD

❑ **Newton Circus:** *At Bukit Timah Road, across from Newton MRT station.* Singapore's most popular hawker center with numerous stalls offering a good varity of hawker foods. Fun atmosphere and fast service. Ignore the touts and only pay the prices listed on the board. Try stalls 64, 68, 72, and 79.

❑ **Chinatown Complex:** *Intersection of North Bridge Road and Smith Road.* Several stalls serve a variety of inexpensive Chinese dishes. Try Stall #02-132 for traditional black sesame and peanut-paste soup, and Stall #02-150 for "Chinese burritos."

❑ **Lau Pa Sat:** *Robinson Road and Boon Tat Street.* This attractively restored old Victorian wet market is a popular 24-hour food center. You can find just about any type of Asian cuisine here. Pick your dishes from dozens of food stalls as well as satay peddlers with their pushcarts. You can easily dine here for under S$10. The place is most popular, festive, and cool in the evening.

SEEING THE SITES

There is much more to Singapore than just shopping. As a totally integrated travel experience, Singapore offers a wonderful array of sightseeing, recreational, entertainment, and gastronomic opportunities. Most of these you can easily do on your own or you can join regularly scheduled tour groups.

As a walking city, you can see most of the interesting sights by taking walks into special areas of the city. The Singapore Tourism Board publishes several useful booklets which enable you to conduct your own 1-3 hour walks in different areas of the city. The maps and accompanying descriptive information will take you to numerous historical sights, peoples, and shops.

❑ **Arab Street District:** Includes the Sultan Mosque along with residences and shops.

❑ **Botanic Gardens:** A beautiful park with 2,500 plants of 250 different hybrids and species located along Napier and Cluny roads near Orchard Road.

❑ **Boat Quay:** South bank of Singapore River, between Cavenagh Bridge and Elgin Bridge. This hip area of once notorious opium dens and coolie shops has been converted to a popular area for restaurants, bars, and nightlife. Dine alfresco along the river as you watch the traffic go by.

❑ **Clarke Quay:** River Valley Road, east of Boat Quay and West of Coleman Bridge. Once a bustling area of warehouses and a pineapple cannery and iron factory, this area is now bustling with shopping and sightseeing. Includes over 150 restored restaurants, warehouses, and shops (Clarke Quay Factory Stores). Its popular flea market draws large crowds on Sunday.

❑ **Chijmes:** *30 Victoria Street.* One of Singapore's most recent heritage projects. Restored buildings of the

Convent of the Holy Infant Jesus. Now converted to restaurants, pubs, and shops with the old chapel serving as a performance center.

❑ **Chinatown Streetwalk:** Includes temples, shrines, noted buildings, shops, architecture, and special streets.

❑ **Colonial Heart Streetwalk:** Covers the General Post Office, Empress Place, Victoria Theatre, Victoria Memorial Hall, Sir Stamford Raffles Landing Site, Parliament House, Supreme Court, City Hall, St. Andrew's Cathedral, Armenian Church of St. Gregory the Iluminator, and Fort Canning Park.

❑ **Little India Streetwalk:** Puts you in Hindu and Buddhist temples, mosques, Parrer Park, and several special streets.

❑ **Sentosa—Singapore's Resort Island:** Take a ferry or cable car to this pleasant recreational island. Visit the Wax Museum, Fort Siloso, Maritime Museum, Coralarium, World Insectarium, Rare Stone Museum. Tourist attractions in this area are being rapidly expanded. Shangri-La's Rasa Sentosa Resort is located here.

❑ **Singapore Art Museum:** *71 Brasah Road, Tel. 332-3222. www.museum.org.sg/nhb.html. Open Tuesday-Sunday, 9am-5:30pm and Wednesday 9am-9pm. Adults $3 and children/ seniors S$1.50.* Housed in a beautiful old historic building (Catholic boys' school) and opened in 1996, this fine museum displays some of the best artists from Singapore and Malaysia.

❑ **Tanjong Pagar Conservation Area:** Located in Chinatown, this newly restored area of historical shophouses consists of over 200 shops, restaurants, and pubs.

❑ **Singapore Zoological** *Gardens: 80 Mandai Alke Road, Tel. 269-3411. Web: www.zoo.com.sg.* Over 1,600 animals representing 170 species on display in 60 exhibits. Operates the popular "Night Safari" from 7:30pm to midnight (adults S$10.30 and children S$4.60) as well as one of Singapore's most popular attractions and activities— "Breakfast or Tea With an Orangutan" (Breakfast daily from 9am and Tea daily from 4pm (except Sundays and public holidays.

❑ **Changi:** This East Coast visit includes the famous POW Changi Prison, Changi Village shopping area, Changi Point, Changi Beach, and Somapah Road.

❑ **Harbor and River Cruises:** Harbor cruises: Chinese junks depart from Clifford Pier every afternoon at 3pm and 4pm for 2½ hour cruises. Twilight cruises take 3 hours and depart at 6pm. River cruises: leave regularly from Clark Quay.

Other self-guided walking tours include Mount Faber, National Museum and Art Gallery, Pernankan Place, Raffles Hotel, and Singapore Science Centre. At night you can attend cultural shows at the Grand Hyatt, Mandarin Hotel, and Raffles Hotel; take a 3-hour dinner cruise; visit Merlion Park; poke through the Night Market on Sentosa Island on Friday, Saturday, and Sunday evenings; take a trishaw tour of Little India and Chinatown; dine at the street stalls along the newly rejuvenated Bugis Street; have dinner at the elegant restored Alkaff Mansion (on Mount Faber Ridge) overlooking the city; or enjoy performances at Victoria Concert Hall and Victoria Theatre (Empress Place). Outside the city proper you will find many additional attractions such as temples, mosques, churches, a crocodile farm, war memorials, gardens, and reservoirs.

Singapore's number one tourist attraction is to have **breakfast or high tea with the Orangutan**—a unique experience guaranteed to be the highlight of many children's (and adult's) visit to Singapore and a photographer's delight!

Another major attraction, and one of our favorites, is the **Night Safari** at the Singapore Zoological Gardens (80 Mandai Lake Road, Tel. 2693411, a 30-minute drive from the City). Operating between 7:30pm and midnight, this tour of the zoo at night is well worth the S$15 admission (S$10 for children 3-12 years). Houses more than 1,200 animals of over 110 exotic species in a natural setting. Great evening activity for both adults and children.

Many tour companies offer relatively inexpensive, convenient, and comfortable half-day to three-day **tours** of Singapore and parts of nearby Malaysia. One of the first tours you may want to join is the "City Tour." This 3-4 hour tour will give you an excellent overview of all the major parts of Singapore. Most tour companies include Orchard Road, Chinatown, Little India, Arab Street, Raffles Place, Shenton Way, Mt. Faber, Botanic Gardens, Raffles Hotel, and several historical sites on their City Tour. Other tours take you to the zoo, harbor, selected night spots, Sentosa Island, and around all of the island. The tour companies also regularly schedule one to two-day trips to the historical city of Malacca on Malaysia's East Coast, Kuala Lumpur, plantations in Malaysia, Desaru (Malaysia's beach playground in the southeast), and Kukup (plantations and unique fishing village in southwestern Malaysia). Other tours can be arranged to the many tourist destinations in Malaysia.

ENTERTAINMENT

Singapore's entertaining **nightlife** includes discos, music clubs, pubs and beer gardens, bars, cocktail lounges, Chinese opera, cultural shows, music, dance, drama, theater, and street stalls. The dress code is usually smart casual and many places have cover charges (from S$15 to S$25) However, after a full day of intense shopping, sightseeing, and dining you may just want to go to bed!

DANCE CLUBS

❑ **Venom:** *Pacific Plaza Penthouse, 12th Floor, 9 Scotts Road, Tel. 734-7677.* Considered Singapore's top dance club. Includes a sushi bar. Cover charge from S$18 to S$25. Wednesday is ladies night where men only pay a S$1 cover charge.

❑ **Zouk:** *17-21 Jiak Kim Street, Tel. 738-2988. Open Wednesday-Saturday 8pm-3am; Happy Hour from 8pm-midnight.* A hip club-bar with great music and celebrity DJs. The unofficial dress code is black, tight, and slinky. Cover charge from S$15 to S$25.

BARS

❑ **Long Bar:** *Raffles Hotel, 1-3 Beach Road.* Long a Singapore institution, this famous bar is now a popular stop for tourists and locals who order the legendary Singapore Sling and listen to live music in the evening. A cozy bar with lots of memorabilia and peanuts!

❑ **Papa Joe's:** *180 Orchard Road, Tel. 732-7012. Open daily, 5pm-3am.* Reputed to offer the best happy hour in town. Also known as the best pick-up place.

❑ **Somerset's:** *The Westin Plaza, 2 Stamford Road, Tel. 338-8585. Open daily 5pm-2am.* Boasts Singapore's longest bar. Includes an excellent jazz band, the Redd Hott Unlimited.

❑ **Hard Rock Cafe:** *#02-01 HPL House, 50 Cuscaden Road, Tel. 235-5232. Open Sunday-Thursday 11am-2am and Friday-Saturday 11am-3am.* Offers the best live music in town by the band Jive Talkin' (after 10:30pm).

WINE BARS

❑ **Les Amis Wine Bar:** *#02-16 Shaw Centre, 1 Scotts Centre, 1 Scotts Road, Tel. 733-2225. Open Monday-Saturday 5pm-1am.* Part of one of the city's best French restaurants that offers over 12,000 bottles of wine priced from S$90 to S$4,000. Popular with businesspeople for power lunches (noon-2pm) and dinners (7:15pm-10pm).

❑ **Beaujolais Wine Bar:** *1 Ann Siang Hill, 224-2227. Open Monday-Thursday 11am-midnight, Friday 11am-2am, and Saturday 6pm-2am.* Located in the Tanjong Pagar area of Chinatown, this charming and romantic bar is popular with local businesspeople.

❑ **Que Pasa:** *7 Emerald Hill Road, Tel. 235-6626. Open daily from 6pm-2am.* This is Singapore's oldest wine bar housed in a swanky shophouse. Also serves tapas.

CABARETS

❑ **The Boom Boom Room:** *#02-04 Bugis Village, 3 Bugis Street, Tel. 339-8187. Open Tuesday-Thursday from 8:30pm-2am and Friday-Saturday from 8:30pm-3am.* Offers stand-up comedy and a humorous cabaret show on life in Singapore.

❑ **Dancers' The Club:** *#03-01 Clarke Quay, 3A River Valley Road, Tel. 335-5535. Open Sunday-Thursday from 6pm-3am and Friday-Saturday from 8pm-3am.* Features scantily clad male and female dancers performing at 10pm, midnight, and 2am.

1 0 1 THINGS TO DO IN SINGAPORE

Les Clefs d'Or Singapore (the International Association of Concierges in Singapore) has identified 101 things visitors can do in Singapore to enjoy their stay. If you run out of things to do in Singapore, use this as your "to do" checklist for fun and entertainment:

1. Dine at a hawker centre, such as Lau Pa Sat.

2. Drink a cool mug of Tiger beer.

3. Have breakfast with the birds at Tiong Bahru.

4. Take a scenic cable car ride from Mount Faber to Sentosa Island.

5. Feast on the local delicacy, chilli crabs.

6. Catch a movie at a cineplex along Orchard Road.

7. Take in a Chinese opera while dining at the Chinese Opera Teahouse (Tel. 323-4862).

8. Try the unique and challenging fruit, the durian.

9. Take a walking tour of Singapore's ethnic enclaves— Chinatown, Little India, and Kampong Glam.

10. Visit the quaint and historic Peranakan Place.

11. Take a bumboat down the Singapore River.

12. Get a foot massage by a qualified reflexologist.

13. Visit the wet markets in Chinatown.

14. Shop till you drop!

15. Buy a kite and fly it at Marina South park.

16. Savour fiery fish head curry at Apollo Banana Leaf restaurant in Little India and chase it with lime juice.

17. Take the MRT to the suburbs to shop for bargains.

18. Sign up for cooking classes at the Raffles Culinary Academy.

19. Take a bumboat ride from Changi Point and explore rustic Pulau Ubin on a rented bike.

20. Take a ferry to the neighboring Indonesian islands of Bintan or Batam.

21. Visit the Long Bar at the Raffles Hotel for the famous Singapore Sling.

22. Try Hainanese Chicken Rice at the Chatterbox in the Mandarin Hotel.

23. Pack a picnic basket and enjoy an outdoor performance at the Botanic Gardens.

24. Take in a local disco.

25. Shop at Mustafa Centre for affordable electronics.

26. Visit "Little Guilin" in the residential suburbs of Bukit Batok. This sand quarry resembles the breathtaking Guilin mountains in China.

27. See the world's largest fountain at Suntec City.

28. Enjoy the sea breeze while dining on black pepper crab or barbecued sting ray at one of the famous seafood restaurants at the East Coast Seafood Centre.

29. Cut your own orchids at Orchidville, Mandai Agrotech Park and have them packed and shipped home (Tel. 552-7003).

30. Wake up early for Tai Chi lessons at the Botanic Gardens (daily from 7-8am).

31. Take a harbor cruise on a Chinese junk and observe the river activity.

32. Between September and March, observe the visiting birds from Siberia at Sungei Bulah Nature Park.

33. Explore the streets of Singapore by trishaw.

34. Pamper yourself at one of Singapore's health spas.

35. Dive with the sharks at the Underwater World (Tel. 275-0030).

36. Go sky diving with other enthusiasts (call Skydive Adventure Ptd. Ltd., Tel. 9731-8873).

37. Go water-skiing at the Kallang Basin.

38. Visit an Indian fortune teller and his "psychic" parrot in Little India.

39. Ask your taxi-driver to take you to a 24-hour coffee shop for a late night supper of *roti prata*.

40. Look for the local ice-cream man along Orchard Road with his cart full of durian, red bean, and corn flavored ice cream.

41. Go treasure hunting for interesting finds at the weekend flee markets at Clarke Quay, Tanglin Mall, or Club Street.

42. Go jogging in the early morning or evening at the MacRitchie Reservoir.

43. Try some colorful *nonya kueh* at the popular confectionery, Bengawan Solo.

44. Visit the local coffee shop (*kopitiam*) at No. 67, Killiney Road for a popular local breakfast of *kaya* (coconut and egg jam) on buttered toast and a cup of *kopi* or traditionally-brewed black coffee with condensed milk.

45. Enjoy freshly ground western-style coffee in one of the many alfresco cafes along Orchard Road, such as Starbucks, Burke's, or Coffee Bean and Tea Leaf.

46. Brace yourself for a tequila shot at the dentist chair at The Jump at Chijmes.

47. Equip yourself with rock climbing gear and scale the sand quarry at the Bukit Timah Nature Reserve.

48. Go on the gourmet safari for a unique itinerant dining experience during the annual Singapore Food Festival.

49. Take a carousel ride at Clarke Quay in the evening.

50. Immerse yourself in the art of tea appreciation at the Tea Chapter in Chinatown.

51. Karaoke the night away at a local pub.

52. Be adventuresome and try some pungent "century eggs" when you have a dim sum meal at a Chinese restaurant.

53. Wander around Holland Village for some souvenir shopping.

54. Try fusion New Asia cuisine at Doc Cheng's at the Raffles Hotel.

55. Shop for rattan products and exotic fabrics at Arab Street.

56. Watch spices being ground in a little shophouse on Cuff Street in Little India.

57. Have your hands ornately painted with henna in Little India.

58. Try night golfing at the Jurong Country Club or Orchid Country Club.

59. Visit the Concourse along Beach Road and get party items and other knick knacks at wholesale prices.

60. Try local grilled kebabs or *satay* that is served with a spicy rich peanut gravy.

61. Attend a classical music concert by the Singapore Symphony Orchestra. Check the local newspapers for details on concert programs.

62. Dare your friends to walk among the wild animals in the still of the night. Welcome to the Night Safari, the first of its kind in the world.

63. Visit the temples at Waterloo Street where Hindu and Buddhist worshipers converge for religious reflection.

64. Toss *yu sheng* (raw fish salad) during Chinese New Year.

65. Take one of the New Asia-Singapore tours. For instance, go on the Painted Faces tour and learn all about the art of Chinese opera.

66. Roller blade at East Coast Park, Pasir Ris Park, or Bishan Park.

67. Spend the afternoon having high tea at the Tiffin Room, Raffles Hotel.

68. Discover the length and breadth of Singapore on an MRT ride.

69. Have breakfast with an Orangutan at the Singapore Zoological Gardens.

70. Try local desserts like *ice-kachang*, cold *cheng tng* and *bubor cha cha*. Perfect for that hot, tropical day!

71. Enjoy a day at the races at the Singapore Turf Club.

72. Rent a canoe and canoe from the People's Association Seasports Centre at Kallang Basin to the East Coast Park.

73. Grab a drink a Charlie's, Changi Village where the dress code is shorts, t-shirts, and flip flops. Your food is ready to be picked up when a beam of light is shone on your table!

74. Enjoy Indian snacks fast food style at Komala's in Little India.

75. Be reinvigorated after a balanced *yin-yang* meal at the Imperial Herbal Restaurant.

76. Have a romantic dinner at the Compass Rose restaurant at the Westin Stamford Hotel.

77. Go fishing at Pasir Ris, Bishan, Changi, Punggol, or East Coast Park.

78. Try the thinly sliced barbecued pork sold at the popular stall, Bee Chun Heng in Chinatown.

79. Look out for the Thaipusam procession in January/February where Hindu devotees walk with enormous *kavadis* pierced to their bodies by spikes and skewers. The procession usually starts from Sri Srinivasa Perumal Temple in Serangoon Road to the Sri Thandayuthapani Temple in Tank Road.

80. Visit the Changi Prison Museum and Chapel for a poignant reminder of Singapore's war history.

81. Try your luck at Toto (local lottery) and go home a millionaire.

82. Watch barefoot Hindu devotees walk across a pit of red hot embers in a show of unflinching faith, at the Sri Mariamman Temple during the Thimithi Festival in October.

83. Go ice skating at Kallang Leisure Park and Fuji Ice Palace at Jurong East.

84. For sun lovers, go windsurfing at Europa East Coast Sailing Centre.

85. Enjoy a charming Rijsttafel dinner on top of a hill at the Alkaff Mansion.

86. Try out the range of exotic soups you can find in Singapore, from Indian mutton soup to Chinese snake blood soup.

87. Buy a day pass from Kart World Pte Ltd and enjoy go-karting in Jurong.

88. Whoever said anything derogatory about "bird brains"! See them at work and play at the world renowned Jurong Bird Park.

89. Order a freshly-cut coconut from one of the fresh fruit stalls in a hawker center. Ask for a spoon to scoop up the sweet, succulent coconut "flesh".

90. Enjoy a 3-D cinematic experience at the Singapore Science Centre's Omnimax Theatre.

91. Enjoy the brilliant lights during Christmas, Chinese New Year, Hari Raya, and Deepavali.

92. Be at one with nature and trek through a tropical rainforest at the Bukit Timah Nature Reserve. Singapore is one of only two cities in the world that has a rainforest within its boundaries, the other being Rio de Janeiro.

93. Check out the Boom Boom Room in Bugis Village for a dose of local saucy humor.

94. Visit the Kong Meng San Phor Kark See Temple, the largest Buddhist temple in Singapore. Local worshipers flock here for the annual Vesak Day procession.

95. Order mock chicken at a Chinese vegetarian restaurant and you will discover that dressing up protein gluten to look like meat is indeed an art itself.

96. Have a *teh tarek*! Ask for a $1 sampler meal at Tiffin Bhavan at the Little India Arcade in Serangoon Road. Your frothy tea comes complete with a dish of two Indian snacks.

97. Check out the latest computer gizmos, gadgets and games at Sim Lim Square. Be sure to compare prices before you buy!

98. For guys, have an affordable and quick haircut at an old barber stand along the back street of Chinatown.

99. Relax at one of the al fresco pubs and restaurants along Boat Quay or Clarke Quay during happy hours.

100. Rub the tummy of the Happy Buddha at Haw Par Villa Tiger Balm Gardens for good luck!

101. Go on a walking tour of museums, historical parks, and other cultural sites in the very heart of the city. Pick up a copy of the "Discovering the Arts" brochure from the Tourist Information Centre at Raffles Arcade.

Singapore offers wonderful shopping opportunities, but it is also a place to relax, pamper yourself, gain a few pounds, and enjoy a bit of Southeast Asian society and culture. A truly international city, Singapore puts you in touch with the rest of the world without having to go through the pain of exploring so many different countries. In Singapore, shopping is one big smorgasbord of high-tech and no-tech opportunities. Spend four days here, and you will not be disappointed. Spend a week in Singapore, and you will be ready to move on to even more exotic shopping places, where you will undoubtedly reminisce fondly about Singapore's shopping convenience and comfort—its cleanliness and orderliness!

PART IV

Exotic Bali

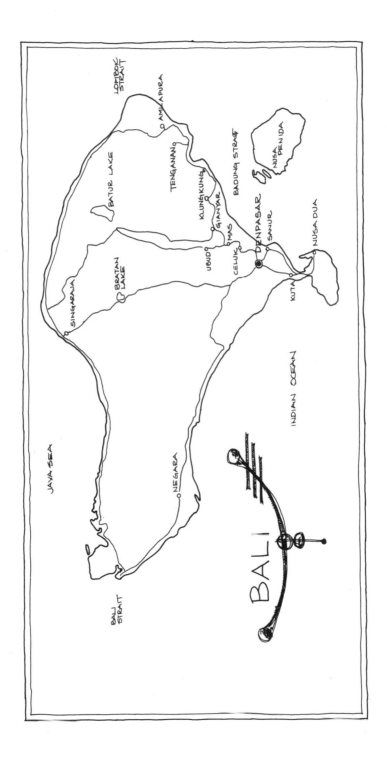

5

Bali

WELCOME TO ONE OF THE WORLD'S MOST unique traveling and shopping experiences. Part of Indonesia, but very different from the rest of Indonesia, Bali is unlike any other place in the world you will ever visit. It's one of the most powerful and seductive travel destinations, a place where many people never want to leave or where they acquire a passion to return again and again to savor Bali's many treasures and pleasures. Unwittingly falling in love with the place, you'll wish you had planned more time in Bali and better prepared for its shopping treasures.

Bali definitely contrasts sharply with high-rise, sanitized, and urbanized Singapore. Compared to modern Singapore, Bali has its own unique character, culture, and class. For many visitors, Bali simply is the closest they will ever get to paradise. Its stunning architecture, landscapes, beaches, ceremonies, people, and crafts immerse you in an exotic world of people, places, and products. Experience alluring and captivating Bali and your travel and shopping may never be the same!

Everything about this place is exotic, from sights to smells to sounds. Bali's highly religious and communal society differs greatly from all other Indonesian societies as well as the rest of Asia. While most Indonesians are Moslems, the Balinese continue to practice their centuries-old Hindu and animistic customs and rituals in the midst of a rapidly developing tourist industry. The lush volcanic island is beautiful and alluring; its nearly 3 million people are delightful; the performing arts are colorful; shopping is centered around workshops, studios, homes, villages, shops, stalls, and hotel shopping arcades; and everything about this place is exotic. In addition to leaving Bali with many purchases, you will have some exciting memories of this very different Southeast Asian, Indonesian, and island experience.

THE BASICS

LOCATION AND PEOPLE

Located off the eastern coast of Java, Bali is a small volcanic island of only 5,561 square kilometers with a population of nearly 3 million. Approximately the size of Rhode Island in the U.S., Bali has a very large presence in the tourism industry because of its rich culture, beautiful landscapes, and expanding tourist infrastructure of fine hotels, restaurants, shops, and inbound travel services.

CLIMATE, SEASONS, WHEN TO GO, PACKING

Being a tropical island, Bali's climate is very similar to that of Singapore's. Its equatorial climate is generally hot and humid year-round. Temperatures range from 78°F to 95°F and humidity averages 75%. Daily temperatures do reach the high 90°s, and the humidity is often in the 90°s. Seasonal variations are slight, normally more or less hot and humid. Nonetheless, at certain times of the year the climate is more pleasant than others.

❑ The best time to visit Bali is during the May to August dry season.

❑ Being a resort island, you can dress casually in Bali; formal attire is seldom required.

❑ A visa is good for 30 days and can be extended for 15 additional days.

❑ Bali is a relatively tranquil and safe haven from the many political, economic, and religious ills besetting the rest of Indonesia.

Bali and much of Indonesia basically have two seasons—wet and dry. The wet season occurs between October and April, with monsoonal January and February being the wettest months. The dry season occurs between May and September. Temperatures are hot, but the humidity is less than during the wet season.

The best time to visit Bali is during the May to August dry season. Temperatures are relatively pleasant, usually in the 80s, and the humidity is less oppressive than during other times of the year. July is an especially good time to visit Bali in terms of weather but this also is Bali's high season for tourists.

Given Bali's hot and humid climate, you need only pack lightweight clothes for your trip. Stay with thin cottons. If you plan to venture into upper inland areas, be sure to take some extra clothes, such as a sweater or jacket, for the cool evenings.

Being a resort island, you can dress casually in Bali; formal attire is seldom required. For men, shirts and trousers are perfectly acceptable for most occasions. For women, dresses, blouses, and skirts and slacks are adequate. In fact, you may wish to pack fewer clothes for Bali since you can purchase plenty of attractive and inexpensive clothes in the Kuta and Ubud areas.

It's also wise to take sunglasses, sun screen, and a hat for handling Bali's bright equatorial light and intense sunshine. Beware of sunbathing for more than an hour at a time in Bali; indeed, it's very easy to get sunburned in Bali without really knowing it, especially on an overcast day. Your photos will turn out better if you take a light filter for your camera.

GETTING THERE

It's relatively easy to get to Bali, although there are fewer flights going into Bali these days than three years ago due to the general economic situation in Indonesia. Direct international flights to Bali originate in Europe, Australia, and Singapore. Airlines servicing Bali include Qantas, Ansett, Lufthansa, KLM, Singapore Airlines, Garuda, Cathy Pacific, Malaysia Airlines, Korean Air, JAL, China Airlines, UTA, Air New Zealand, Thai International Airways, and Royal Brunei. Daily connections between Bali and Jakarta and Jogjakarta are frequent. On our most recent flights to and from Bali, after flying Northwest Airlines from the U.S. to Singapore, we took Singapore Airlines from Singapore to Bali and Ansett from Bali to Darwin, Australia. Both airlines do a superb job in handling these relatively short routes. The flight from Singapore to Bali takes just over 2 hours. The flight from Bali to Darwin took nearly 4 hours.

DOCUMENTS

Entry into and exit from Indonesia and hence Bali is relatively easy in terms of documentation as long as you plan a normal trip. A normal trip is to enter and exit from one of the gateway airports: Jakarta, Denpasar (Bali), Pontianak, Medan, Biak, Pekanbaru, Padang, and Balikpapan. You are not required to have a visa if you enter at these points, and if you are a citizen of the United States, Canada, or most European and Asian countries. You only need a passport valid for at least six months beyond the date you enter Indonesia. Upon arrival you will be issued a tourist pass valid for a two-month stay.

If you are uncertain about your entry or exit points, or wish to attempt an entry or exit from Irian Jaya, play it safe by getting a visa before arriving in Indonesia. You cannot enter or exit Indonesia at other than the eight gateway cities without one of these visas. A visa is good for 30 days and can be extended for 15 additional days.

Health documents are not required except in certain situations. If you arrive within six days from an area infected with smallpox, yellow fever, or cholera, you must produce international certificates showing that you have received the appropriate vaccinations. Also, be aware that some areas in Indonesia do have occasional outbreaks of these infectious diseases. If you visit these areas, you may have to be inoculated before visiting other countries.

ARRIVAL

Bali has both international and domestic airports which are adjacent to one another. Assuming you are arriving at the Ngurah Rai International Airport, go to the tourist information booth for literature on Bali or assistance with accommodations. During the high season (May-August), you should have hotel reservations since Bali tends to be fully booked at this time of the year. Many hotels run mini-vans between the airport and the hotel. If your hotel does not provide this service, take a taxi from the airport to your hotel. Go directly to the taxi counter where you will pay a fixed amount for a taxi. Next, take your receipt to a driver who will take care of you and your bags. The domestic airport has similar services.

CUSTOMS

Indonesian Customs regulations are similar to Custom regulations in other Asian countries. You are permitted to enter with no more than two liters of alcohol, 200 cigarettes or 50 cigars or 100 grams of tobacco, and a reasonable amount of perfume. You are prohibited from bringing into Indonesia arms and ammunition, TV sets, tape/radio cassette recorders, pornographic objects and publications, printed matter in Chinese characters, and Chinese medicine. You need prior approval to carry transceivers. And you need to have any developed movie film or video cassettes censored by the Film Censor Board. You go directly to jail for drugs.

Indonesian Customs normally go through the motions of checking your baggage. Unless you are Chinese, chances are your baggage check will be pro forma. If you normally travel with a small radio and CD or cassette player as part of your travel gear, chances are it will go through Customs with no difficulty. In fact, you are permitted to bring in photographic equipment, laptop computers, and radios as long as you take them out with you.

AIRPORT TAX

In Indonesia, each airport levies an airport tax on departing passengers, even on domestic flights. The airport tax on international flights in Bali is Rp. 50,000 or US$6.80. The airport taxes on domestic flights in Bali is Rp. 11,000 or US$1.50. These taxes are payable after check-in but before passing through immigration and security.

CURRENCY AND CREDIT CARDS

Money can become a real problem or nuisance in Bali. The value of Indonesian currency has fluctuated greatly during the past two years due to the collapse of the Indonesian economy and its currency. Consequently, the value of this currency may change significantly from the time we go to press to when you visit Indonesia. For now, Indonesia remains one of the best tourist buys because of the favorable exchange rate with the U.S. dollar.

You will feel rich in Indonesia since you will be carrying literally thousands of the local currency. The Indonesian currency is called the rupiah (Rp.). The banknotes come in denominations of 50,000, 20,000, 10,000, 5,000, 1,000, 500, and 100. Coins are issued in denominations of 100, 50, 25, 10, and 5. Since at present 7,365 rupiah (Rp. 7,365) equals US$1, you must carry a great deal of Indonesian cash when shopping. Indeed, the largest bill is only equivalent to US$6.79!

The best places to exchange your money are at banks and with money-changers; both give similar rates. The airport branch banks give the same rates as the banks elsewhere in Bali. In Kuta and Ubud you should have no problem exchanging money. But outside major tourist areas you may have problems cashing traveler's checks or using credit cards. In addition to carrying a pile of Indonesian rupiah, you should carry U.S. dollars into these areas. The $10, $20, and $50 banknotes are good choices. Everyone seems to recognize the U.S. dollar and will honor it similarly to the local currency. Be sure to count your rupiah when dealing with money-changers. We've had experiences, which we caught, where we were shorted by 20 percent. Other travelers report similar experiences—money changers purposefully miscounting transactions. Be especially on guard when given many small denomination bills, such as 1,000, 5,000, and 10,000 rupiah notes. There's a high probability not everything will add up properly! Also, money changers may try to pawn off many worn, torn, and filthy banknotes. Refuse to accept them since they are a nuisance.

Credit cards are widely accepted in major hotels, restaurants, and shops. However, outside the major shopping and resort areas, you will have difficulty using your plastic money. In addition to the local currency, expect to use traveler's checks and U.S. dollars to get you through Bali. A money belt may be a wise investment, but you may find it uncomfortable to wear in Bali's heat and humidity. As elsewhere in the world, bargained prices in Bali are generally "cash only" prices—not credit card prices.

Getting change is a constant problem in Bali. In some shops, you may be given gum or some cheap item in lieu of Rp. 100 or Rp. 500 change (equivalent to 1¢ to 6¢). Indeed, on one memorable hot day in Kuta, after stopping several times to purchase cool drinks at convenience stores, we accumulated so much gum as small change that we actually began paying parts of our next bills with gum! Be sure to stock up on small change, especially Rp. 100 coins and Rp. 1,000, 2,000, 5,000, and 10,000 banknotes. This small change comes in handy for telephones and tips for taxi drivers, porters, bellhops, and waiters. Few people will have change for your Rp. 10,000 and 20,000 banknotes and hardly anyone will change a Rp. 50,000 banknote. Yes, this means weighing yourself down with a great deal of dirty cash!

SECURITY

Indonesia's airport security system is very tolerable to lax. Security personnel X-ray and hand check luggage with relative ease and not much attention to detail.

Until recently, Indonesia has been a relatively safe country for travel. However, with the collapse of the Suharto military regime in 1998 and subsequent student and separatist protests, riots, and killings in many parts of Indonesia, the country is now on the U.S. Department of State warning list, and for good reasons: *http://travel.state.gov/travel_warinings.html*. While you should avoid those parts of Indonesia that are obvious political trouble spots, don't mistakenly think that Bali is in the same security category as the rest of Indonesia. Bali is very different. Above all, it remains a relatively tranquil and safe haven from the many political, economic, and religious ills besetting the rest of Indonesia. If you have questions about the security situation in Bali, we recommend posting a question on this very active and informative Bali discussion forum:

www.balitravelforum.com

Chances are you should get immediate feedback from expats and recent travelers about the current situation for safety and security in Bali—plus a great deal of other useful information on Bali. You'll find this forum to be more useful and reliable than U.S. Department of State's travel warnings which are often overly broad and alarmist.

This does not mean you can let your guard down in Bali. Like many other places in the world, and compounded by Indonesia's poverty and recent economic ills, Bali has its share of pickpockets, thieves, crooks, and other unsavory characters to upset your otherwise wonderful holiday in Bali. Remember, Bali is part of a poor country where all foreigners appear rich; thus you may become a target for petty thievery. Take the normal precautions you would elsewhere—keep valuables out of sight; watch where you carry your purse or wallet; hold on to your valuables in restaurants and bars (the lights sometimes go out and valuables disappear during the so-called power failure!); and don't wander off the beaten path at night. The main safety warning in Bali remains the traffic—watch where you walk, look both ways when you cross a street or road, and don't try to drive on your own.

TIPPING

Tipping is gradually becoming an acceptable practice in Bali and other parts of Indonesia. Most major hotels and restaurants add a 10 percent service charge to your bill. Where no service is added, a 5 to 10 percent tip would be adequate. Drivers like to receive tips. Leave them some loose change of no more than Rp. 2,000. Hotel and airport porters expect to receive Rp. 1,000-1,500 per bag. In many cases airport porters will also take care of your baggage and ticket and thus save you the hassle of having to push and shove your way through the masses that converge at counters. This additional service should be rewarded with Rp. 3,000 to 4,000.

Be sure to carry plenty of small change for tips. The Rp. 1,000 and 2,000 banknotes often come in handy as small tips. Rp.100 and 500 tips are inappropriate for most situations—amount to an insulting US$.014 and US$.068 respectively.

Language and Communication

While the national language is Bahasa Indonesia, not everyone speaks this language within Indonesia where over 300 languages are spoken. Most Balinese can speak both Balinese (at home and with friends) and Indonesian (in public). Many also speak some English. Most people you encounter in Bali, especially in shops, understand and speak some English. Their grammar and pronunciation may at times be difficult to understand, but you will be able to communicate in most situations.

❏ If you only learn one word in Bahasa Indonesia, make sure it's *jalan jalan*. It will come in handy when approached by strangers and/or touts.

❏ Expect to frequently encounter communication problems that may test your patience and tolerance.

❏ As you will quickly discover, customer service is not a Balinese virtue.

❏ We hesitate to recommend shippers given our recent problems in shipping from Bali. Take what you can with you.

If you only learn one word in Bahasa Indonesia (after "thank you" or *terima kasi*), make sure it's *jalan* which means "street". When you repeat the word by saying *jalan jalan*, it means "just walking". It's our favorite response to touts and other strangers who approach us with the idea of getting our business. When they ask us *"Where are you going?"*—which usually means do you need transportation or do you want them to take you shopping—we usually reply *jalan jalan*.

In most cases they understand we want to be left alone (we're having a "private moment") and usually they smile and go away. You'll find *jalan jalan* comes in very handy in Kuta and Ubud where many touts tend to congregate and pester tourists about transportation and shopping.

While English is widely spoken and understood in the major hotels, resorts, restaurants, and shopping areas, you may have difficulty communicating with drivers. In many cases you may think you have a language problem, because the driver takes you to the wrong place, you get bad directions, or you receive the wrong restaurant order. This may not be the case. Indeed, it's a constant problem amongst Indonesians rather than just between tourists and the locals.

There is a general communication problem in Indonesia which is related more to education and culture than to language. When asked for information, many drivers and waiters, for example, are simply confused, lack information, or are uneducated to begin with, regardless of whether you speak the local language or not. They may be polite in giving what may appear to be knowledgeable information, but more often than not, they will give you incorrect information! Expect to get lost several times in Bali, because of incorrect information you receive from well-meaning people.

Expect to frequently encounter communication problems that may test your patience and tolerance. While frustrating, most are minor problems and somewhat amusing. The problem is that most people are very polite and accommodating, but they often lack accurate information. Rather than tell you "I don't know" in response to your questions and thus disappoint you, they proceed to give you an answer which is inaccurate. When they say "yes," they sometimes mean "no." Consequently, you frequently get wrong directions, and communication can become very frustrating at times. Keep in mind that this is not a problem just for foreigners. Indonesians in general have problems communicating with each other. They may say "yes" when they mean "no," and they give and get confusing directions and instructions. You must be tolerant to survive this seemingly irrational element in Indonesia. Better still, get answers to your questions from three different sources before venturing off in any direction.

BUSINESS HOURS AND TIME

Most shops are more or less open from 8am to 9pm. Many close on Sunday, or are open only part of the day, since Sunday is a public holiday.

Banking hours are usually from 8am to 2pm, Monday through Friday, and from 8am to 11am on Saturday. Some banks remain open until 3pm. However, banks in hotels and money-changers have longer hours. Post offices have similar hours as banks.

Government offices are open 8am to 3pm Monday through Thursday, from 8am to 11:30am on Friday, and from 8am to 2pm or 3pm on Saturday.

But be prepared for the ubiquitous *jam burapa*, or "rubber time," as well as "day-lighting." Indonesia does not operate according to a Western clock, and punctuality is not a national virtue. Shops which are supposed to be open are sometimes closed with no explanation. Sometimes they explain the closure

by telling a neighboring shop that they are attending a ceremony or they had to visit Java or Lombok. Consequently, you
may have to visit some shops several times to find them open.
This is particularly irritating, especially if you traveled a long
distance to get to a shop. And even if a shop or office is open,
you may enter to find no one around to help you. If you wait
awhile, someone eventually will show up to announce whether
or not they are doing business. As you will quickly discover,
customer service is not a Balinese virtue. At other times you
may visit an office or shop to see a particular person; or a bank
or government office may require you to wait for the signature
of their boss. If the person is not in, you may be told he or she
will be back in a few minutes or "soon." The person may be out
on personal business or "day-lighting"—working a second job
on official time. If so, you will probably have to wait, wait, and
wait. The longer you wait, the more irritated you may get.
Unfortunately, there is little you can do other than wait, wait,
and wait. Take a good book with you so you are adequately
equipped to kill time. Welcome to the land of *jam barapa* and
"day-lighting."

TOURS AND TRAVEL AGENTS

Before you depart for Indonesia, you may want to contact
several travel agencies that specialize on travel to Indonesia.
Most of these agencies offer a complete group tour package.
Some of them can arrange individualized tours or connect you
with specialized local tours. Contact a few of these companies
and ask for their brochures on Indonesia: **Bolder Adventures**
(800-642-2742), **Innovasian Travel** (800-553-4665), **Natrabu**
(800-628-7228), **The Pacific Explorers** (800-972-6632),
Passport to Indonesia (800-303-9646), **Select Tours International** (800-356-6680), **Sita World Travel** (800-421-5643),
Vayatour (800-999-8292), and **Zegrahm Expeditions** (800-
628-8747). Your local travel agent should have information on
tours to Indonesia sponsored by many of the large international
tour groups, such as **Abercrombie and Kent**, **American
Express**, **Globus**, and **Travcoa**.

If you arrive in Bali on your own, you may want to use the
services of a travel agency for seeing the island. Most travel
agencies can provide a car and driver on an hourly, daily, or
weekly basis. Unless you prefer setting your schedule in
advance or are arriving during peak season, you can usually
arrange your tours and travel needs once you arrive in Bali. Just
contact your hotel for information, and you will be directed to
a travel agent that offers a variety of tour options, from

regularly scheduled group tours to custom-designed tours to meet your particular needs. These firms have English-speaking guides and drivers. Firms such as **Panorama Tours Bali** (Jl. By Pass Ngurah Rai No. 76, Sanur, Tel. 281511 or Fax 281515) and **Bali Griyasari** (Tel. 461910 or 461131) provide half-day and one and two-day sightseeing tours; **Sobek Bali Utama** (Jl. Tirta Ening No. 9, Bypass Ngurah Rai, Sanur, Tel. 287059 or Fax 289448) provide adventure (rafting, kayaking, trekking, cycling) tours of Bali. Alternatively, you can find several travel agencies along the street in Kuta that provide a variety of tour and driving options. We've used, for example, **Top Holiday Tour & Travel** (Jl. Legian Kaya No. 465 Kuta, Tel. 763087 or Fax 761312) for hiring a car and driver by the day. We hesitate to recommend many companies due to the recent Indonesian economic collapse that has created several upheavals in tourism. If you make local arrangements before arriving in Bali, do not prepay for such services. Many companies continue to experience serious economic problems that question the wisdom of prepaying for services. Also, most tour companies are willing to negotiate their asking prices. For example, if a company says a car and driver will cost US$80 a day, offer them US$40. Chances are they be willing to lower their prices, especially if you arrive during the off season. During the high season, cars and drivers may be at a premium.

TRANSPORTATION

Transportation in Bali is convenient. You can rent bicycles, motorbikes, and self-drive cars, or hire a car with driver. While driving yourself is relatively easy, it may not be safe given the continuing traffic congestion, especially in the southeastern section of the island; even expats living in Bali do not recommend driving on your own! If you drive and get into an accident, you most likely will end up in jail and your departure will be delayed. A car with driver is most convenient and relatively inexpensive. You can arrange your transportation at the airport or your hotel or visit the many rental offices dotting the main roads near the major tourist areas. The Blue taxis, which are metered and air-conditioned, also are an inexpensive way to get around the island (US$10-15 for half a day!).

FOOD, DRINK, AND RESTAURANTS

Indonesia is another one of our favorite destinations for food. The Indonesian cuisine is somewhat similar to Malay and Thai cuisine, although regional varieties are quite diverse. Indonesian food tends to be very spicy. Peanuts, coconut milk, curries, and coriander are used generously in much of Indonesian cooking.

Some favorite **Indonesian dishes** for Western travelers are *satay* (grilled skewered beef, chicken, or lamb dipped in a spicy peanut sauce), *gado gado* (a special Indonesia salad with a peanut dressing), *rendang* (curried beef with coriander in coconut milk), *ayam goreng* (fried chicken), and *nasi goreng* (fried rice). The *rijsttafel*, or Dutch "rice table," is a mini-buffet consisting of various Indonesian foods served at your table. Padang food, from western Sumatra, is also popular, especially the mini-buffet served with numerous small dishes. The Indonesia *satay* is served by numerous vendors along the streets. When in doubt what to order, you seldom can go wrong by ordering *nasi goreng* and *satay*.

You'll find several Chinese and western restaurants in Bali. Most major hotels serve buffets which combine western, Chinese, and Indonesia foods.

Indonesia offers a great variety of tempting **fruits**, similar to those found in Thailand and Malaysia. Our favorites include *pisang* (bananas), *nanas* (pineapple), *mangga* (mango), *manggis* (mangosteen), *nangka* (jackfruit), and oranges.

Indonesia also offers a wide variety of **drinks**. Tap water is not safe to drink, but you can buy bottled water in small plastic containers. These are convenient to carry and are found in most small convenience stores. You also will find a large variety of soft drinks, such as Coca Cola, 7-Up, Sprite, and Fanta, in bottles and cans. Local beers—Bintang and Anker—are very good, although they are expensive and often served warm or diluted with ice. Beer production has definitely been influenced by the Dutch. Fruit juices are a real treat in Indonesia. You can buy several varieties of fruit juices in small paper cartons or cans which can be conveniently carried. The Indonesian guava and orange juices are very good.

You must acquire a taste for Indonesian coffee and tea. The coffee is served sweet and the granules are included in your cup or glass—most often floating on top! Many westerners prefer not drinking everything in the cup or glass. If you let the granules settle and leave the final 1/4 inch behind, the coffee is not bad. Most major hotels and restaurants also serve western varieties of coffee—both brewed and instant. You might want to pack your own instant coffee, additives, cup, and heating element to make your own coffee first thing in the morning.

Indonesian tea is very different from teas elsewhere. Many visitors love it whereas others find it too unique. Much of the tea is served strong and very sweet.

As in most other Third World countries, you need to be careful about where you eat and avoid consuming the local ice which may or may not be made with bottled water. You will find small restaurants and food stalls everywhere you go in Bali. Much of the food is safe, especially the *satay* and *nasi goreng* which are made before your eyes. But be careful about many of the other dishes which may sit out in the open all day absorbing the heat, dust, and flies. Be wary of dishes made with eggs or milk products, especially if they appear not to have been refrigerated for long periods of time. Most restaurants in major hotels as well as those recommended in this chapter (pages 234-236) should be fine—if you're careful.

ACCOMMODATIONS

Bali offers a wide variety of alternative accommodations from expensive deluxe hotels and resorts to inexpensive bungalows, *wisman* and *losmen* (Indonesia's version of bed and breakfast accommodations). Such hotels as the Four Seasons, Ritz-Carlton, Amandari, Grand Hyatt, and Bali Hyatt are outstanding in terms of service, ambience, convenience, and comfort. They also include quality shops on their premises. These hotels cost US$180 and up per night, double occupancy. Other hotels in the first-class and deluxe range cost US$100-150 a night.

Bali also has numerous inexpensive hotels and bungalows that go from US$25 to US$65 a night. However, many lack such amenities as air-conditioning and swimming pools.

ELECTRICITY AND WATER

Electricity in Bali is 220. If you travel with appliances or a computer, you may need an adapter for the Indonesian configured outlets as well as an extension cord to reach the limited number of outlets in your room.

Tap water is unsafe to drink, as is ice made from tap water. Most hotels provide bottled water in plastic bottles or in a thermos. Also use this water to brush your teeth. Given the heat and humidity of Bali, you may dehydrate quickly or frequently want to quench your thirst. For these occasions, carry a small plastic container of bottled water, purchase fruit juices in cans or cartons, or stop at a restaurant for a soft drink (without ice), coffee, or tea. Bottled water and fruit juices packaged in such containers are readily available at most stores throughout Bali. You may want to occasionally shop at these stores to replenish your supply of drinks.

Useful Resources

You can now find lots of useful information about Bali on the Internet, from tour operators and local news to discussion groups involving expats and tourists. Some of the best sites include:

www.bali-paradise.com	www.travelbali.com
www.balitravelforum.com	www.bali1.com
www.indo.com/home.html	www.baliwww.com
www.balipost.com	www.balihotels.com
www.balinetwork.com	

The Bali Travel Forum discussion group—*www.balitravelforum. com*—is especially interesting since it brings together expats and tourists, both seasoned and new to Bali. If you have a question, just post it to this very active forum. Also, use several standard search engines to locate useful information on Bali, such as *www.yahoo.com, www.google.com* and *www.altavista.com.* Several of these gateway travel sites also yield useful information on Bali:

www.citynet.com	www.travel-guide.com
www.kasbah.com	www.Travel-Library.com
www.mytravelguide.com	www.vtourist.com
www.opinionatedtraveler.com	www.travel.com
www.travel.com	www.web-travel-secrets.com
www.travelnotes.org	

If you plan to spend a few days or a week or two in Bali, we highly recommend getting a copy of Bill Dalton's *Bali Handbook* (Moon Publications) and Lonely Planet's *Indonesia.* Both of these excellent guidebooks are detailed, informative, and well written. They cover everything from history, art, and culture to hotels, restaurants, and sightseeing; they include some information on shopping. The sections on arts, crafts, and culture will give you a good background on many items you will likely purchase on Bali. Also, check out the message boards, discussion groups, and newsgroups relating to Indonesia and Bali at *www.lonelyplanet.com*, *www.fodors.com*, and *www.deja.com* as well as our international shopping site: *www.ishoparoundtheworld.com*

Shipping

We have successfully shipped numerous times from Bali. However, since the economic collapse in 1998, we've been hesitant to recommend shippers because of a major problem recently encountered in Bali. One shop (Sonata) and shipper (Bali Niki) have literally taken our money without delivering the goods. This is the first problem with shipping we have ever encountered in over 20 years of international travel. Unfortunately, we may never see our shipment of art, antiques, and furniture despite numerous calls, faxes, and local contacts.

Our best shipping advice for Bali at present is to take as much as you can carry with you. If you are shipping a large container, plan to ship it "Collect." In the case of smaller shipments, most shippers require prepayment in full for all shipping charges. And therein lies a potential problem. As in our case, the shipper may take your prepayment to pay off his other debts—literally "steal from Peter to pay Paul"—and thus you may never see your shipment. Make sure you have complete documentation on everything to be shipped—and then pray you are dealing with someone with honesty and integrity!

Since experiencing this shipping problem, we have located one company that appears to be very reputable and extremely service oriented. Operated by a former employee of the Ritz-Carlton Resort, who reputedly operates his shipping company according to Ritz-Carlton's exacting service standards, the company can be contacted as follows:

> Indosakti Cargo
> ATTN: Dewa Krisna
> Jl. Raya Kerobokan No. 2, Kuta
> Denpasar, Bali, Indonesia
> Tel. 62-361-730-272
> Fax 62-361-731-917

We also recommend contacting an affiliated trading company, Bali Nita Trading Corporation, for handling custom-made purchases as well as the whole shipping process. Indeed, this company may be able to take care of your major shopping and shipping needs. You can visit them and their catalog online:

> *www.angelfire.com/ns/balinita/index.html*

They also can be contacted by mail or fax:

> Bali Nita Trading Corporation
> ATTN: Krisna or Nita
> Taman Griya
> Jl. Danau Buyan Barat Dalam Gg. I Blok E5 No. 3
> Jimbaran, Bali 80361, Indonesia
> Tel./Fax 62-361-777-454

For updates on reliable shipping in Bali, visit our international shopping Web site: *www.ishoparoundtheworld.com*. Because shipping is such an important issue in the case of Bali, and for us personally, we also would appreciate hearing from you about your particular experiences, either good or bad. You can e-mail use directly as follows: *krannich@impactpublications.com*.

LIFE IMITATES ART

Bali has the best developed tourist facilities in all of Indonesia. Air connections to Bali are frequent. The island boasts many fine hotels and resort complexes. You will have plenty to do, be it lying on the beach, sailing, scuba diving, observing village ceremonies and dance performances, exploring the island, or "shopping 'til you drop!" Indeed, many visitors make Bali their only Indonesian stop. With the recent collapse of the Indonesian economy and attendant political violence on Java, Sumatra, Ambon, Timor, and Lombok, Bali has become a haven for tourists who have largely abandoned other parts of Indonesia. It remains Indonesia's major center for tourism. Falling in love with this island of beauty, art, and tradition, many visitors yearn to return to further experience the pleasures of a place where time appears to have stopped and life seems so unreal.

The Balinese are master craftspeople and artists. Everywhere you go on this island, you see people producing arts and crafts. Villages specialize in particular products. If, for example, you are interested in woodcarvings, then you should visit the village of Mas, which is Bali's woodcarving center. If you are interested in clothes, leather goods, souvenirs, jewelry, furniture, antiques, and textiles, Kuta Beach and Legian should be your destinations. For stone carvings and additional furniture, Batubulan is the place to visit. Silver production is concentrated around the village of Celuk. For paintings, you should go to Ubud.

CHOOSING THE PERFECT PLACE

The best way to organize yourself for the Bali experience is to select a hotel from which you will drive to the various villages to observe craftspeople and shop. As soon as you arrive at the international airport in Bali, you can contact several hotels through the information counter. Hotels, bungalows, and losmen range in price from US$5 to US$700 a night, depending on how you wish to experience Bali.

There are essentially six major areas where you can stay in Bali: Denpasar, Nusa Dua, Jimbaran, Kuta Beach, Sanur Beach, and Ubud. Each has its own character as well as certain advantages and disadvantages for shopping and sightseeing.

DENPASAR

Denpasar, a bustling, crowded, and congested city of 300,000, is the major city on Bali. Similar to many other provincial cities in Indonesia, there is nothing particularly Balinese about this utilitarian city. Downtown Denpasar is not an exciting place to stay, and the shopping here is limited to a few small antique, batik, and handicraft shops along **Jl. Gadah Mada, Jl. Arjuna, Jl. Dresna, Jl. Veteran**, and **Jl. Gianyar**. Nonetheless, a shop such as **Arts of Asia Gallery** (Jl. Thamrin 27-37, Blok C.5, Tel. 23350) is one of the best places in Bali for quality arts, antiques, and textiles. Denpasar also has a few central markets, a wholesale crafts market, and cooperative arts market that offer a wide range of inexpensive products of interest to both tourists and dealers.

SANUR BEACH

Most visitors to Bali stay in one of the remaining five areas. Sanur Beach is located along the southeast coast. This is one of the older and quieter hotel and resort areas. Three of Bali's best hotels are found here: Bali Hyatt, Bali Beach, and Tanjung Sari. Shopping is largely confined to the shopping arcades in the Bali Hyatt and Bali Beach hotels as well as in a few shops along the main road, Jl. Tanjung Sari. The beaches are not as expansive as those in the south, but Sanur Beach is a very peaceful and pleasant area to stay and stroll along the beach and roads. This also is a relatively expensive area to stay in comparison to Kuta Beach, Ubud, or Denpasar.

KUTA BEACH

Kuta Beach in the south is a popular area for budget travelers and young people looking for a good time. You'll either love or hate this place, depending on your travel interests. Very noisy, chaotic, congested, and touristy, it has a free-wheeling, frontier town feel to it. Kuta Beach does have a good beach and offers inexpensive accommodations (some for US$5) along with a few deluxe and first-class hotels and an occasional good restaurant. One of the best located hotels in this area is the **Bali Padma Hotel** (Jl. Padma No. 1, Legian, Kuta, Tel. 52111). Its beautiful grounds and well appointed rooms provide an oasis from the maddening crowds in the nearby streets. This is our favorite hotel in the Kuta area. At the very end of the long and narrow main street—Legian Road—you will discover one of Indonesia's best hotels—the **Bali Oberoi**. This is an oasis of class and ambience at the end of what is unquestionably Indonesia's most chaotic shopping street. However, the Oberoi is not within most people's conception of "walking distance" of Kuta's shopping areas. Kuta Beach also has spectacular sunsets. Bars, restaurants, car and motorbike rental offices, and clothing and souvenir shops and stalls line the main roads in Kuta; hawkers pester tourists everywhere. It's usually "party-time" in this fun area where budget-traveling Australians have long preferred its cheap pleasures. If you like bar hopping, crowds, people watching, surfing, and abusing another culture, this is the place to go.

But Kuta is full of contradictions. While it has lots of tourist knickknack and t-shirt shops lining both sides of Legian Road, here you also can find some excellent shops offering clothes, jewelry, textiles, antiques, and ethnographic art. Overall, however, the quality of products available here largely reflects the spending habits of Kuta's youthful traveling-on-a-shoestring clientele—mediocre to low. More than any other place, Kuta Beach symbolizes why quality shopping in Bali tends to be found in resort shops and other locations throughout the island or in the Indonesian capital of Jakarta. This place is not for everyone. Indeed, for many visitors Kuta Beach merely confirms the worst effects of tourism on paradise. On the other hand, many visitors love the festive atmosphere of Kuta, and they come away with some exciting shopping discoveries. See for yourself if this is your style.

NUSA DUA

Nusa Dua is Bali's largest self-contained resort area just southeast of Kuta Beach. Set away from the hustle and bustle of chaotic Denpasar and Kuta Beach, the style here is strictly luxury. Its expansive grounds, beautiful landscaping, gorgeous resorts, convention facilities, safe water supply, reliable electrical system, and tout-free environment especially appeal to convention groups and packaged tours. If your idea of traveling is "having it better than back home," and you're not particularly interested in mingling with the locals, then this area is for you. It's expensive here, but a great place to pamper yourself.

JIMBARAN BAY

Jimbaran Bay, located between Kuta and Nusa Dua on the northeast tip of Bukit peninsula and within 15 minutes of the airport, is Bali's newest area for upscale hotels and resorts. Here you will find the fabulous Four Seasons Resort, Ritz-Carlton Bali, and the Inter-Continental Bali Resort. We consider the **Four Seasons Resort** (Tel. 62-361-701010 or Fax 62-361-701020) to be Indonesia's best hotel/resort, and possibly the best in all of Asia. You simply can't do better than this place. It's an incredible resort with 147 private villas which include plunge pools, outdoor pavilions, and knock-your-socks-off views of Jimbaran Bay and Bali's sacred Mount Agung. The sleeping, bathing, and dressing pavilions in each of the quest quarters are spacious as is the outdoor dining and lounging pavilion. The restaurants here (The Dining Room, Pantai Jimbaran Restaurant, Pool Terrace Café) are outstanding. Indeed, we had two of the best meals we have ever enjoyed in Bali at the Four Seasons. The resort also provides one of the best upscale shopping boutiques with a dazzling array of quality antiques as well as good quality, but lesser priced, handicrafts. If you really want to pamper yourself and experience the best of the best in Indonesia, stay here for a few days. You won't want to leave! If you only stay at one five-star hotel in Indonesia, make sure it's the Four Seasons Resort in Jimbaran.

For families, the nearby **Ritz-Carlton Bali** (Tel. 62-361-702222 or Fax 62-361-701555) offers similar outstanding accommodations accompanied with the legendary Ritz-Carlton service. The Ritz-Carlton offers a range of guest rooms from a luxurious low rise hotel facility with wonderful beach views to individual villas on the beach.

UBUD

Ubud is fast becoming a popular place to stay. Indeed, many travelers regret not staying here or spending more time in Ubud. Located in a picturesque inland area north of Sanur Beach, Ubud is a center for artists and world travelers. It's a favorite destination for budget travelers who prefer a local cultural alternative to Kuta Beach and upscale travelers who seek an inland alternative to the fabulous resorts in Jimbaran and Nusa Dua. With the arrival of electricity, telephones, deluxe hotels, such as the Four Seasons Sayan and the Amandari, the character of Ubud is quickly changing. Nonetheless, many travelers still prefer staying in Ubud, because it is less "touristy" and closer to the "real Bali" they remember than any of the other major areas. The best hotels/resorts here are the world famous **Four Seasons Sayan** (Ubud, Gianyar, Bali 80571, Tel. 62-361-977577 or Fax 62-361-977588) and **Amandari** (P.O. Box 33, Ubud, Bali, Tel. 62-361-975333 or Fax 62-361-975335). If you really want to pamper yourself in Bali, spend a few days at the Four Seasons Resort in Jimbaran and then move to the Four Seasons Sayan in Ubud for a few days. While the resorts are very different, they are the best of the best in Indonesia.

TACKLING THE ISLAND

Getting around Bali is relatively easy given the good road system and maps available for visitors. Regardless of where you stay, your shopping adventure requires traveling from one area to another. In this sense it really doesn't make much difference—perhaps 15 minutes—where you stay in relation to the shopping. We still prefer the Jimbaran, Sanur, and Ubud areas for their quiet, ambience, and central location for shopping, restaurants, hotels, and beaches. Except in Kuta, do not plan to walk from your hotel to most shops!

SOUTHERN BALI

One of the first things you should do is look at a map of Bali. The island is best viewed in terms of regions: South, Central, East, North, and West. **Southern Bali**—including Denpasar, Kuta Beach, Jimbaran, Sanur Beach, and Nusa Dua—is the most urbanized and least Balinese. Most tourists stay here to enjoy the beaches and tourist facilities. Ironically, the Balinese prefer the upland areas and are not particularly keen about one of the favorite pastimes of tourists—the beaches. The upland central region, just to the north of Denpasar and Sanur Beach, is where most of the major arts and crafts villages are found. Your village-centered shopping will take place within a 10-mile radius of the noted artist village and tourist center of **Ubud**. Village after village perform dances and produce the arts and crafts Bali is so well noted for.

EASTERN BALI

Eastern Bali is perhaps the most beautiful part of Bali with its picturesque volcanos, terraced rice fields, quaint villages, and interesting temples. For centuries this region has been the center for Bali's major kingdoms. You travel here to view the scenery, especially Mt. Agung, and tour various temple complexes. You also will pass through **Gianyar**, Bali's famous textile center where you can tour the factories and workshops and also shop for local jewelry; **Klungkung**, a market town noted for basketry; and **Kamasan**, a village with wayang paintings and gold and silver products.

NORTHERN BALI

Northern Bali is one of the most peaceful sections of the island. It's largely devoid of tourists. Since trips from the south to the northern coast take a long time, you may wish to stay overnight if you visit this area. This area is best noted for its spectacular scenery—volcanos, lakes, hot springs, and beaches—and temples. You will find several nondescript market towns, such as Singaraja and Kubutambahan, in this area. Go here for the scenery, peace and quiet, but don't expect to do any quality shopping.

WESTERN BALI

Western Bali is the largest region. Several villages in this area are noted for temples, music, dancing, bull races, and textiles. This is the region of the famous seaside temple Tanah Lot, the monkey forest, and snake caves.

WHAT AND HOW TO BUY

Shopping is one of the big surprises for visitors to Bali who thought they were coming to the island to primarily spend time on the beaches, tour Hindu temples, and see picturesque villages. At times, you may think you are in the midst of one big shopping bazaar in one of the world's most beautiful settings! If you are like many other visitors to Bali, you'll quickly get caught up in shopping for unique and inexpensive items. Like Bali's seductive culture, its shopping will quickly seduce you.

Bali offers an incredible variety of arts, crafts, antiques, jewelry, and clothing. Of particular interest to visitors are the Balinese woodcarvings, paintings, gold, silver, and pottery as well as antiques, furniture, ethnographic pieces, and textiles from other areas in Indonesia, especially from Sulawesi, Madura, Lombok, Timor, and other eastern islands. Numerous shops also sell the latest in resortwear, leather products, fashion clothes, home decorative items as well as surfboards, backpacks,

CDs, cassettes, and a wide assortment of tourist kitsch. Shopping is found in hotel shopping arcades, shopping centers, markets, roadside stalls, small shops and boutiques, home factories and galleries, and among hawkers. Less well known to visitors, but of most importance to the Balinese, are the **ritual arts**. These consist of many beautiful sculptures made as ceremonial offerings. Most last no more than two weeks and are usually destroyed as part of a ceremony—cremations being the most spectacular. These are the real Balinese arts. For the Balinese, art is used as offerings to the demons and gods—not collectibles for decorating homes. In the meantime, the Balinese produce other forms of art primarily for tourists. Like the tourist preference for the beaches, this permanent art is designed to satisfy the Western concept of arts and crafts used primarily for display.

While Bali offers a great deal in terms of shopping, it also offers some of the worst aspects of tourist shopping. Much of what you find in the small shops, roadside stalls, factories, and galleries is simply tourist junk. Most of the Balinese woodcarvings and paintings are copies of each other. You will enter galleries and literally see hundreds of "busy" Balinese oil paintings that look the same. After visiting two or three of these shops, you will probably never want to see another Balinese painting the rest of your life! Many of the woodcarvings have a similar fate—hundreds of the same figures assault your eyes. You will have to dig around in many different shops to find unique pieces which appeal to your sense of quality shopping.

Bali offers quality shopping, but you have to work to find it. The problem with quality shopping in Bali is readily apparent by observing the type of tourists who frequent this island. Bali has a reputation for attracting budget travelers and backpackers who come here for cheap accommodations, inexpensive food, and free fun. They are not big spenders with a taste for quality shopping. When they shop, they look for small inexpensive items they can either wear or fit into their backpacks. Large numbers of quality shops simply cannot survive amongst many of these types of tourists. What quality shops do exist tend to be found in and around the deluxe hotels or they sell primarily to dealers who purchase their products for resale. Bali is especially a shopping paradise for foreign dealers who purchase inexpensive carvings and jewelry.

You should also be prepared for hawkers, commissions, rip-offs, and mangy dogs on Bali. In many areas hawkers will pester you with their tacky goods. Just say *jalan jalan* and keep moving if you want to rid yourself of this annoyance. Since many sellers are used to dealing with rich and naive tourists, they are not above taking advantage of you. Be careful about claims of items being "old" and "antique," and bargain everywhere for a 30 to 60 percent discount according to our rules on pages 45-50. Indeed, some antiques dealers in Singapore have been known to unwittingly buy antique reproductions in Bali. After discovering they have been cheated, their only recourse was to send them back to Bali where they can be sold to tourists who think they are getting a real bargain! Not surprisingly, you may discover prices for some items made in Bali to be higher than those found abroad for the same item. Be especially careful of antique shops which have recently experienced a tremendous increase in acquisition of so-called antique items.

The commission game in Bali is almost as bad as the notorious commissions that gouge tourists in Chiangmai, Thailand and in many parts of India (Agra, Jaipur, New Delhi). Most guides and drivers steer tourists to particular shops that give them commissions on everything you purchase. Merchants, of course, pass this commission charge on to the purchaser. Most commissions range from 10 to 20 percent. However, commissions on silver purchases in the famous village of Celuk range as high as 30 to 35 percent. If you want to reduce your price as well as your driver's commission, some merchants may suggest that you lie to your driver/guide. Instead of telling the driver that you actually paid US$100 for an item, tell him you only paid US$20. Remember, top quality shops in Bali don't pay commissions, because they have a steady clientele based on their reputation. Many guides and drivers will not want to take you to such shops because there is no payoff for them in doing so. For example, the **Ida Bagus Tilem** gallery shop/workshop in Mas—Bali's top woodcarver—is not popular with tour guides and drivers. If you don't tell your guide or driver that you want to visit this place, chances are you will miss what is the most important woodcarver in Bali as well as Indonesia. In fact, some guides and drivers may bad-mouth this place as being "very expensive," which it is, and then try to take you to one of their recommended shops where in fact they get a commission. The prices will most likely to cheaper at this other shop, but you will see a definite difference in the quality of products.

The old saying that *"You get what you pay for"* is doubly valid in Bali where you also get to pay a hidden commission for poor and mediocre quality items. Shops that are frequented by tour buses invariably pay commissions to guides. In addition, many of the shops targeted by guides and drivers offer mediocre products. If you visit such shops on your own, when bargaining over the price, remind the salesperson that you are not with a guide or driver and thus you expect a substantial discount for your lone efforts. Consequently, you may want to direct your guide or driver to many of the quality shops recommended in this chapter. While not all of these shops are commission-free, at least you get quality for your money.

Keep clear of the mangy dogs that roam the streets throughout Bali. They are not cute, so don't pet or feed them, unless you want to risk rabies shots!

SHOPPING STRATEGIES

A good approach to shopping in Bali is to visit the Bali Museum, the Mandera Giri Art Center, and Central Market (Pasar Padung) in Denpasar to get an overview of Balinese arts and crafts. Next, survey a few antique, textile, and curio shops along Jl. Gajah Mada, Jl. Arjuna, Jl. Dresna, Jl. Veteran, and Jl. Gianyar in Denpasar. After that, survey some of the hotel shops in the major resort hotels, such as the Bali Beach, Bali Hyatt, and the Nusa Dua Beach Hotel, and stroll along the main streets in Kuta Beach (Legian Road) and Sanur Beach. Plan to return to these areas after visiting several arts and crafts villages in central Bali. If you want to see what real quality shopping is, visit the shops at the Four Seasons Resort in Jimbaran and the Amandari resort in Ubud as well as several shops we recommend under the "Best of the Best." You'll know quality when you see it in comparison to much of the tourist kitsch that dominates shopping in Bali.

We recommend hiring a car with driver who speaks some English to make the village shopping tour. Know though that many drivers or guides will make known to the shop owners that they brought you there (even though you may have selected the shop) in order to collect commissions on your purchases. Alternatively, armed with a good map, which may be difficult to find, you may want to rent a self-drive car. But doing so is hazardous and you may get lost since roads are not well marked in Bali. While motorbikes are fun for sightseeing, they are not very safe nor convenient for shopping.

You might develop a checklist of villages for planning your shopping adventure into central Bali. Most villages tend to specialize in producing one or two particular products. If you're interested in woodcarvings, for example, you go to one village. If its silver or paintings, you go to another village or villages that only specialize in these items. Indeed, some villages only specialize in producing carved doors, banana trees, and flowers. In addition to factories and shops, many villages will have dance and musical performances and ritual ceremonies going on

during your visit. You will probably immerse yourself in the
local culture while shopping. Within a 20-kilometer radius of
Ubud, the most important arts and crafts villages are:

Village	Specialty
Celuk	Bali's silver and gold center. Family factories produce the unique Balinese filigree jewelry which is largely an acquired taste (shops in Kuta and Ubud offering contemporary silver jewelry may be more appealing). Expect deep discounting since most shops pay high commissions (as much as 35 percent) to tour guides and drivers.
Batuan	Famous village for Balinese paintings and dance and musical performances. Great place to first observe the performances and then shop.
Batubulan	In addition to being the popular center for dance performances, the shops, factories, and warehouses along both sides of the main road that cuts through this village are noted for their stone carvings, furniture, and antiques. This is a popular place for dealers who come here to buy container-loads of products.
Mas	Famous village of woodcarvers with numerous galleries to explore. World famous woodcarvers live and work here. The mecca for carved figures and masks.
Ubud	This town used to be Bali's best kept shopping secret, until recently. The island's creative art center, it's linked to a cluster of artistic villages, such as Campuan, Penestanan, Juti, Pujung, Sebatu, Taro, and Pengosekan. The streets are lined with shops and stalls selling woodcarvings, masks, paintings, clothes, leather goods, textiles, and a variety of knickknacks. Many famous Indonesian and expatriate artists live in and around this town and have homes and galleries open to the public. Ubud is a great place to stroll for shopping, dining, and viewing

the countryside. Fast becoming a major tourist destination in Bali for both budget and deluxe travelers and an especially pleasant shopping alternative to Kuta Beach. If there is one place in Indonesia visitors really regret not having spent more time visiting, it definitely is Ubud. Plan to spend two or three days in this area. Trust us. You'll be glad you came and spent some time, and money, here.

Outside the central region, you will find several other villages specializing in the production of colorful arts and crafts. Most of these villages are within a 15 to 25 minute drive of the major towns and villages. Some of the most important arts and crafts villages include:

Village	Specialty
Blayu	A textile village noted for producing good quality songket. Located northwest of Mengwi.
Gianyar	Famous for its cottage textile industry and architecture. Located 18 miles northeast of Denpasar.
Kamasan	Center for producing wayang style painting as well as large silver bowls and gold jewelry. Located just south of Klungkung.
Peliatan	Famous dance and gamelan orchestra village with a gallery displaying the works of artists from nearby Pengosekan, a village less than one mile from Mas.
Pengosekan	Famous village with some of Bali's finest painters. Located just south of Ubud.
Sukawati	Bali's wayang center. Has a popular and congested market selling colorful masks, woodcarvings, batik, and ikat. Located 8 miles northeast of Denpasar.

| Tenganan | Extremely traditional and conservative walled village noted for producing *gringsing* cloth. |

You will also find small shops and souvenir stalls near some of the major tourist sites, such as the Elephant Cave (Goa Gajah). Most of these places sell woodcarvings, baskets, leather goods, and a variety of knickknacks which you may or may not want to acquire.

Another way of approaching Bali is to seek out particular shops specializing in quality arts and crafts. The real shopping problem in Bali is how to go beyond much of the boring copy-cat tourist junk to find quality items. Thousands of artisans continue to produce copycat arts and crafts solely for the tourist market. If you are looking for quality products, be sure to explore the following locations:

Items	Location
Textiles	**Arts of Asia** in Denpasar and several shops in Kuta Beach, along Legian Road, have good selections. Kuta is also a good place to shop for batik beachwear. Try the towns of Gianyar (visit **Chili** and **Togog**) and Ubud and the villages of Tengganan (for unique double ikat, or "gringsing," cloth), Sideman, Batuan, Blayu, Gelgel, and Mengwi. **Argasoka Textile Gallery**, **Kamar Sutra**, **Tomboya**, **Wardani Fabric**, and **Jani's** in Ubud are well worth visiting for good quality and reasonably priced textile selections.
Clothes	Bali is fast becoming a center for fashionable sports and casual wear using batik and ikat materials. Numerous shops along Legian Road in Kuta Beach as well as in the major hotels offer locally designed clothes. One of the best such shops is **Nogo** on Jl. Legian (Kuta Beach) and Jl. Tanjung Sari 173 (Sanur). Also look for the **Keris Gallery Department Store** (Nusa Dua) for batik clothes and fashionable shops at the two-storey **Plaza Bali** near the airport. In Ubud, **Lotus Studios**, **Mutiara Art Bali**, **Toko**, and the **Bamboo Gallery** (see their

adjacent clothing shop) offer uniquely designed clothes.

Jewelry

While Celuk is the center for traditional Balinese filigree silver jewelry, there's a lot more to jewelry in Bali that what is found in Celuk. In Kuta, be sure to visit **Jonathan Gallery**, **Mario Silver**, and **Ratu Silver** for contemporary silver jewelry. In Ubud, be sure to visit **Treasures** for contemporary gold jewelry and **Seraphim** for beautifully designed jewelry using opals, amber, and pearls.

Paintings

Head for Ubud and the nearby villages of Mas, Batuan, Sangginyan, Pengosekan, Penestanan, and Peliatan. Visit the **Neka Museum**, **Gallery Munut**, and the **Pengosekan Community of Artists**. Klungkung is the center for traditional wayang style paintings. In Peliatan, visit the **Agung Rai Gallery**. Several world-renowned artists in Ubud have galleries in their homes: Arie Smit, Hans Snel, Wayan Rendi, Antonio Blanco, Rainer Anderle, and I Gusti Nyoman Lempad. In Ubud, be sure to visit the **Neka Gallery** (established artists) and the **Bamboo Gallery** (young, promising artists).

Wood-carvings

Woodcarvings, both old and new, are found in several shops in Kuta, Sanur, and Klungkung. The major woodcarving center is Mas. Be sure to stop at the **Ida Bagus Tilem Gallery**, **Ketut Puja**, and the **Tantra Gallery** in Mas. Ubud also is a woodcarving center as are the villages of Pujung, Batuan, and Jati. They produce a large variety of woodcarvings using teak, ebony, and jackfruit woods. Each town and village tends to produce its own unique styles.

Stone-carvings

Batubulan is the center for sandstone carvings. You'll see stonecarving shops lining both sides of the road. Stop by **I Made Suasa** and **Made Kakul** for a nice range of selections. This is a great place to buy traditional Balinese figures and animals carved in sandstone for fountains and garden pieces. The shops are experienced in packing and shipping abroad.

Gold/silver	Celuk, Kamasan, and Kuta are the centers for gold and silver work. Shops in Denpasar along Jl. Sulawesi and Jl. Kartini offer a good selection of traditional Balinese jewelry. One of the best shops in Celuk is **Melati Silver**. Watch out for guides and drivers who steer you into mediocre shops which give them 20-30 percent commissions on everything you buy.
Pottery & porcelain	Be sure to visit the village of Pejatan (12 miles west of Denpasar) for a distinctive style of contemporary Balinese terra-cotta pottery. You will find glazed ceramics in Batu Jimbar, Sanur. Visit **Djody** in Mas for porcelain.
Antiques	The best locations for antiques are the major hotel shopping arcades and shops in Kuta Beach, Sanur, Denpasar, Klungkung, Batubulan, and Singaraja. In Kuta Beach (Jl. Legian), one of Bali's best antique shops is **Polos**. Also, look for **Agung Rakas, Timor Art, H. Sjamsuddin Art, Anang's Place, Kaliuda Gallery,** and **Jonathan Gallery**. In Batubulan and Celuk, stop at **Puri Sakana, Polis,** and **Sonata**. In Denpasar, visit one of Indonesia's oldest and most reputable antique shops—**Arts of Asia**. In Sanur a few antique shops are found along Jl. Sanur. For excellent one-of-a-kind treasures, try the gallery shops at the **Four Seasons Resort** in Jimbaran and the **Amandari** in Ubud. When in Ubud, be sure to visit **Shalimar** for top quality antiques, furniture, and home decorative items as well as **Rococo Antiques, Dayu Collection,** and **Kamarkini Gallery**.
Furniture	Numerous shops offer a wide assortment of furniture. Most furniture is either from the nearby island of Madura or produced locally. Probably Bali's best furniture shop is **Warisan Gallery** north of Kuta on Jl. Raya Krobokan (Tel. 730710). Many other shops are found in the same area (see **Andy's Gallery** and **Jonathan's Bali Furniture**) as well as along the road near Celuk and Batubulan, especially **Polis, Puri Sakana,** and **Sonata**. In Ubud, visit

Rococo Antiques, Shalimar Gallery, and Kamarkini Gallery.

Home decorative	Many of the antique and furniture shops, such as **Warisan** and **Shalimar**, also offer many lovely home decorative items. **Konsep Lama Kini** in Kuta includes a unique collection of contemporary and ethnic pieces popular with interior designers. **Casa Lina**, on the main road to Ubud, offers a wonderful collection of interior decorating accessories.
Gifts	One of Bali's nicest gift shops is found across the street from one of Ubud's best restaurants, Café Wayan—**Archipelo**. Also in Ubud look for **Toko** and **Lingsir** for unique gift selections.
Handicrafts	You will find handicrafts everywhere, in souvenir shops, markets, and stalls. For baskets, visit **Bona, Bedulu**, and **Goa Gajah**. For bone carvings, visit **Tampaksiring**. For numerous inexpensive woodcarvings, batik, ikat, and tourist kitsch, visit the popular handicraft market in **Sukawati**. For good quality handicrafts, visit the shops at **Plaza Bali** near the airport.

To shop Bali properly, you need at least four days, but preferably a week to absorb other aspects of this wonderful island. Bali is not a big island, but its narrow and winding roads and numerous shops that command your attention along the way make going slow. Indeed, your best laid shopping plans for the day may quickly be altered as you engage in a serendipitous shopping adventure that ends up in places you never intended to visit. That's the true joy of shopping in Bali! Hopefully, your shopping adventure will take you to some wonderful places we have yet to discover.

WHERE TO SHOP

Shopping in Bali seems to be everywhere, from hotel shopping arcades to village workshops. You'll encounter numerous shops along main streets as well as alongside the major roads connecting one village to another. Above all, you need a car, driver, good map, and time to explore the many shopping cities, towns, villages, and roads.

DENPASAR

Denpasar is no one's favorite city, but it does have its own treasures and pleasures. Functioning as the major city on Bali, it is typical of so many Indonesian cities—large, crowded, congested, polluted, worn, and ugly. It's an administrative and commercial center rather than a major tourist destination. Most visitors pass through this city on their way to the major tourist areas—Nusa Dua, Jimbaran, Kuta Beach, Sanur Beach, or Ubud.

Yet, you should not overlook shopping in Denpasar. The city does have some noted shopping opportunities. It has a few markets worth exploring. The three-storey market along the river in downtown Denpasar, **Pasar Badung**, has everything from fish, fruit, vegetables, and hardware to clothing, textiles, and baskets. On the opposite side of the river the **Kumbasari Shopping Centre** functions as an arts, crafts, and clothing market. Here you will find a large number of small stalls on the second and third floors selling woodcarvings, textiles, bags, hats, T-shirts, masks, and batik. This is a good place to purchase inexpensive gift items. The center is open until 8pm each night. Denpasar also has a night market—**Pasar Malam**. Located just south of the Kumbasari Shopping Centre, this lively market consists of brightly-lit food stalls as well as vendors selling inexpensive clothes, shoes, batik fabric, and other items. Good buys on arts and crafts can be found at the **Pasar Satria**, Denpasar's version of an art dealer's wholesale market. Located at the corner of Jl. Nakula and Jl. Veterans (two streets north of Jl. Gajah Mada), Pasar Satria's two upper floors are devoted to wholesaling woodcarvings, paintings, and other craft items.

Denpasar also has a few good art and antique shops. One of the best antique shops is **Arts of Asia** (Jl. Thamrin 27-37, Blok C.5, Tel. 23350). A well established and reputable shop, Arts of Asia offers excellent quality textiles, furniture, Chinese porcelain, Dayak and Balinese masks, jewelry, wayang puppets, Batak gables, drums, and paintings. The owners—a husband and wife team—are very knowledgeable about antiques and textiles and only offer top quality. However, stock fluctuates. During our most recent visit, we were disappointed in finding so little in the shop. You will also find several arts shops along Jl. Thamrin, Jl. Supraman, Jl. Arjuna, and Jl. Gratot Kaca. Jl. Gadjamata has a few clothing and gift shops. **"Mega" Art Shop** at Jl. Gajah Mada No. 36 has an excellent selection of woodcarvings, wayang, paintings, silver, ceramics, leather purses, kris, and textiles. Its larger shop—**"Mega" Gallery of Arts** on the outskirts of Denpasar (Jl. Gianyar, Km. 5.7, Denpasar, Tel. 28855) is a huge emporium for Indonesian arts and crafts. In fact, this was the first shop established in Bali. One section of this shop includes the owner's private collection of textiles and kris which, of course, are not for sale but well worth a visit if you're interested in these items. **Popiler** (Tel. 35162, 35180), which is located next to "Mega" Gallery of Arts, is a good shop for batik clothes and paintings. Good quality batik paintings are located in the back of the shop as well as upstairs. If you are interested in traditional Balinese jewelry, visit the gold shops along Jl. Hasanudin.

If you visit the suburb of Tohpati, you'll find an art cooperative supervised by the Department of Industry—**Sanggraha Kriya Asta**. Consisting of five buildings, each displaying particular crafts, this cooperative offers woodcarvings, garments, batik, silver, and paintings, and all at fixed prices. This is a good place to come for comparative pricing information.

NUSA DUA

Nusa Dua is Bali's resort and convention center. Here you will find several excellent hotels relatively isolated from the rest of the island. Both the **Nusa Dua** and **Melia Bali Sol** hotels have small shopping arcades where you will find a few excellent quality shops offering everything from resort clothes to jewelry and handicrafts. On the ground floor of the Melia Bali Sol Hotel, you'll find several arts and crafts stalls selling everything from Balinese paintings to woodcarvings. The **Hyatt Regency Nusa Dua** includes a shopping arcade with small boutiques and an art gallery/museum exhibiting examples of Balinese culture and history. Outside these hotels, be sure to visit the well appointed **Galeri Keris** which is a large handicraft emporium and department store at Galleria Nusa Dua (Tel. 771303 or 771304); it's open daily from 9am to 10pm. This is a good place to buy a large range of Indonesia handicrafts and clothes at fixed prices.

KUTA BEACH/LEGIAN

What a wild, wild place! For some, Kuta Beach is a shopper's paradise. For others, it's paradise lost, having succumbed to bright lights, noise, congestion, tourist kitsch, and pestering touts. Whatever your opinion, Kuta Beach at the least has the largest concentration of shopping found anywhere on Bali. It's non-stop shopping from 9am to 9pm. Shop after shop line the main street—Legian Road—and a few adjacent streets selling everything from T-shirts, used books, surf board covers, batik patchwork quilts to jewelry, designer clothes, art, and antiques. Here you'll find a real mixture from junk to treasures. Restaurants, bars, and guest houses are interspersed amongst the many shops and are found along lanes and side streets.

Kuta Beach is an extremely crowded and congested place, reminiscent of a honky-tonk strip development or a frontier town run amok. It especially appeals to $7-a-day youthful world travelers who are looking for an inexpensive fun time. And many of the shops reflect the spending habits of Kuta Beach's primary clientele—lots of cheap clothes and eats. Yet, Kuta also draws other types of travelers and age groups to make this a truly eclectic collection of visitors who enjoy Kuta's unique atmosphere and inexpensive prices.

However, amongst the many eateries and T-shirt shops are several shops offering good quality clothes, jewelry, and antiques. In fact, during the past 10 years Legian Road has blossomed with the arrival of several shops selling ethnographic pieces from Kalimantan, Sulawesi, Lombok, Timor, and other eastern islands. While many of the so-called antiques are suspect, you will find some genuine old pieces here.

Quality shops are not readily apparent in any one area of Kuta Beach. You literally need to start at one end of Legian Road and walk to the other end, including side trips into the lanes and adjacent streets, in order to discover quality shops. You'll most likely begin at Jl. Bukungsari which bounds Legian Road. Along the way you are likely to become exhausted from the long walk as well as irritated by transportation hawkers who pester you by repeatedly shouting that they have a very "special price" on rides along the street, which is usually five times the going rate! Three thousand rupiah, or about US$.45, is plenty to pay for the journey along this street, which you will probably want to take advantage of for the return trip once you get to the end of the road and need to go back to where you started, which is three kilometers away!

You can easily spend a half day or more shopping along Legian Road and its adjacent streets and lanes. The street is most lively in the evening from 6pm to 9pm when everyone comes out to have a good time, eating and drinking in open-air restaurants and roaming the narrow, congested streets and lanes. And you'll do a lot of walking since Legian Road is very long—approximately three kilometers of shops on both sides of the street. This road eventually leads to Kuta Beach's great oasis—the Bali Oberoi Hotel—where you can escape from all the crowds, clutter, and noise. Going further north, along Jl. Raya Seminya, takes you to numerous furniture, antique , and home decorative shops, including Bali's best furniture and home decor shop, **Warisan**.

If you are looking for arts and antiques, especially ethnographic items, you'll find numerous shops offering good selections of textiles, masks, carvings, beads, porcelain, kris, old silver, doors, boxes, baskets, chests, pottery, and furniture along Legian Road and the adjacent streets: **Agung Rakas, Timor Arts, Letros Art Shop, Konsep Lama Kini, Apo Kayan, H. Sjamsuddin Art, Mahakam, Kaliuda Gallery** (best stuff is at the owner's house, Eddy Laurens), **Anang's Place, Asmat Kamoro**, and **Polos**.

For nicely designed contemporary silver jewelry, be sure to visit **Jonathan Gallery, Mario Silver, Ratu Silver**, and **Runa Jewelry**. Other good shops to look for are **Rama Collection** for leather bags using ikat designs; **Biak Biak** for uniquely designed clothes in cotton, silk, and rayon; **Gretha Leather** for handbooks and luggage; **Gecko** for nice leather coats, vests, shoes, and belts; **Ikar** for colorful and fashionable clothes and bed linens; and **Gallery Copper** for copper pieces that make nice gifts or home decorative items.

SANUR

Compared to Kuta Beach, Sanur's shopping is much more limited and sedate. This relatively quiet, beach front resort area has two major hotels with nice shopping arcades—the Bali Hyatt and Bali Beach—as well as several shops that line the main street in Sanur, Jl. Tanjung Sari. Although the shops are limited in number, the quality of shopping here is generally better than in Kuta Beach. A few of the restaurants here tend to be some of the best in Bali.

The **Bali Hyatt Hotel** is one of Bali's loveliest hotels. A few small but excellent quality boutiques, craft, and jewelry shops are found on the ground floor just below the lobby. **Tilem Gallery**, for example, offers fine quality Balinese carvings by one of Bali's top carvers who also has a gallery shop in Mas. **Djody Art, Curio, and Antiques** has good quality silver and antiques. For stylish sportswear, visit **Taman Boutique, Sari Bali Boutique**, and **Lila Shop**.

The **Bali Beach Hotel** has the largest hotel shopping arcade on Bali, although it is still small by most standards. For excellent quality Balinese woodcarvings, visit both **Njana Tilem Gallery** and **Bali Indah**. For good quality silver, visit **Mahesa** and **Ardana**. **Djody** has a good selection of antiques, woodcarvings, and kris.

Jl. Tanjung Sari is the main beach-front road that connects most major hotels, restaurants, and shops in Sanur Beach. Running for approximately two kilometers, a one kilometer stretch between the Bali Hyatt Hotel and the Tanjung Sari Hotel is where you will find most of Sanur's shops. Both sides of this road have a smattering of good quality shops offering a wide range of clothes, textiles, home furnishings, carvings, ceramics, gifts, and antiques.

If you visit the Bali Beach Hotel on Jl. Segara, just across the street is the **Beach Market I Sanur** which is filled with stalls selling beachwear, handicrafts, antiques, and tourist kitsch. One shop—**Lukman**—may look like a typical tourist shop, but it has some genuine antiques and old textiles amongst the handicrafts. If you are a serious antique buyer, Lukman will invite you to his home in Denpasar (Jl. Serma Made Pil 22) where he will show you his latest collection of antique jewelry, silver, kris, and textiles acquired from nearby islands. All items, of course, are for sale. Do be sure to bargain for everything.

UBUD

Plan to spend some time in this pleasant town—preferably 2-3 days. You won't be disappointed. It's inexpensive and you'll have a great time shopping, dining, and sightseeing. Located approximately 8 miles north of Sanur Beach, Ubud is fast becoming a choice location for travelers—both budget and deluxe—who wish to get closer to the real Bali that largely disappeared years ago in Nusa Dua, Denpasar, Kuta Beach, and Sanur Beach. Indeed, after spending a few hours shopping in chaotic Kuta Beach, you'll think you've discovered a paradise in Ubud!

A small inland town that only recently acquired electricity (1976) and telephone lines (1987), Ubud is a well noted art center in Bali. Here you will find many of Bali's famous Balinese, Indonesian, and expatriate artists who have galleries displaying their distinctive paintings. This also is a center for inexpensive clothes, textiles, handicrafts, and antiques. It boasts a few good restaurants, too.

It's easy to shop in Ubud since this is a small town with most shops found along two main streets—**Main Road**, or Jl. Raya Ubud, and **Monkey Forest Road**. It's best to start at one end of Main Road—preferably at the north end adjacent to the bridge and **Murni's Warung**—and walk this two kilometer stretch of road. If you start here, you may want to begin by visiting one of Ubud's best restaurants and shops. Murni's

Warung is literally a small hole-in-the-wall restaurant overlooking a ravine, but it serves some of the best milkshakes in Indonesia! Its adjacent two-storey shop has some very nice handicrafts and gift items, including textiles and carved bowls. Just a few doors away is **Kunang Kunang I** (Tel. 95716), an upscale and stylish shop offering excellent quality textiles, pottery, purses, jewelry, clothes, wayang golek puppets, musical instruments, pillows, and furniture—the most fashionable boutique and gift shop in Ubud. Across the street and up a few shops is **Kunang Kunang II** an upscale shop selling antiques, jewelry, textiles, baskets, boxes, puppets, and clothes. The remainder of this street is lined with small shops selling arts, crafts, silver, jewelry, batik patchwork quilts, masks, antique, and clothes shops. Some of the best shops along this road are **Rococo Antiques** (Tel. 974805) for furniture, textiles, and handicrafts; **Dayu Collection** (Tel. 975428) for a nice selection of antiques, textiles, and carvings; **Treasures** (Tel. 976697) for uniquely designed gold jewelry by three different Western designers; **Lotus Studios** (Tel. 975363) for textiles, clothes, paintings, and gift items; and **Shalimar Gallery** (Tel. 977115, located across from the Central Market, for some of the best quality antiques, furniture, textiles, and home decorative items in all of Bali. The **Central Market**, a two-storey building with numerous vendor stalls, is similar to many other central markets on Bali. You'll find everything from clothes, fans, and bags to jewelry here. Across the street from the Central Market you'll find several clothing, handicraft, and art shops. Further along this road you will come to Ubud's two best art galleries, **Neka Gallery** and the **Bamboo Gallery** (Tel. 975037). Neka Gallery is adjacent to the Neka Museum which includes paintings from well known artists. The Bamboo Gallery represents the paintings of young promising artists. The remainder of this road has several art galleries displaying the paintings of local artists.

At this point, you might want to turn around and go back toward the Lotus Café. Be sure to turn left onto **Monkey Forest Road** which is lined with numerous arts, crafts, clothing, jewelry, and gift shops. This is a very long road which may take several hours to cover on foot. Indeed, you can easily spend the whole day shopping and dining along this road. Some of the best quality shops along this road include **Oleh Oleh** (Tel. 973466) for ethnic (Asmat) carvings and textiles; **Seraphim** (Tel. 973287) for outstanding quality designer jewelry and antiques—and air-conditioning on a hot day! Also, look for **Tomboya** (Tel. 977372) for textiles, clothes, and antiques; **Argasoka Textile Gallery** (Tel. 973231) for uniquely designed batik cloth by Isnia of Jokja; **Kamar Sutra** (Tel. 977109), next to the popular Café Wayang, for excellent quality, and expensive, textiles and scarves; **Toko** (Tel. 95046) for lots of nice gift items, from batik to jewelry; **Lingsir** (Tel. 97984), a small hole in the wall, for many small gift items, especially rice paper, books, and candles; **Archipelo** for a very tasteful collection of gift items; and **Floren Art Shop II** for arts, antiques, and textiles from Timor. Just outside Ubud, on the road to the Four Seasons Resort at Sayan (Jl. Raya Lungsiakan, is **Kamarkini Gallery** (Tel. 975296) for good quality antique furniture and crafts.

VILLAGES AND ROADS

You'll discover numerous workshops, shop houses, factories, and shops lining the roads between the major towns and villages. While many of these places offer similar products, occasionally you will find exceptional quality shops amongst the mediocre. If you are interested in furniture and antiques, be sure to visit the many shops lining Jl. Gianyar at the village of **Batubulan** just a few kilometers north of Sanur. We particularly like the unique selections available at **Puri Sakana** (Tel. 298205). This huge shop/warehouse is located on both sides of the road and includes an extensive collection of furniture and ethnographic pieces. Other good antique and furniture shops in this area include **Kadek Nedhi** (Tel. 298105) and **P.T. Sonata** (Tel. 298259).

Most of the silver shops in the famous silver village of **Celuk** look the same and business here is highly competitive. They all seem to produce similar types of silver filigree jewelry and figures which may or may not appeal to your tastes. Shop around, compare prices, and bargain hard in every shop you visit. Remember, many shops here are used to paying 20 to 35% commissions to tour guides and drivers for steering customers their way. One of the largest factory shops offering a good selection of silver jewelry, including gold and silver combinations, is **Rama Sitha**. A similar shop that also offers some handicrafts along with silver products is **Dewi-Murmi**. The best silver shop is **Melati Silver**. Also look for **Polis** (Tel. 298684 for directions), one of Bali's best antique and furniture shops. This is where many foreign dealers come to make their selections.

Be sure to visit two galleries in the famous woodcarving village of **Mas**. The **Ida Bagus Tilem Gallery** (Tel. 975099) produces and sells the works of Indonesia's premier wood carvers—Ida Bagus Njana and his son Tilem. This is a beautiful gallery consisting of a large compound with woodcarvers at work and a two-story shop-gallery. One section of the gallery is actually a museum with gorgeous carvings which, of course, are not for sale. While the carvings here are very expensive, they are all exquisite works of art. Tilem is now considered to be Bali's best carver. To own a carving from this place is to be a true connoisseur of Bali's finest woodcarving tradition. To a very large extent Ida Bagus Njana made Balinese carvings world famous for their graceful and elongated lines and carved in hibiscus wood. Tilem is well noted for his wonderful carved birds. Across the street is the **Tantra Gallery**, owned by the younger brother of Tilem. The quality of carvings here is also excellent. This large gallery actually consists of two shops, one selling woodcarvings and the other offering carved Balinese doors (carved on both sides), masks, paintings, ikat, and batik.

The area in and around the town of **Gianyar** has numerous factory shops selling textiles and woodcarved banana trees, cactus, and garudas. You can easily spend a half day in this beautiful area browsing from one factory shop to another.

If you are interested in shopping at a large market for inexpensive arts and crafts, be sure to visit the **Sukawati Art Market** in the village of Sukawati. Here you will find an extremely crowded and congested two-story market with numerous stalls crammed with textiles, woodcarvings, jewelry, and T-shirts produced in home factories. This can be a fun market for those who enjoy bargain hunting and friendly haggling rather than for quality shopping. Be sure to carefully examine your purchases since some items may be seconds. Given the very dark and crowded conditions inside the market, you may need to take an item outside the market in order to carefully examine it in the light! Across the street from the Sukawati Art Market is the fresh market which also has numerous vendors selling locally produced baskets.

Quality Shopping

As we noted earlier, quality products are hard to find in Bali given the two types of buyers drawn to this island: the $7-a-day budget travelers and dealers. The first group spends little on shopping for items other than what they can wear—T-shirts, bags, costume jewelry, and cassettes. Dealers primarily look for inexpensive items they can resell abroad. Indeed, Bali is a dealer's heaven, especially for cheap silver jewelry, clothes, leather goods, and woodcarved masks, animals, banana trees, and flowers. Such items end up in numerous gift and handicraft shops around the world at five to 10 times the prices found in Bali. Consequently, Bali offers a good range of inexpensive clothes, jewelry, and woodcarvings to meet the needs of these two groups. Quality shoppers and collectors will probably do better shopping in Jakarta.

More and more quality shopping is moving into what used to be the sleepy artist village of **Ubud** as well as the road north of Kuta, **Jl. Raya Kerobokan**, and along the road to Nusa Dua, **Jl. By Pass Ngurah Rai**. When in Ubud, remember the two main streets are often referred to in both English and Indonesian. The Main Street is called **Jl. Raya Ubud** and Monkey Forest Road is called **Jl. Wanara Wana**.

As the same time, you can find excellent quality products in the midst of all the tourist kitsch if you know where to go for quality. Some of Bali's best shops—several of which were mentioned earlier—include the following:

BEST OF THE BEST

ANTIQUES

☐ **Polos:** *Jl. Legian 319, Kuta, Tel. 751316.* This is one of Bali's very best antique shops. Here you will find excellent quality furniture from Java and the island of Madura as well as many ethnographic carvings, boxes, and artifacts. While this is a small shop, be sure to see additional items in the back room and the back yard. Better still, get directions to visit their huge warehouse in Celuk near Batubulan. Many international dealers in search of quality antiques and furniture only buy at Polos when visiting Bali.

☐ **Shalimar:** *Ubud Main Street, Ubud, Tel. 977115.* Located across the road from the huge Central Market, this relatively new shop is a real find in Ubud. Tastefully decorated in air-conditioned comfort, it includes a fine collection of antiques, carvings, textiles, and decorative pieces. Well organized with price lists and displays.

☐ **Anang's Art Shop:** *Jl. Legian 50, Kuta, Tel. 752480.* Includes a very unique collection of ethnic arts and antiques from throughout Indonesia: carvings, boxes, baskets, pottery, and textiles. Anang also operates a large furniture shop and warehouse on the road to Nusa Dua (Jl. By Pass Ngurah Rai No. 3X, Tel. 755281).

❑ **Kaliuda Gallery:** *Jl. By Pass Ngurah Rai 107, Suwung Kauh, Tel. 724460.* Operated by Fenny Laurens, the daughter of Eddy Laurens, this expansive shop includes lots of furniture, art, and antiques. However, the really unique antiques are found at Eddy Laurens' residence. You'll need to go to this shop first and ask to talk with Eddy about seeing his collection. If he's available, you'll be taken to his house where you will see an incredible collection of ethnographic art and antiques from Timor and Sumatra (Batak), everything from old carvings to huge stone carved pieces. Be sure to bargain hard here. His prices can be outrageous—fit for the New York Metropolitan Museum! Offer him one-third of the asking price and be willing to walk away. A very special place to shop.

❑ **Asmat Kamoro:** *Jl. Patih Jelantik 175, Kuta, Tel. 755625.* Located on the corner near Jl. Majapahit, you can't miss this shop; it has a character of its own. This very crowded and cramped shop specializes in tribal artifacts from Irian Jaya. While you can find lots of junk here, if you dig enough, you may find an occasional treasure. Look for long carved Asmat poles, shields, drums, penis sheaths, axes, and bows and arrows.

❑ **Floren Art Shop II:** *Monkey Forest Road, Ubud.* Located across the street with the popular Café Wayan, this shop specializes in antiques, furniture, and textiles from Timor. Also has four other branch shops in Ubud, Kuta, Gianyar, and Benoa. Offers some very unique pieces.

❑ **Rococo Antiques:** *Main Road (Jl. Raya Ubud), Ubud, Tel. 974805.* Offers a nice selection of antique handicrafts as well as textiles, baskets, and furniture. Be sure to visit the building in the rear of the compound which houses colonial style furniture.

FURNITURE

❑ **Warisan Gallery:** *Jl. Raya Kerobokan, Kuta, Tel. 730710.* Located north of Kuta and Legian, beyond the Oberoi Hotel and on the left side of the road, this is Bali's best furniture and furnishings shop. Its expansive two-storey showroom nicely displays old and new Indonesian furniture, accessories, decorative pieces, fabrics, textiles, ceramics, and jewelry reflecting the Italian influences of its

owner. Warisan also has a factory which produces reproduction furniture. Ask to see their catalog of model
furniture from which to order pieces. Known for quality
and reliability. Works with many dealers worldwide. If
you're looking for only one place to purchase furniture, be
sure to first visit Warisan. You won't be disappointed.
The long trip through Kuta and Legian to get here is well
worth the trouble. One added bonus: the French restaurant just off the showroom which is outstanding for both
lunch and dinner. At least plan your visit so you can have
lunch at the pleasant outdoor restaurant near the back of
the shop.

❑ **Puri Sakana Gallery:** *Batubulan, Tel. 298205.* Located on
both sides of the main road, this huge emporium of
furniture and antiques is one of our long-time favorites.
Owned and operated by Mr. Wayan, who has a keen eye
for collecting quality antiques, especially ethnographic
pieces, you definitely should stop here for at least 30
minutes of browsing through the many rooms of furniture
and antiques. Includes both antique and reproduction
furniture which is produced in its factory-shop. The place
where Sylvester Stallone, Steven Seagal, and their celebrity friends come to shop for custom-made furniture and
antiques.

❑ **Jonathan Bali's Furniture:** *Jl. Kerobokan 10, Br. Taman,
Kuta, Tel. 739563.* This is the furniture showroom owned
by the same people who own Jonathan Gallery in Kuta,
one of Bali's best gold and silver shops. Offers good
quality tables, chests, beds, chairs, and cabinets which are
nicely displayed both inside and outside the main showroom. Will make furniture to your specifications. Works
with many dealers in exporting furniture abroad.

❑ **Kamarkini Gallery:** *Lungsiakan, Ubud, Tel. 975296.*
Located on the road to the Amandari Resort. Offers good
quality antique furniture, silver, jewelry, textiles, and
wayang puppets in a pleasant country setting

❑ **Anang:** *Jl. By Pass Ngurah Rai 3X, Tuban, Tel. 755281.*
Offers a good selection of quality Indonesian colonial and
ethic antique furniture. Will custom-make furniture using
old woods.

❑ **Sri Sedana:** *Jl. By Pass Ngurah Rai Km. 30 (Sebelah Planet Bali), Tel. 776608 or Fax 777558, Jimbaran.* Offers excellent quality furniture accompanied by good service. Specializes in antique colonial and ethnic Indonesia furniture as well as produces reproduction furniture. Popular with furniture shoppers in Bali. Ask for Mrs. Palupi or Mr. Handoyo. For more information, visit *www.angelfire.com/ns/balinita/index.html.*

❑ **Teck Coco:** *Jl. Pura Petitenget 110 X, Kerobokan, Kuta, Tel./Fax 730170.* Another shop offering excellent quality furniture accompanied by good service. Specializes in producing reproduction antique colonial and ethnic Indonesian furniture. Can combine coconut and teakwood materials. Popular with furniture shoppers. Ask for Mr. Budi Artha. Visit *www.angelfire.com/ns/balinita/index.html* for more information.

❑ **Sonata Antik:** *Jl. Raya Batubulan 45, Batabulan, Tel. 298259, Web: www.SonataAntiques.com.* Offers excellent quality antique furniture but primarily focuses on producing new teakwood furniture for export. Has factories in Jakarta, East Java, and Bali producing lots of new furniture for dealers abroad. Nice quality and designs. Ask for a copy of their full color catalog which includes examples of their work. But be very careful in buying here. While ostensibly a reputable place, we've encountered some major problems with their shipping and customer service. We hesitate recommending Sonata for shipping. Do so only on a "collect" basis. Better still, find someone else who has a good reputation for reliable shipping and work with them on shipping goods purchased at Sonata Antik.

❑ **Kadek Nadhi:** *Jl. Raya Batubulan, Batubulan, Tel. 298105.* Located near both Puri Sakana and Sonata Antik, this cramped factory-shop offers both antique and reproduction furniture as well as masks and bowls. Excellent prices compared to most other places producing similar furniture. Folding teak chairs, for example, go for US$30 here whereas many other shops sell the identical chair for over US$60.

❑ **Mariyah Jaya:** *Jl. Tunjung Mekar 87, Br. Plase, Kuta, Tel. 754259.* Deals in good quality Indonesian ethnic furniture. Excellent workmanship and reputable.

❑ **Gong:** *Jl. Batuan, Ubud, Tel. 298269.* Offers a large collection of antique and reproduction furniture along with lots of carvings and handicrafts. Huge complex with a demonstration area for visitors.

❑ **Andy's Gallery:** *Jl. Raya Br. Taman Kerobokan No. 15, Kuta.* Offers an eclectic mix of furniture and carvings nicely displayed on two levels. Includes both antique and reproduction furniture. Has attractive wedding chests.

JEWELRY

❑ **Jonathan Gallery:** *109 Legian Road, Tel. 54209.* What a pleasant change from the helter-skelter shops that tend to dominate this street. If you are looking for inexpensive as well as good quality gold and silver jewelry, be sure to stop at this fine shop. You'll find a good selection of neckpieces, rings, bracelets, pins, and flatwear nicely displayed around primitive and folk art pieces. Many dealers come here to buy for their shops in Australia, Europe, and North America. The wholesale section is on the second floor.

❑ **Treasures:** *Main Street (Jl. Raya Ubud), Ubud, Tel. 976-697.* Located next to Ari's Warang and across the street from the Lotus Café, this small and inviting (if you can squeeze through the small Balinese door!) shop showcases the attractive gold jewelry creations of three expat designers: Carolyn Tyler, Penny Berton, and Jean-Francois.

❑ **Seraphim:** *Monkey Forest Road (Jl. Wanara Wana), Ubud, Tel. 973287.* Truly a surprising oasis, especially on a hot and tiring day walking along Monkey Forest Road! Entering this air-conditioned small jewelry shop reminds one of a different place—perhaps a shop in Sydney. Displays the creations of a talented Australian jewelry designer who works with opals, amber, and pearls.

❑ **Mario Silver:** *Jl. Raya Seminyak, Kuta, Tel. 730977.* Nicely displayed silver jewelry, from rings to necklaces. Wholesalers are escorted upstairs where they can negotiate a deal of bulk purchases. Has four shops in Legian with "Antonio Silver" being the largest shop.

TEXTILES/CLOTHES

❑ **Arghasoka Gallery**: *Monkey Forest Road, Ubud, Tel. 973231.* Offers a unique collection of batik cloth designed and produced by Isnia of Jokjakarta. The textiles make attractive wall hangings and can be used as shawls.

❑ **Tomboya**: *Monkey Forest Road, Ubud, Tel. 977372.* This nicely appointed shop includes a good collection of clothes, textiles, ethnic art, and antiques.

❑ **Kamar Sutra**: *Monkey Forest Road, Ubud, Tel. 977109.* Located next door to the popular Café Wayang, this shop specializes in fine quality Chinese silk and handmade batik. Look for nicely designed and displayed textiles and scarves. Expensive but top quality.

❑ **Kunang Kunang I & II**: *Main Road, Ubud, Tel. 975714 and 975 716.* Located within 600 meters of each other, these two shops offer a wide selection of arts, crafts, antiques, textiles, jewelry, and gift items. Both shops carry similar lines of products with very few antiques in their midst. Most items can easily be packed in a suitcase. These two shops also are operated by the owner of the nearby restaurant and shop—Murni's Warung

❑ **Nogo**: *Jl. Raya Kuta 47, Kuta, Tel. 754335.* Offers a nice collection of Ikat fabrics, clothes, and crafts. Look for a small loom in the front of this sometimes hard to find shop. If you're looking for a shipper, ask the shop about the owner's brother, Iwan Sumichan, who also has a passion for ethnic art, especially Asmat art.

ARTS AND CRAFTS

❑ **Galeri Keris**: *Galleria Nusa Dua, Tel. 771303. Open daily 9am - 10pm.* If you're looking for a one-stop-shop for all your arts and crafts needs, this is the place to visit. Also known as the Indonesian Handicraft Centre and Department Store, Galeri Keris has a wide selection of arts, crafts, and clothes that make inexpensive and fun gifts. A good place to kill a half hour checking out prices and choices.

❑ **Sukawati Art Market**: *Sukawati.* Located in the village of Sukawati, this is an extremely crowded and congested two-storey market with numerous stalls crammed with textiles, woodcarvings, jewelry, and T-shirts produced in home factories. This can be a fun market for those who enjoy bargain hunting and friendly haggling rather than for quality shopping. Be sure to carefully examine your purchases since some items may be seconds. Given the very dark and crowded conditions inside the market, you may need to take an item outside the market in order to carefully examine it in the light! Across the street from the Sukawati Art Market is the fresh market which also has numerous vendors selling locally produced baskets.

❑ **Wardani's Shop:** *Monkey Forest Road, Ubud, Tel. 975538.* Located near Café Wayang, this shop offers a large selection of baskets, boxes, textiles, and furniture. If you're look for very big baskets, this is the place to visit.

❑ **Toko:** *Monkey Forest Road, Ubud, Tel. 95046.* This upscale shop offers a nice selection of gift items, from batik and jewelry to books and purses.

GIFT ITEMS/HOME DECORATIVE PIECES

❑ **Four Seasons Resort Shop:** *Jimbaran, Tel. 701010.* Offers an excellent collection of tasteful arts, crafts, antiques, jewelry, clothes, and books in a lovely resort setting.

❑ **Amandari Gallery and Amandari Gift Shop:** *Amandari Resort, Ubud.* Located on the grounds of the Amandari resort, these two adjacent shops offer a nice collection of antiques, silver, jewelry, textiles, and wayang puppets. The Gallery is especially worth visiting, although its hours are sometimes unpredictable.

❑ **Archipelo:** *Monkey Forest Road, Ubud, Tel. 975120.* Located across the street from Café Wayan, this nice gift shop offers tastefully designed bags, ceramics, lamps, napkin rings, coconut products, and place mats.

❑ **Kunang Kunang I & II:** *Main Road, Ubud, Tel. 975714 and 975716.* See comments above (page 241) under "Textiles/ Clothes" sections.

❑ **Murni's Warung:** *Campuan, Ubud, Tel. 975233.* Located at the foot of the Main Street, just a few shops from

Kunang Kunang I, this is actually a restaurant with a small two-storey shop attached to it. The shop includes lots of gift items, from textiles to handicrafts.

❏ **Gallery Copper:** *Jl. Raya Legian 477, Kuta, Tel. 761319.* A very small but classy shop offering uniquely designed contemporary home decorative pieces, such as candle holders, lamps, and mirrors.

❏ **Transit Bali:** *Jl. Raya Seminyak 35, Kuta, Tel. 732260.* A nice small gift shop offering candles, carved figures, bags, trays, and more.

WOODCARVINGS

❏ **Ida Bagus Tilem:** *Mas, Ubud, Gianyar, Tel./Fax 975099.* Also known as Njana Tilem Gallery, this gallery represents the works of Indonesia's premier wood carvers—Ida Bagus Njana and his son Tilem. This is a beautiful gallery consisting of a large compound with woodcarvers at work and a two-storey shop-gallery. One section of the gallery is actually a museum with gorgeous carvings which, of course, are not for sale. While the carvings here are very expensive, they also are all exquisite works of art. Tilem is now considered to be Bali's best carver. To own a carving from this place is to be a true connoisseur of Bali's finest woodcarving tradition. To a very large extent, Ida Bagus Njana made Balinese carvings world famous for their graceful and elongated lines and carved in hibiscus wood. Tilem is well noted for his wonderful carved birds.

❏ **Tantra Gallery:** *Mas, Ubud, Gianyar.* Located across the street from Ida Bagus Tilem Gallery, Trantra Gallery is owned by the younger brother of Tilem. The quality of carvings here are also excellent. This large gallery actually consists of two shops, one selling woodcarvings and the other offering carved Balinese doors (carved on both sides), masks, paintings, ikat, and batik.

❏ **Gong Art Gallery:** *Mas, Ubud, Gianyar, Bali. Tel. 975242 or Fax 975242.* This huge complex, complete with a demonstration area, includes lots of woodcarvings, from figures to panels. They also do, as their sign announces, "Antiques—Made to Order".

PAINTINGS

❑ **Neka Gallery**: *Main Road, Ubud*. Adjacent to the Neka Museum, this is one of the premier galleries representing some of Bali's top artists.

❑ **Bamboo Gallery**: *Main Road (in front of BCA Bank), Ubud, Tel. 975037*. Known for representing many of Bali's most promising young artists. Less traditional and more innovative than most other galleries in Bali.

❑ **Komaneka Gallery**: *Monkey Forest Road, Ubud, Tel. 976090*. Represents new generation paintings of local and foreign artists.

❑ **Agung Rai Gallery**: *Jl. Raya Peliatan, Ubud, Gianyar, Tel. 975449*. Representing a community of artists, this gallery offers paintings of some of Indonesia's best young artists.

❑ **Seniwati Gallery of Art by Women**: *Jl. Sriwedari 2b, Banjar Taman, Tel. 975485*. Represents the works of Bali's best female artists. Includes a permanent collection for those interested in tracing the history of female artists.

ART/SCULPTURE

❑ **Konsep Lama Kini**: *Jl. Legian 427, Kuta, Tel. 761167*. An unusual shop for Kuta with a decided "expat artist" look to it. Includes unique sculptures, architectural pieces, boxes, pillows, bowls, jewelry, baskets, old carvings, and textiles. Good quality, well presented, with excellent framing and mounts.

ACCOMMODATIONS

Few places in the world offer such a wide range of excellent resort accommodations as Bali. The very best accommodations will be found in the Jimbaran Bay and Nusa Dua areas. Ubud is fast becoming a center for top quality accommodations. Kuta Beach, as well as parts of Sanur Beach, still remains the center for budget accommodations, although it does boast some excellent quality hotels and resorts. You'll have no problem finding places to fit your particular budget. Here we identify the "best of the best" which also tend to be the most expensive. Treat yourself to at least a night or two in one of these places:

JIMBARAN BAY

❑ **Four Seasons Resort Bali at Jimbaran Bay**: *Jimbaran, Bali 80361, Indonesia, Tel. (62) 361-701010 or Fax (62) 361-701020, or toll-free from U.S. 800-815-5053 or Canada 800-819-5053. Web: www.fourseasons.com*. Whatever may be said of luxury properties anywhere in the world, no superlatives are too great to be used when describing The Four Seasons Resort Jimbaran. The villas, each with its own private plunge pool, huge dressing and bathing areas, open air sala, comfortable beds enclosed in decorative gauze-like mosquito netting, beautiful landscaped gardens of lush tropical vegetation, and sea views of Jimbaran Bay would be enough to convince even the most jaded traveler he had found paradise. Add to these creature comforts, impeccable service including a "buggy" to take you from your villa to anywhere on the property that your heart desires, some of the best restaurants on Bali, a wonderful spa, not to mention the library or Ganesha Art Gallery to promote island art—once you visit Four Seasons you may not want to leave! It is no wonder Four Seasons, Jimbaran, has been a frequent award winner including the coveted *Travel & Leisure's* #1 Resort in Asia and #6 Resort worldwide. The resort is large enough to offer a wide choice of activities, but has the feel of a smaller, boutique resort. The villas (147 units) are airy and spacious. The one-bedroom villas contain expansive indoor and outdoor living areas. Each unit is comprised of three thatched-roof pavilions: an open-air, yet private, two-enclosed sided living and dining area overlooking the private plunge pool and the sea beyond; and two enclosed air-conditioned pavilions which house the sleeping area—also overlooking the sea—and the dressing/closet area and marble bath area replete with an oversized soaking tub, double vanities, separate shower and toilet areas, and an outdoor shower in the adjacent secluded garden. There are two bedroom villas as well as two-unit Royal Villas available. All villas are equipped with compact disc sound system discreetly concealed along with the television and VCR in an amoire, a minibar, make-up/shaving mirror, hairdryer, in-room safe, and an expansive selection of Four Season amenities—including lotion for those who tarry too long in the tropical sun! Mineral water and a tropical fruit selection are provided in the villas daily. Want to shop, but can't tear yourself away from the resort? The on-site shopping boutique and gallery are first rate. The spa facilities have been expanded, and a choice of Balinese, Aroma, Orient and Reflex massage therapies are offered. An aerobic studio, separate gym, two floodlit "Wimbledon" tennis courts, free form swimming pool, beach and watersport equipment including windsurfers, catamarans, surf skis, boagie boards, surf boards, hobie cat, laser sailing boat and snorkeling equipment assure that guests can stay fit and enjoy their stay. Two championship golf courses are nearby. Want to have your wedding or renew your vows in Bali? Four Seasons will help you make arrangements for your special event. Taman Wantelan Restaurant located 98 feet above the bay serves a sumptuous breakfast with a spectacular view. In the evening a candlelight ambience prevails. We have enjoyed many of our best meals in Bali here. The Warung Mie, set in an exotic water garden serves traditional noodle dishes from a variety of Asian cuisines. PJ's beachside restaurant serves seafood specialities and pizzas in a casual setting. Other venues serve light fare or try dining one evening in your villa! When departing Bali, order your meal "to go" two hours in advance of your departure from the resort and it will be delivered to your villa conveniently packaged for easy traveling and eating during your flight. Better yet, take advantage of Four Season's complimentary transfer to their Sayan Resort near Ubud for the inland, tropical highland equivalent of your wonderful oceanfront resort at Jimbaran! Special programs available for corporate meetings, incentive groups and children's activities.

❑ **Ritz-Carlton Bali**: *Jl. Karang Mas Sejahtera, Jimbaran, Bali, 80364, Indonesia, Tel. (62) 361-702222 or Fax (62) 361-701555 or toll-free from U.S. 800-241-3333. Web: www. ritzcarlton.com.* Here's one of Bali's newest surprises—a fabulous resort that manages to deliver the legendary Ritz-Carlton service with the grace and beauty only found in Bali! If there were a contest for the best hospitality service in Asia, the Ritz-Carlton Bali would be at the very top of the list. It simply doesn't get much better. Set on a bluff above Jimbaran Bay, The Ritz-Carlton Bali offers a choice of well-appointed rooms in a four story hotel setting or beautifully appointed villas—each set in its own private compound. Almost all rooms boast a view of the Indian Ocean. The regular guestrooms are comfortable and nicely decorated and provide a balcony with a seating area—a pleasant spot to sit early in the morning and listen to the birds and watch the ocean. But the piece de resistance are the villas, each with its carved Balinese doors leading to your own private compound. Each contains a separate living area and bedroom which adjoins a spectacular bathroom with a tub big enough for two in a setting that gives an outdoor feel even though you are still in air-conditioned comfort. Outside is your private plunge pool and a bale bengong—a gazebo-like structure with huge cushions for lounging outside or you can have the hotel masseuse ease your muscles after a busy day of shopping in Kuta or enjoying the sports facilities of the resort. Although a perfect spot for a wedding or honeymoon—the resort has a honeymoon consultant that will help couples plan their wedding or custom tailor their honeymoon activities—the Ritz-Carlton literally has something for everyone. The two bedroom villas make bringing the children a breeze. The resort has activities planned especially for children with "The Ritz-Carlton Kids"—a daily program of supervised activities especially chosen to share the world of Balinese art, drama, and traditions for children ages four to ten. Children can make masks, decorations and batik paintings with the help of Balinese staff artists. They learn Balinese dance under the shade of coconut trees. They can stage their own performance for parents at the amphitheater. Adults may choose to learn more about island culture through both on-site and off-site daily activities programs called "Cultural Pathfinder." The Bali Club Floor provides guests with a wide range of service amenities. In addition to five complimentary food and beverage presentations daily, Ritz-Carlton Club guests receive unlimited play on the 18-hole golf putting course; one hour use of the tennis pavilion; laundry and pressing complimentary for the first four pieces per room; and late check-out privileges to 4:00pm. In addition to the Fitness Center, a full range of water sports are available: swimming—a two-tiered infinity-edged pool overflows into the lower level via a waterfall—boating, rafting, diving, deep-sea fishing among them. Conference Facilities are available and memorable theme parties can be organized from an elegant "Royal Rijstaffel Dinner" to a lively "Jungle Night". With so many choices of luxurious accommodation, the expected Ritz-Carlton service, beautiful grounds, and variety of activities, it is little wonder the Ritz-Carlton Bali was named one of the top five Asian resorts by *Conde Nast Traveler*.

❑ **Inter-Continental Hotel**: *Jl. Uluwatu 45, Jimbaran, Bali 80361, Indonesia, Tel. (62) 361-701888 or Fax (62) 361-701777.* From a distance this Inter-Continental could be almost anywhere. Only the grounds covered with tropical foliage and the large lotus pond at the entrance, flanked by large stone garudas convey to the guest he is in exotic Bali. From the carefully detailed large pavilions that house the public areas to the interior decor of its 214 guest-rooms decorated with Balinese ornamentation, the subtle Balinese features are evident. Restaurants, Health/Fitness facilities and Business/Conference facilities.

KUTA/LEGIAN

❑ **Oberoi Hotel**: *Jl. Laksmana, Legian Beach, Denpasar, Bali 80033, Indonesia, Tel. (62) 361-730361 or Fax (62) 361-730791.* A member of the Leading Hotels of the World and the Small Luxury Hotels of the World, the Oberoi Bali features luxurious accommodations in traditional Balinese style in a peaceful, oceanside setting of 15 acres of tropical gardens. The 60 thatched-roof Lanai cottages—each with private balcony—are built in clusters of four around a central rock pond. The bathroom is set in a private walled garden appointed with a marble sunken tub and double vanity. Some units have a separate shower stall as well as a walk-in closet. The 15 villas have a walled courtyard ensuring absolute privacy, a dining pavilion for intimate dining. Each of the villa bathrooms has a walk-in closet and luggage storage area, two vanity counters, separate stalls for shower and toilet, and a sunken bath-tub. Several villas have their own pool. Royal Villas have two open air garden bathrooms and a kitchenette. All rooms have minibar, in-room safe, daily fruit basket, hairdryer, IDD telephone, satellite television, video CD player. Try the Kura Kura Restaurant for Indonesian, Asian and continental cuisine or the Frangipani Café for fresh seafood and light meals. The recently opened Lotus Arts de Vivre boutique offers true haute couture jewelry and objets d'art. Open air massage pavilions are a popular feature of the Health Spa, complimentary sauna, gym-nasium, and tennis court. Business Center/Conference Room.

❑ **Bali Padma Hotel**: *Jl. Padma 1, Legian, Bali, Indonesia, Tel. (62) 361-752111 or Fax (62) 361-752140.* Located on Legian Beach, and a few steps away from the main road of Kuta with its myriad shopping venues, the Padma incorporates traditional Balinese architecture in a low rise hotel. Expansive and comfortable open air public areas and large guestrooms furnished in typical island decor. Ample bathrooms, minibar, IDD telephone, international and local channel television. Guestrooms on the ground level have patios and upper levels have private balconies. Nicely landscaped tropical grounds with greenery and lotus ponds—the Padma logo incorporates the lotus flower. Restaurants feature Asian cuisine and a separate restaurant serves Japanese selections, a pizzeria and a café with an a la carte international menu. Large swimming pool, fitness center, business services. A bit less spectacular than some of the other featured hotels and less expensive, the Padma represents good value. It is just off the main road so as to be quiet and peaceful, but a few minutes walk puts the guest smack-dab in the hustle of Kuta.

SANUR

❏ **Bali Hyatt**: *Jl. Danau Tamblingan, Sanur, Denpasar, Bali 80228, Indonesia, Tel. (62) 361-281234 or Fax (62) 361-287693. Web: www.hyatt.com* Set on the beachfront in Sanur, from the large airy reception entrance pavilion with its large Indonesian chests and typical island decor to its 390 guestrooms with marble baths and balconies set in low-rise four story buildings accented with local crafts, the guest experiences tropical Bali. Regency Club rooms are an upgrade and offer complimentary breakfast, coffee, evening cocktails and newspapers. The lower level features a nice shopping arcade with some quality shops. Grounds are neatly manicured with ponds set amidst the tropical greenery. Great breakfasts are served amidst the tranquil setting of the lower level coffee shop which shares indoor and outdoor spaces. More tranquil than the newer, larger Grand Hyatt in Nusa Dua, this property in Sanur should not be confused with the other. There is a shuttle service between the two Hyatt properties. Health/Fitness facilities and Business Facilities. It is possible to walk to many restaurants and shops along Jl. Tamblingan.

❏ **Tandjung Sari**: *Jl. Danau Tamblingan #41, Sanur, Denpasar, Bali 80228, Indonesia, Tel. (62) 361-288441 or Fax (62) 361-287930.* The Tandjung Sari is the first of the boutique hotels in Bali and perhaps in Southeast Asia.

Comprised of 29 separate bungalows created from traditional Balinese materials and constructed in typical Balinese style. From the moment the ceremonial welcome gong is struck to announce his arrival, the guest enters a tranquil enclave watched over and attended to by a staff of nearly 100. There are a variety of bungalow sizes and styles featuring both one and two level living. The largest, a family bungalow, has two bedrooms. Each bungalow is individual in its design and set in its own private garden. All provide king or queen size beds, IDD telephones, refrigerators and hairdryers and of course, all are air-conditioned and provide expected amenities. Set in tropical gardens on Sanur beach, the Tandjung Sari retains the ambience of a private resort. Small stone temples with the ubiquitous pagoda shape and thatched roof discreetly dot the grounds. Stone statues of deities are framed in niches. The grounds are truly beautiful and peaceful, and you can feel Bali before the crush of tourism here. Both Balinese and Dutch colonial antiques are set in the backdrop of Balinese traditional architecture. Though an older property in a climate that is not a friend to dwellings constructed by man, the Tandjung Sari has been well maintained. It is possible to walk to several restaurants and shops along Jl. Tamblingan. Tandjung Sari has established a foundation to study, revive, and nurture the traditional culture in all its forms with the initial program focusing on Balinese dance and music.

Nusa Dua

❑ **Amanusa**: *Nusa Dua, Bali 80363, Indonesia, Tel. (62) 361-771 267 or Fax (62) 361-771266 or toll-free from the U.S. & Canada, 800-447-7462. Web: www.amanresorts.com/ nusa_m. html.* Perhaps not as well known as its sister highland resort in the center of the island—Amandari—Amanusa is the Amanresort's most central hideaway–not far from Kuta, Sanur and Legian. From its hilltop location overlooking the sea, Amanusa enjoys tropical island views and tradewinds. The 35 thatched roof suites are set behind traditionally designed attractive stone walls. Each suite is divided into a large living area and spacious bathroom. The living area includes a four-poster bed, a table for private dining and a TV and stereo system. There is also a balcony with an oversized daybed under a canopy. The bath features a marble-tiled tub enclosed in a glass wall recessed into a lily pond. Sliding doors lead to an outside shower built into a high stone wall. Several suites have their own private swimming pools. The main pool is smashing. The Terrace Restaurant offers Indonesian and Thai cuisine; The Restaurant specializes in Italian cuisine. The Gallery and Gift Shop maintain a select range of Balinese and Indonesian crafts and antiques. Large pool, two all-weather floodlit tennis courts, beach club, nearby Bali Golf and Country Club. Boardroom can accommodate up to 30 people. With Amanresorts and its three, distinctly different island resorts: Amandari, Amankila and Amanusa, the guest has the choice of enjoying one or trying all three!

❑ **Grand Hyatt Bali**: *Nusa Dua, Bali 80363, Indonesia, Tel. (62) 361-771234 or Fax (62) 361-772038*. Reminiscent of a Balinese water palace and set amidst 40 acres of lagoons, tropical gardens and several swimming pools, this low rise resort on the beach in NusaDua is convenient by vehicle to Sanur, Kuta and Legian. Rooms are large with balconies and are decorated in traditional Balinese style. Bathrooms have separate shower stall. All rooms have satellite TV, IDD phone, in-room safe, and hairdryer. The self-contained Regency Club Village's lounge offers complimentary continental breakfast, all day tea and coffee service, evening cocktails, and its own private swimming pool. Restaurants serve a variety of cuisines: Indonesian, Italian, Japanese and European. There is a shopping village; fitness and health center; water sports; convention facilities.

❑ **Bali Hilton International**: *Jl. Raya Nusa Dua, NusaDua, Bali 80363, Indonesia, Tel. (62) 361-771102 or Fax (62) 361-771616, or toll-free in U.S. 800-445-8667*. Located on the beach and set amid 30 acres of landscaped tropical gardens, the five story buildings form a "U" around the large reception pavilion and Balinese styled courtyards. Exteriors have a decided Balinese appearance and the large waterfall makes a definite statement. Good sized rooms are decorated in an island resort style and have balconies. Club rooms are slightly larger and feature a separate guest registration. Several restaurants offer a variety of cuisine choices. Fitness facilities and water sports; business and conference facilities.

❑ **Sheraton Laguna Nusa Dua**: *Nusa Dua, Bali 80363, Indonesia, Tel. (62) 361-771327 or Fax (62) 361-771326.*

Web: www.luxurycollection.com. The "Laguna" in the name says it all. How many hotels allow you to step directly from your room into the pool? Not just any pool, but one that winds its way through the property. Rooms are spacious with an island decor. The large wood and marble bathrooms offer all the amenities. Guestrooms have IDD telephone, cable TV, minibar, and in-room safe. Several restaurants offer a choice of menus: seafood and a variety of regional and European cuisines. Fitness facilities and water sports. Business Center.

UBUD

❑ **Four Seasons Resort at Sayan:** *Sayan, Ubud, Gianyar, Bali 80571, Indonesia, Tel. (62) 361-977577 or Fax (62) 361-977588 or toll-free from U.S. 800-815-5053 or Canada 800-819-5053.* A stunning and unusual property, the Four Seasons Sayan near Ubud overlooks the Ayung River as it flows through the central highlands of Bali. Whereas the Jimbaran Four Seasons Resort features traditional Balinese architecture, Sayan is contemporary, yet blends seamlessly into its lush tropical riverside setting. Architecturally the two resorts are worlds apart, but the same attention to detail and impeccable service pervade both properties. Enter Sayan across a wooden bridge to the elliptical reception hall—topped by a large lotus pond. The lotus pond rests on the roof of the resort's three-level central building. As you descend the stairway to the reception and lounge level, the 180 degree vista of lush, tropical vegetation opens up and surrounds you. Sayan features 46 beautifully appointed units including suites as well as one and two bedroom private villas, plus the Royal Villa. Extending from the top of the hillside down to the river's edge, Sayan offers one of the most impressive views of the "sacred" Auyung River valley. The villas are literally tucked into the landscape, with lily ponds and lush vegetation covering most signs of the luxurious accommodations that lie beneath. The villas include private plunge pools and afford total privacy, yet offer views of the river valley. The peaceful sounds of the running river can be heard from plunge pools of the villas closest to the river. All accommodations feature custom-made furnishings fabricated in Java and Bali. Each guest unit features a selection of local art skillfully displayed and perfectly lighted. Each suite and villa feature both spacious indoor and outdoor living space, dual line telephone with computer/fax connection capabilities, CD sound system, televison with satellite reception and a VCR is available on request. The marble baths feature separate shower and soaking tub, and a separate toilet enclosure. Large walk-in closets provide an in-room safe, plenty of space for hanging clothing as well as drawers for folded items and space for luggage. A make-up/shaving mirror, hairdryer, and Four Seasons amenities provide all the comforts of home—and then some! Three resort boutiques provide a variety of items from textiles and clothing, home decorative items, antiques and artwork, oils and bath salts, and incense, paper products, and jewelry. The spa offers various therapeutic massage and aromatherapy treatments which focus on preparations authentic to villages of Bali. An exercise facility, endless outdoor activities in the area—trekking, cycling, river rafting, kayaking or swimming in Sayan's pool—will keep the activity enthusiast occupied. Sayan has two restaurants–Ayung Terrace for elegant dining and breathtaking views and Riverside Café for casual, poolside dining. The Jati Bar is a comfortable lounge with a panoramic view. Meeting facilities available.

❑ **Amandari**: *Kedewatan, Ubud, Bali 80571, Indonesia, Tel. (62) 361-975333 or Fax (62) 361-975335, or toll-free from U.S. & Canada 800-447-7462.* The Amanresorts were one of the first to use local materials and art as well as indigenous architectural styles combined with luxury and all the modern amenities a guest could want. They are still one of the best and receive constant accolades from guests and top awards from travel magazines' reader surveys. Amandari was the first of three Amanresorts on Bali. It is set among rice terraces on a hillside overlooking the Ayung River gorge below. Tall stone walls enclose gardens that surround thatched roofed villas laid out like a traditional Balinese village. The lush tropical foliage and lotus ponds provide a sense of tranquility that pervades this boutique hotel. Its 30 suites have spacious rooms and baths decorated with comfortable and attractive furnishings and textiles from the Indonesian islands. A chest from Madura that doubles as seating, accents and adds warmth to the rooms. The baths have a large indoor shower and separate toilet area, and a sunken outdoor soaking tub is a wonderful place to draw a bubble bath and relax under the stars! The duplex suites feature a spiral staircase which leads to the upstairs sleeping area. CD players and satellite TV in guestrooms, cordless phones, minibar and hairdryers. The restaurant serves delicious food—some of the best—but the magical night setting is the most memorable. The restaurant overlooks a fan-shaped infinity edged pool that appears by day, to drop off into the river gorge below. At night, a single musician plays under a lone palm tree situated on a small island set near the center of the edge of the pool. A beam of light shines on the musician giving an almost ethereal quality to the moment. Amandari translates as "peaceful spirits" in Sanskrit, if you stay here, you will soon be a believer! Shoppers will find the Gift Shop and Gallery provide quality shopping. Old and antique wood figures, textiles, and jewelry are available. You are only minutes by vehicle from Ubud and its wonderful shops for art and crafts. Service is exceptional. Health club, spa with options of traditional Balinese treatments, resort sport activities, tennis courts, trekking and that wonderful pool! Spend all your time here, or spend some time at one of their beach resorts: Amanusa or Amankila.

MANGGIS

❑ **Amankila**: *Manggis, Bali, Indonesia, Tel. (62) 363-41333 or Fax (62) 363-41555 or toll-free from U.S. & Canada 800-447-7462.* The third of the Amanresorts located on Bali, Amankila is set on a cliffside overlooking the Lombok Strait in East Bali. This resort is also a frequent award winner. The suites are elevated to take advantage of the spectacular views to the sea. The 35 free-standing suites with thatched roofs each feature a large bedroom with wide window views, a canopied, four pillared bed, a writing desk and music system. The bathroom is dominated by double terrazzo vanities fitted with seashell-finished taps. A separate shower is located next to the tub and the toilet is in a separate enclosed space. Large dressing areas paneled with coconut wood lay at both ends of the terrazzo-tiled combination bath. The outdoor terrace of each suite provides a large daybed, a terrazzo table and chairs. Seven suites, including the Amankila suite come with private pools. The Restaurant, which is open only for dinner. serves European and Asian cuisine. It overlooks stunning views of the ocean. The Terrace, serves breakfast and lunch and offers selections from both East and West. Amankila's Gallery sells a quality selection of local products, as well as arranges trips to nearby villages famed for their crafts for those guests who prefer to shop at the source! The triple tiered swimming pool is spectacular. Spa treatments available. Water Sports, cruising, trekking, touring.

RESTAURANTS

Bali may impress visitors with its arts, crafts, culture, landscapes, and outstanding resorts, but it does not abound in outstanding restaurants. It does have many inexpensive eateries that cater to budget travelers. It also has many good restaurants, but few that are truly outstanding. The best restaurants tend to be found in the top hotels and resorts and offer Western cuisine. Indeed, many of the chefs are French, Italian, British, and American. We are increasingly finding good restaurants in Bali. Most dining takes place in open-air restaurants. Among our favorites are:

JIMBARAN BAY

❑ **The Dining Room** and **Pantai Jimbaran (PJ's) Restaurant**: *Four Seasons Resort, Jimbaran.* Two fine restaurants overlooking Jimbaran Bay. The Dining Room overlooks the bay and is very romantic in the evening. PJ's is the beachfront restaurant serving excellent seafood; especially good for lunch.

❑ **Ko Japanese Restaurant:** *Bali Intercontinental Hotel Jimbaran, Tel. 701888, 6:30pm to 11pm.* Tenpanyaki and Tatami.

❑ **La Indonesia:** *Jl. Raya Uluwatu 108, Jimbaran, Tel. 701-763, 11am to 11pm.* Several excellent Indonesian cuisine.

❑ **Jimbaran Fish Markets:** Several open-air restaurants serve excellent grilled seafood on the beach.

NUSA DUA

❑ **Terrace Restaurant:** *Amanusa Resort, Tel. 772333, 11:30am to 11pm.* International and Thai cuisine.

❑ **Italian Restaurant:** *Amanusa Resort, Tel. 772333, 6:30pm to 11pm.* Italian cuisine.

❑ **Lagoona:** *Bali Hilton Hotel, Tel. 771102, 11am to 11pm.* Seafood and grill.

❑ **Lotus Garden:** *Jl. Bypass Ngurah Rai, Tel. 771710, 9am to 11pm.* European and Indonesia cuisine.

❑ **Ikan Restaurant:** *Nusa Indah Sheraton Hotel Nusa Dua, 10am to 11pm.* Specializes in seafood and local Balinese cuisine.

SANUR

❑ **Kul Kul:** *Jl. Tanjung Sari, across from Penida View Hotel, Sanur, Tel. 88038.* Elegant outdoor dining.

❑ **Telaga Naga Restaurant:** *Jl. Tanjung Sari, across from Bali Hyatt Hotel, Sanur.* Elegant outdoor dining. Chinese.

❑ **Tanjung Sari Hotel Restaurant:** *Jl. Tanjung Sari, Sanur.* Excellent Indonesian cuisine in a romantic setting.

❑ **Spice Islander:** *Bali Hyatt Hotel, Sanur.* Elegant indoor dining.

UBUD

❑ **Amandari Resort Restaurant:** *Amandari Resort, Ubud.* Fabulous for both lunch and dinner. Reserve a day ahead since restaurant only seats 66 people. Great ambience—often magical and accompanied terrific service—at night.

❑ **Cafe Wayan:** *Monkey Forest Road, Ubud, Tel. 975447, 7am to 10;30pm.* Our favorite restaurant in Ubud and centrally located for shopping. Very pleasant outdoor dining. Excellent selections, service, and location. Serves both Western and Indonesian dishes. Always reliable. The friendliest and most helpful service in Bali.

❑ **Casa Luna:** *Jl. Raya Ubud, Tel. 96283, 9am to 11pm.* Serves Mediterranean and Balinese cuisine. Offers many innovative dishes plus wonderful Western desserts.

❑ **Ary's Warung:** *Jl. Raya Ubud, Tel. 975053, 9am to midnight.* Centrally located, this pleasant restaurant offers Western and Indonesian dishes. Both downstairs and upstairs dining areas.

❑ **Lotus Café:** *Jl. Ubud, Ubud.* A long-time favorite of travelers in a pleasant downtown setting. Offers both Western and Indonesian dishes.

Kuta/Legian

❑ **Warisan:** *Jl. Raya Kerobokan, Seminyak, Tel. 731175, open for lunch and dinner.* Offers excellent French and Italian cuisine at Bali's top home decorative and furniture shop. Great place to both shop and eat!

❑ **Kura Kura Restaurant:** *Oberoi Hotel, Legian, Tel. 730361, 7am to 10pm.* Serves International and Indian cuisine in a wonderful and romantic outdoor setting.

❑ **Kin Khao:** *Jl. Kartika Plaza 170, Tel. 757808, 11am to midnight.* Serves Thai cuisine.

❑ **Ketupat:** *Jl. Legian 109, Tel. 654209, 12noon to 11pm.* Located behind Jonathan Gallery, this attractive restaurant serves excellent Indonesian dishes. Great please to both shop and eat.

❑ **La Lucciola:** *Jl. Kayu Aya-Peti Tenget, Seminyak, Tel. 261047, 8am to midnight.* Serves wonderful Italian cuisine on the beach.

❑ **Made's Warung:** *Jl. Pantai Kuta, Kuta, Tel. 751923, 8:30am to midnight.* Serves Indonesian and European dishes.

❑ **Yanies Restaurant & Bar:** *Jl. Tunjung Mekar, Legian, Tel. 751292.* This pleasant corner restaurant and bar is great place to escape from the heat of the day. Don't play with the cute cockatoo swinging on its open perch—it really bites!

❑ **Poppies:** *Off Jl. Legian, Poppies Lane 1, Kuta, Tel. 751059, 6:30am to 11pm.* Literally an institution in Kuta. Inexpensive Indonesian and European cuisine.

❑ **Hard Rock Café:** *Jl. Legian, Kuta, Tel. 755661, 11am to 11pm; live hand from 11pm to 2am.* Serves best hamburgers in Bali.

ENJOYING YOUR STAY

There's plenty to see and do in Bali in addition to shopping. You can easily spend weeks lying on beaches, scuba diving, sailing, visiting temples and villages, observing art performances and ceremonies, learning to make arts and crafts, or touring the countryside and taking pictures. Of all places in Indonesia, Bali has the largest variety of things to see and do.

Some of the most popular sightseeing attractions and things to do in Bali include:

❑ **Touring the island:** Many tour groups provide half or full-day tours of Bali's many regions. Alternatively, you can hire a car and driver to see the major highlights of the island. Most tours include time to shop since crafts are so important in Balinese life. Most will stop at major towns and villages, such as Celuk (silver), Sukawati (art and handicraft market), Mas (woodcarvings), and Ubud (paintings and crafts). You are also likely to visit a few of the major temples, such as Besakih, Pura Taman Ayun, and Tanah Lot, see the elephant cave (Goa Gajah) and monkey forest, stop at a palace, and view Lake Batur. You'll find many travel agencies located in Denpasar, Kuta, and Sanur. Most major hotels will have a tour desk, and other hotels can arrange group or private tours.

❑ **Temples:** Bali has nine major temples. The three most popular ones are the Pura Besakih, Pura Taman Ayun, and Tanah Lot. Pura Besakih, known as the mother temple, is Bali's holiest place. The trip here takes you through some spectacular countryside of terraced rice fields and mountains. Once at the base of the temple complex, you may want to ride on the back of a motor-bike (Rp. 1,000) for the long trip to the temple gates. Otherwise, it's a long hot walk. Pura Taman Ayun is considered the most beautiful temple in Bali. Tanah Lot is an intriguing temple built on a small rock island which is connected to the main island during low tide. This is a popular place to watch spectacular sunsets. Try to arrive around sunset time when you should be able to get some wonderful photos.

❑ **Museums:** Bali has a few public and private museums throughout the island. The major one is the Bali Museum in Denpasar (Jl. Surapatwith its extensive collection of traditional Balinese art. The Puri Lukisan ("Palace of Paintings") museum in Ubud displays some of the best examples of modern Balinese paintings, drawings, and sculptures. Several galleries also have museum sections which display top quality art. While many pieces may not be for sale, others may; it's best to ask when you visit these museums. Njana Tilem Gallery in Mas, for example, has a museum of exquisite woodcarvings on the second floor. Neka Museum in Ubud displays many of Indonesia's famous artists.

❑ **Beaches:** Many visitors to Bali just want to lie on the beach and relax for a few days. The best beaches are found in the Nusa Dua, Kuta, and Sanur areas. If you like beaches, you might prefer staying at a beachfront hotel. However, lying on the beach does not necessarily take you away from shopping. In Sanur, for example, you will find a market (Beach Market I Sanur) fronting the beach next to the Bali Beach Hotel as well as many hawkers and masseuses approaching sun bathers. One word of caution: be very careful how long you stay on the beach and use a good sun screen product. Bali's equatorial sunlight can quickly give you a bad case of sun burn, even on overcast days.

❑ **Water sports:** Most of the major beach front hotels have a full range of water sports organized for guests. Outrigger sailboats are very popular with visitors and are readily available for rental along the beaches. You can also charter yachts and deep-sea fishing boats as well as go water skiing and wind-surfing. If you like scuba diving, the water around Bali is beautiful. In fact, you may want to stay at the Hotel Club Bualu in Nusa Dua, since this is the only hotel especially organized for scuba divers. They are fully equipped, including PADI instructors, to take care of all your scuba diving needs.

❑ **Performances and ceremonies:** Bali is alive with cultural activities. Everyday somewhere you will discover a colorful village ceremony, be it a cremation, wedding, or other rite of passage. Musical and dance performances are regularly staged at the major hotels as well as at the popular village of Batubulan. A major activity for tour groups, every morning at 9:30am an outstanding group of musicians, dancers, and actors perform the Barong and Kris dances in an open-air theater on the main road in Batubulan.

While staged just for tourists, this performance is very well done and worth seeing. It's a great photo opportunity. You may want to arrive a half-hour early (9am) in order to get a good seat.

Index

SINGAPORE

The Authors

W inston Churchill put it best—*"My needs are very simple—I simply want the best of everything."* Indeed, his attitude on life is well and alive amongst many of today's adventuresome travelers. With limited time and careful budgeting, many travelers seek both quality and value as they search for the best of the best.

Ron and Caryl Krannich, Ph.Ds, discovered this fact of travel life 16 years ago when they were living and working in Thailand as consultants with the Office of Prime Minister. Former university professors and specialists on Southeast Asia, they discovered what they really loved to do—shop for quality arts, antiques, and home decorative items—was not well represented in most travel guides that primarily focused on sightseeing, hotels, and restaurants. While some travel guides included a small section on shopping, they only listed types of products and names and addresses of shops, many of which were of questionable quality. And budget guides simply avoided quality shopping altogether.

The Krannichs knew there was much more to travel than what was represented in most travel guides. Avid collectors of Thai, Burmese, Indonesian, and South Pacific arts, antiques, and home decorative items, the Krannichs learned long ago that one of the best ways to experience another culture and meet its talented artists and craftspeople was by shopping for local products. Not only would they learn a great deal about the culture and society, they also acquired some wonderful products, met many interesting and talented individuals, and helped support local arts and crafts.

But they quickly learned shopping in Asia was very different from shopping in North America and Europe. In the West, merchants nicely display items, identify prices, and periodically run sales. At the same time, shoppers in the West can easily do comparative shopping, watch for sales, and trust quality and delivery; they even have consumer protection! Americans and Europeans in Asia face a shopping culture based on different principles. Like a fish out of water, they make many mistakes: don't know how to bargain, fail to communicate effectively with tailors, avoid purchasing large items because they don't understand shipping, and are frequent victims of scams and rip-offs. To shop a country right, travelers need to know how to find quality products, bargain for the best prices, avoid scams, and ship their purchases with ease. What they most need is a combination travel and how-to book that focuses on the best of the best.

In 1987 the Krannichs inaugurated their first shopping guide to Asia—*Shopping in Exotic Places*—which covered Hong Kong, South Korea, Thailand, Indonesia, and Singapore. Receiving rave reviews from leading travel publications and professionals, the book quickly found an enthusiastic audience amongst other avid travelers and shoppers. It broke new ground as a combination travel and how-to book. No longer would shopping be confined to just naming products and identifying names and addresses of shops. It also included advice on how to pack for a shopping trip (take two suitcases, one filled with bubble-wrap), comparative shopping, bargaining skills, and communicating with tailors. Shopping was serious stuff requiring serious treatment of the subject by individuals who understood what they were doing. The Krannichs subsequently expanded the series to include separate volumes on Hong Kong, Thailand, Indonesia, Singapore and Malaysia, Australia and Papua New Guinea, the South Pacific, and the Caribbean.

Beginning in 1996, the series took on a new look as well as an expanded focus. Known as the Impact Guides and appropriately titled *The Treasures and Pleasures . . . Best of the Best*, new editions covered Hong Kong, Thailand, Indonesia, Singapore, Malaysia, Paris and the French Riviera, and the Caribbean. In 1997 and 1999 new volumes appeared on Italy, Hong Kong, and China. New volumes for 2000 cover India, Australia, Thailand, Hong Kong, Egypt, Brazil, Singapore and Bali, Israel and Jordan, and Brazil.

Beginning in 2000, the Impact Guides became the major impetus for launching the new *i*ShopAroundTheWorld Internet site for international shoppers and travelers:

www.ishoparoundtheworld.com

While the primary focus remains shopping for quality products, the books and Web site also include useful information on the best hotels, restaurants, and sightseeing. As the authors note, *"Our users are discerning travelers who seek the best of the best. They are looking for a very special travel experience which is not well represented in other travel guides."*

The Krannichs passion for traveling and shopping is well represented in their home which is uniquely designed around their Asian and South Pacific art collections. *"We're fortunate in being able to create a living environment which pulls together so many wonderful travel memories and quality products,"* say the Krannichs. *"We learned long ago to seek out quality products and buy the best we could afford at the time. Quality lasts and is appreciated for years to come. Many of our readers share our passion for quality shopping abroad."* Their books also are popular with designers, antique dealers, and importers who use them for sourcing products and suppliers.

While the Impact Guides keep the Krannichs busy traveling to exotic places, their travel series is an avocation rather than a vocation. The Krannichs also are noted authors of more than 30 career books, some of which deal with how to find international and travel jobs. The Krannichs also operate one of the world's largest career resource centers. Their works are available in most bookstores or through the publisher's online bookstore: *www.impactpublications.com*

If you have any questions or comments for the authors, please direct them to the publisher:

Drs. Ron and Caryl Krannich
IMPACT PUBLICATIONS
9104 Manassas Drive, Suite N
Manassas Park, VA 20111-5211
Fax 703-335-9486
E-mail: *krannich@impactpublications.com*

More Treasures
and Pleasures

The following travel guides can be ordered directly from the publisher. Complete the following form (or list the titles), include your name and address, enclose payment, and send your order to:

IMPACT PUBLICATIONS
9104 Manassas Drive, Suite N
Manassas Park, VA 20111-5211 (USA)
Tel. 1-800-361-1055 (orders only)
703/361-7300 (information) Fax 703/335-9486
E-mail: *singapore@impactpublications.com*
Online bookstores: *www.impactpublications.com* or
www.ishoparoundtheworld.com

All prices are in U.S. dollars. Orders from individuals should be prepaid by check, moneyorder, or credit card (we accept Visa, MasterCard, American Express, and Discover). We accept credit card orders by telephone, fax, e-mail, and online (visit Impact's two online travel bookstores). If your order must be shipped outside the U.S., please include an additional US$1.50 per title for surface mail or the appropriate air mail rate for books weighting 24 ounces each. Orders usually ship within 48 hours. For more information on the authors, travel resources, and international shopping, visit *www.impactpublications.com* and *www.ishoparoundtheworld.com* on the World Wide Web.

Qty.	TITLES	Price	TOTAL
__	Click & Easy Travel Planning on the Internet: The Top 1,000 Sites Worldwide	$19.95	_____
__	Treasures and Pleasures of Australia	$16.95	_____
__	Treasures and Pleasures of the Caribbean	$16.95	_____
__	Treasures and Pleasures of China	$14.95	_____

__ Treasures and Pleasures of Egypt	$16.95	_____
__ Treasures and Pleasures of Hong Kong	$16.95	_____
__ Treasures and Pleasures of India	$16.95	_____
__ Treasures and Pleasures of Indonesia	$14.95	_____
__ Treasures and Pleasures of Israel & Jordan	$16.95	_____
__ Treasures and Pleasures of Italy	$14.95	_____
__ Treasures and Pleasures of Paris and the French Riviera	$14.95	_____
__ Treasures and Pleasures of Rio and São Paulo (Brazil)	$13.95	_____
__ Treasures and Pleasures of Singapore and Bali	$16.95	_____
__ Treasures and Pleasures of Thailand	$16.95	_____

SUBTOTAL ------------- $ _____

■ Virginia residents add 4.5% sales tax $ _____

■ Shipping/handling ($5.00 for the first
   title and $1.50 for each additional book) $ _____

■ Additional amount if shipping outside U.S. $ _____

TOTAL ENCLOSED ---------- $ _____

SHIP TO:

Name _____

Address _____

_____

_____

PAYMENT METHOD:

❑ I enclose check/moneyorder for $ _____
   made payable to IMPACT PUBLICATIONS.

❑ Please charge $ _____ to my credit card:

❑ Visa ❑ MasterCard ❑ American Express ❑ Discover

Card # _____

Expiration date: _____/_____

Signature _____

Experience the "best of the best" in travel Treasures and Pleasures!

Emphasizing the "best of the best" in travel and shopping, the unique Impact Guides take today's discerning travelers into the fascinating worlds of artists, craftspeople, and shopkeepers where they can have a wonderful time discovering quality products and meeting talented, interesting, and friendly people. Each guide is jam-packed with practical travel tips, bargaining strategies, key shopping rules, and recommended shops, hotels, restaurants, and sightseeing. The only guides that show how to have a five-star travel and shopping adventure on a less than stellar budget!

New for 2000!

▶ *The Treasures and Pleasures of Australia: Best of the Best.* April 2000. ISBN 1-57023-060-9

▶ *The Treasures and Pleasures of Hong Kong: Best of the Best.* April 2000. ISBN 1-57023-115-X

▶ *The Treasures and Pleasures of Singapore and Bali: Best of the Best.* April 2000. ISBN 1-57023-133-8

▶ *The Treasures and Pleasures of Thailand: Best of the Best.* April 2000. ISBN 1-57023-076-5

▶ *The Treasures and Pleasures of India: Best of the Best.* January 2000. ISBN 1-57023-056-0

Order Online! www.impactpublications.com

Rave Reviews About The Impact Guides:

Travel and Leisure: *"An excellent, exhaustive and fascinating look at shopping."*

Travel-Holiday: *"Books in the series help travelers recognize quality and gain insight to local customs."*

Washington Post: *"You learn more about a place you are visiting when Impact is pointing the way. The Impact Guides are particularly good in evaluating local arts and handicrafts while providing a historical or cultural context."*

▶ *The Treasures and Pleasures of China: Best of the Best.* 1999. 317 pages. ISBN 1-57023-077-3

▶ *The Treasures and Pleasures of the Caribbean.* 1996. 371 pages. ISBN 1-57023-046-3

▶ *The Treasures and Pleasures of Indonesia.* 1996. 243 pages. ISBN 1-57023-045-5

▶ *The Treasures and Pleasures of Italy.* 1997. 271 pages. ISBN 1-57023-058-7

▶ *The Treasures and Pleasures of Paris and the French Riviera.* 1996. 263 pages. ISBN 1-57023-057-9

▶ *The Treasures and Pleasures of Singapore and Malaysia.* 1996. 282 pages. ISBN 1-57023-044-7

Authors: Drs. Ron and Caryl Krannich are two of America's leading travel and career writers with more than 40 books to their credit. They have authored 10 books in the Impact Guides series, including volumes on Hong Kong, Singapore, Malaysia, Indonesia, Italy, and France.

Order Toll-free! 1-800/361-1055

*i*ShopAroundTheWorld

Travel the World for Treasures!

Welcome to *i*ShopAroundTheWorld, an Internet site that brings together the best of the best in shopping and traveling around the world. If you enjoy shopping, be sure to visit our one-stop-shop for great advice, resources, discussion, and linkages to make your next trip a very special adventure. Discover how to:

- Prepare for a shopping adventure
- Find quality shops and products
- Bargain for the best prices
- Identify local shopping rules
- Order custom-made goods
- Handle touts and tour guides
- Avoid shopping and travel scams
- Pack and ship goods with ease
- Select the best hotels and restaurants
- Use the Internet to travel and shop
- Find inexpensive airfares and cruises
- Travel independently or with tours
- Hire cars, drivers, and guides
- Schedule times and places
- Choose the best sightseeing
- Enjoy terrific entertainment

…and meet talented, interesting, and friendly people in some of the world's most fascinating destinations. Join our community as we travel to the intriguing worlds of artisans, craftspeople, and shopkeepers in search of fine jewelry, clothing, antiques, furniture, arts, handicrafts, textiles, and numerous other treasures to grace your home and enhance your wardrobe. Best of all, shop and travel online before and after your next trip!

www.ishoparoundtheworld.com